EXECUMÉ™

It's More Than A Resume, It's A Reflection of You

Interactive Resume-Building Workbook and CD-ROM

by Gayle Oliver-Leonhardt

Empower-U Publishers
Atlanta, Georgia

Take Control of Your Career and Take Control of Your Life

Published by
Empower-U Publishers
3400 Peachtree Road, N.E.
Suite 549
Atlanta, Georgia 30326

ISBN: 0-9672358-0-4

Cover design: Total Graphics, Inc.
Cover concept: Julie White
Book design: Jill Dible
Editor: Erica Fox
CD-Rom development: Ryan Chapple

* Please note that any examples in this workbook and CD-ROM are included only to guide you in developing your own resume. Please be sure to substitute your own information when completing the exercises throughout the resume-writing process.
Printed in Canada

EXECUMÉ™

It's More Than A Resume, It's A Reflection of You

Believe in Yourself and Success Will Follow

To my immensely talented and adoring husband, Michael Leonhardt,
for his innumerable contributions and relentless support,
without which this book would not have been possible.
You really are the Gingerbread Man, and I'll love you forever.

CONTENTS

ACKNOWLEDGMENTS

Special thanks to an exceptional editor, Erica Fox, for helping to nurture this project through many transformations into a book that makes me proud, and to my sister, Julie White, for reminding me that trusting ourselves is the natural beginning of all great things.

I also extend the deepest gratitude to the many others who encouraged and assisted me during the journey of this creation. I would particularly like to thank each of my clients who have shared their accomplishments, aspirations, and hope for the future while entrusting me to memorialize their professional histories.

Imagine having less than a minute to convince a perfect stranger to meet with you about the job of your dreams. You'd want to make the best impression possible, wouldn't you? One of the most effective ways to get a job interview is by having a well-designed, accomplishment-rich resume—one that clearly, concisely, and strategically presents your qualifications. A powerfully written resume and cover letter can definitely make the difference between your success and failure in the job market.

For example, when one job seeker named John sent a company his resume and cover letter in response to a classified ad, they landed in a pile of resumes with those of hundreds of other job applicants. After receiving a rejection letter explaining that his qualifications didn't match the company's requirements, John took the time to rewrite and significantly improve his resume. He faxed a copy of the revised resume, which clearly, concisely, and strategically highlighted his skills and accomplishments, to the same company. Guess what? He received a phone call within two hours from a manager who explained that although the advertised position had been filled, the company was expanding and needed additional people with John's qualifications. Amazingly, the same qualifications, presented in two different ways, led to two totally different responses. The obvious conclusion is that an effective resume can open doors that might otherwise be closed. Having a powerful, well-written resume can also help you better communicate your qualifications during the interview process. The choice is yours—either write a resume that sells you short or write one that presents you in the best light possible.

So, the question is, how do you write a resume and cover letter that get results? First, it's important to recognize that resumes have changed fairly dramatically. In the past, a resume provided only a general commentary on a person's job history and personal background. It was similar to a biography, frequently long and often boring. Today, a resume still includes a job history, but it also lists the person's professional accomplishments and related skills. In our competitive job market, your resume must read more like an advertisement with active and dynamic language that grabs the reader's attention. More specifically, it must quickly and convincingly highlight the unique skills you can offer an employer. It should also make you feel self-confident about your capabilities throughout the job search.

The challenge is learning how best to present your skills and related qualifications. If you're like most people, you've been searching for an easy way to write a resume that will get you interviews and give your career momentum. We believe that this step-by-step workbook and CD-ROM are just the right tools to help you create a resume that will get you the results you're after.

Once you better understand the psychology behind what people look for and respond to in a resume, you will find the process of resume writing to be not only quick but worthwhile in preparing you for interviews. The purpose of the workbook and the CD-ROM is to provide you with user-friendly assistance in preparing your resume and cover letter by walking you through a variety of helpful exercises. These tools will help you describe your qualifications and background both powerfully and persuasively. Used together or separately, the workbook and CD-ROM will eliminate potential frustration while speeding up the entire resume-building process. The result will be a high-quality, high-response resume and cover letter that will help you better compete in the global job market and reach your highest career goals. Just remember, your possibilities are endless when you recognize and promote your full potential to others. Let Execumé help you take charge of your career and proactively direct your professional future.

Congratulations on taking action toward achieving professional empowerment by learning how to market yourself.

EXECUMÉ will teach you how to:

▌ Highlight and document your successes and accomplishments

▌ Sharpen your visual presentation

▌ Showcase your expertise

▌ Demonstrate your professional value

▌ Put power in your words

▌ Identify your marketable talents

▌ Prepare a strategically designed resume that capitalizes on proven resume-writing strategies

STEP 1

IDENTIFYING YOUR MARKETABLE SKILLS AND CHARACTERISTICS

Every person is valuable to his or her employer and plays a critical role in his or her respective position. Identifying your talents and what makes you unique is the first step in writing an effective resume. This is true whether you want to advance in your current field or get a position in another industry. Writing a resume is no time to be modest. It's the time to highlight your value to previous employers so others can understand what you could contribute to their organizations. It's critical that your resume shows you possess the skills required in the position you're pursuing.

Many people sell themselves short by underestimating their skills. The *Skills Inventory* on pages 2-11 lists the skills and characteristics typically associated with a variety of careers and provides examples of how these skills could be described in a resume. Review this section so you can begin to identify your own marketable skills and talents.

> **Now turn to Worksheet One entitled *My Job History and Skills I've Acquired*, on pages 111-113.**

This exercise will help you identify the skills you currently possess, many of which may be transferable to other industries if you'd like to move in a new direction.

If you're like many people, you may be considering making a career change but feel uncertain about how to do it. The secret to writing a resume that will be valuable in launching a new career is to find a way to present your experience in a new light. By examining the *Skills Inventory* carefully, you'll notice that many of your existing skills are transferable and probably overlap with those required in many jobs you might be interested in but have never held. Perhaps you gained skills from volunteering or other nonwork-related activities. Skills gained outside the workplace can be extremely valuable, so don't discount them. Jobs that require these skills may very well be ones you should pursue. Seek out information about the skills required for the positions that interest you. If possible, speak to people in the jobs you want to secure or consult career guides that list the skills and qualifications required for the jobs you really want.

If your job or career is no longer appealing or challenging to you, there's no reason you must continue in it. Remember, all change begins with a desire and a willingness to take action. Don't be afraid to think big and to take some risks, and don't limit yourself by limiting your thoughts. Completing Worksheet Two, *New Careers I'm Considering and the Skills They Require*, on pages 114-116, is an excellent first step toward making a career change. And if you've identified your skills carefully, you'll probably find that you're better prepared to make a career change than you thought you were.

SKILLS INVENTORY

(The information below is grouped into 16 major professional categories.)

ADMINISTRATION

Skills

- Organization
- Meeting coordination
- Information management
- Business administration
- Document production
- Needs identification
- Word processing
- Process-building
- Calendar planning
- Deadline management
- Multitasking
- Records management
- Reception
- Telephone
- Filing
- Planning

Personal Traits

- Resourceful
- Reliable
- Efficient
- Precise
- Task-oriented
- Consistent
- Team-oriented
- Conscientious
- Flexible
- Swift
- Proficient
- Detail-oriented
- Supportive
- Decisive
- Thorough
- Focused

Phrases That Describe These Skills and Traits

- Managed high-traffic, 13-line communications system for a multifaceted, 80-employee firm.
- Successfully handled over 500 business transactions daily in fast-paced environment.
- Adept at developing and controlling annual sales and marketing reports and budgets.
- Fielded up to 90 incoming calls daily, resolving problems and addressing diverse matters.
- Demonstrated highly effective telephone skills and resourceful research capabilities.
- Displayed an outstanding ability to comprehend and assimilate detailed data/information.
- Possess crucial needs-identification skills vital to providing strong administrative support.
- Demonstrated ability to creatively reorganize existing systems to improve operational efficiency.
- Highly effective in a detail-oriented atmosphere that involves efficient records management.
- Self-directed individual who has demonstrated an ability to effectively perform in fast-paced settings.
- Exceptional organizational and prioritization skills regarding all facets of administration.
- Outstanding data-entry skills enhanced through intensive training and practical job applications.

CONSULTING

Skills

- Needs assessment
- Procedural development
- Leadership
- Business development
- Process improvement
- Cost control
- Problem solving
- Marketing
- Project coordination
- Deadline management
- Solutions-building
- Staff motivation
- Financial
- Retraining
- Organizational
- Client relations

Personal Traits

- Efficiency-minded
- Technically astute
- Finesse
- Resourceful
- Quality-focused
- Meticulous
- Forward-thinking
- Persuasive
- Analytical
- Accuracy-driven
- Insightful
- Investigative
- Detail-oriented
- Organized
- Diplomatic
- Communicative

Phrases That Describe These Skills and Traits

• Adept in operational reengineering requiring effective strategic planning and implementation skills.

• Demonstrate proactive process management and production modification strategies that maximize yields.

• Experienced in all phases of quality control and program implementation to facilitate internal efficiency.

• Extensive experience in all phases of project management within a multitiered organization.

• Skillfully utilize vast knowledge of total quality and change management principles to produce results.

• Successfully conceived and implemented reengineering programs to reduce costs and increase profits.

• Exceptionally talented at team-building, training, and rallying staff support of revised operations.

• Capable of providing effective consultative direction related to technical execution of key projects.

• Revitalized underperforming locations through strategic reorganization of marketing and business plans.

• Possess skills in quality improvement, as well as strengths in business-opportunity identification.

• Maintain in-depth knowledge of operations management, including total quality practices, work process/operations analysis, production supervision, and customer retention.

• Proven ability to devise and implement strategies that improve front-line organizations.

COUNSELING / SOCIAL WORK

Skills

▮ Treatment planning	▮ Crisis intervention	▮ Observation	▮ Listening
▮ Situation assessment	▮ Counseling	▮ Emergency response	▮ Mentoring
▮ Rehabilitation management	▮ Decision making	▮ Client evaluation	▮ Coaching
▮ Progress mapping	▮ Case management	▮ Programming	▮ Action planning

Personal Traits

▮ Psychologically astute	▮ Empathetic	▮ Compassionate	▮ Intuitive
▮ Inquisitive	▮ Open-minded	▮ Multiculturally aware	▮ Analytical
▮ Nonjudgmental	▮ Emotionally sensitive	▮ Team-oriented	▮ Patient
▮ Discrete	▮ Trustworthy	▮ Resourceful	▮ Ethical

Phrases That Describe These Skills and Traits

• Conceived and implemented numerous program enhancements in student advisement counseling.

• Extensive experience in educating staff to quickly handle crisis and special-needs scenarios.

• Utilize superior development skills to create successful activity and treatment programs.

• Implement a reality therapy approach providing extensive special-needs training for clients with serious eating disorders, diabetes, abuse, abandonment, neglect, and behavior problems.

• Dual expertise in nursing and counseling, facilitating healing using integrated modalities.

• Talented at initiating, developing, and implementing educational and counseling services.

• Strong counseling skills used to rehabilitate families and improve family systems functioning.

• Adept in providing extensive crisis intervention and ongoing individual and family counseling.

• Skilled in treatment plan development outlining clients' needs, goals, and corrective steps.

• Experienced in all phases of the counseling process from client intake to treatment implementation.

CREATIVE

Skills

▮ Interior design	▮ Marketing	▮ Advertising	▮ Public relations
▮ Campaign development	▮ Promotions management	▮ Event planning	▮ Production
▮ Graphic design	▮ Theme development	▮ Conceptualization	▮ Computer
▮ Project-oriented	▮ Deadline coordination	▮ Detail management	▮ Brainstorming

Personal Traits

▮ Multifaceted	▮ Clever	▮ Innovative	▮ Unique
▮ Versatile	▮ Individualistic	▮ Leading edge	▮ Artistic
▮ Technically proficient	▮ Originality	▮ Broadminded	▮ Flexible

Phrases That Describe These Skills and Traits

- Vastly talented in interior design involving both residential and commercial projects.
- Highly skilled in all aspects of event coordination, implementation, and management.
- Expertise encompasses event marketing development and production for national corporations.
- Capable of developing theme interiors and event decorations, including floral designs.
- Talented in creating multitiered advertising campaigns and sponsorship programs.
- Strong public relations abilities combined with promotional campaign design/execution skills.
- Demonstrated success in originating diverse forms of advertising on a national scale, including four-color newspaper and magazine, television, billboards, brochures, and collateral materials.
- Conceptualized program content and supervised the production of video montages and PSAs.
- Skilled in audio and video post-production procedures, including final edits prior to airing.
- Created press kits that involved continuous contact with the media regarding company events.
- Strategically planned and placed company media advertising to include both print and radio ads.

CUSTOMER SERVICE

Skills

▮ Troubleshooting	▮ Problem solving	▮ Relationship management	▮ Interpersonal
▮ Rapport-building	▮ Needs analysis	▮ Solution identification	▮ Organizational
▮ Decision making	▮ Follow-up	▮ Grievance management	▮ Documentation
▮ Remedy planning	▮ Process compliance	▮ Escalation prevention	▮ Support

Personal Traits

▮ Diplomatic	▮ Resourceful	▮ Team player	▮ Empathetic
▮ Task-oriented	▮ Service-oriented	▮ Responsive	▮ Prompt
▮ Articulate	▮ Efficient	▮ Thorough	▮ Analytical
▮ Supportive	▮ Judicious	▮ Understanding	▮ Proactive

Phrases That Describe These Skills and Traits

- Consistently received superior ratings in all categories that emphasized outstanding customer satisfaction, ongoing productivity, procedural compliance, and overall professional effectiveness.
- Demonstrate in-depth understanding and accurate interpretation of changing corporate policies, ultimately ensuring prompt management of all customer requests within diverse departments.

- Extensive skills in planning and follow-up, complying with protocol and managing critical time lines.
- Served as a liaison between employees and management, presenting and resolving employee grievances.
- Utilize keen analytical abilities/problem-solving techniques in identifying plausible solutions.
- Proven interactive capabilities utilized to communicate effectively with all levels of personnel.
- Key contributor in establishing superior customer relations due to expedient problem resolution.
- Remarkably capable of handling irate customers and resolving problems efficiently.
- Consistently achieve exceptional customer service evaluations and client satisfaction ratings.
- Adeptly managed time-critical, client-related record-keeping and administrative functions.
- Extremely diplomatic individual with responsive decision-making and key troubleshooting skills.

ENGINEERING

Skills

Accurate	Deductive reasoning	Drafting	Computation
Research	Computer	Project analysis	Prioritization
Quantitative	Process mapping	Scheduling	Design
Precise	Critical thinking	Problem solving	Mathematical

Personal Traits

Analytical	Conscientious	Thorough	Inventive
Deadline sensitive	Intellectually astute	Creative	Systematic
Accurate	Technically inclined	Disciplined	Detailed

Phrases That Describe These Skills and Traits

- Proven project management experience involving architectural, mechanical, and electrical engineering.
- Excellent ability to cost effectively manage multimillion-dollar, multidiscipline design projects.
- Experienced in supervising contractors, engineers, architectural representatives, and clerical staff.
- Effectively negotiate business solutions with cross-functional consulting and engineering teams.
- Extremely experienced in the enforcement of quality control and quality assurance standards.
- In-depth architectural and structural engineering background combined with a proven design expertise.
- Adept at value engineering and fiscal planning with an ability to devise cost-effective design strategies.
- Effective in specification planning, contractor bid development, permitting, scheduling, and inspections.
- Demonstrate astute drafting abilities as well as strong deductive reasoning and critical-thinking skills.
- Vast experience in project design and management functions, including utilizing AutoCAD extensively.
- Inventive problem-solving skills combined with advanced process mapping and system design abilities.

FINANCE / ACCOUNTING

Skills

Financial	Analytical	Planning	Computer
Mathematical	Deductive reasoning	Research	Organizational
Cash management	Reporting	Business administration	Budgeting
Forecasting	Project management	Problem solving	Record-keeping

Personal Traits

▪ Logical	▪ Detail-oriented	▪ Accurate	▪ Efficient
▪ Methodical	▪ Precise	▪ Objective	▪ Consistent
▪ Deadline-oriented	▪ Ethical	▪ Interpretive	▪ Technical

Phrases That Describe These Skills and Traits

• Exhibited astute financial decision-making skills managing a $10M annual supply/equipment budget.

• Highly skilled in cash and records management and in preparing daily activity and forecasting reports.

• Possess proven accounting and organizational skills key to managing diverse record-keeping functions.

• Instituted financial controls to ensure efficiency and compliance in strictly regulated lending areas.

• Develop strategies and tactics that control costs related to labor, inventory, and production.

• Effective negotiation and cost-control capabilities used to maximum profit margins.

• Proven ability to enhance critical computer information, financial, and manufacturing control systems.

• Excellent financial and strategic decision maker with an emphasis on planning and budgeting.

• Formulate, develop, and interpret complex financial models that serve as key decision tools.

• Extremely analytical and logical individual with precise mathematical and astute interpretive abilities.

HUMAN RESOURCES

Skills

▪ Documentation	▪ Information management	▪ Rapport-building	▪ Communication
▪ Team-building	▪ Career pathing	▪ Skills identification	▪ Training
▪ Performance monitoring	▪ Reengineering	▪ Change management	▪ Follow-up
▪ Organization design	▪ Policy making	▪ Troubleshooting	▪ Planning

Personal Traits

▪ Diplomatic	▪ Empathetic	▪ Pioneering	▪ Resourceful
▪ Multifaceted	▪ People-focused	▪ Creative	▪ Conscientious
▪ Nurturing	▪ Assertive	▪ Accurate	▪ Understanding

Phrases That Describe These Skills and Traits

• Display a genuine ability to capitalize on manpower and resources at all organizational levels.

• Consistently perform all administrative and reporting functions with critical timeliness.

• Utilize superior team-building and employee relations skills to create a cooperative environment.

• Proven training, professional development, career pathing, and succession planning techniques.

• Adept in creating processes and practices that positively impact organizational effectiveness.

• Proven ability to hire talent and maximize their performance through appropriate job placement.

• Highly skilled in strategic acquisition planning, change management, and organization design.

• Vastly talented in the initiation, integration, and enforcement of diverse corporate policies.

• Created human resources departments from ground zero, requiring development and implementation of recruitment, training, employee policies, regulatory compliance, and payroll functions.

• Possess over 10 years of experience in management development, union avoidance, performance management, staffing, training, employee relations, communications, compensation, and benefits.

INFORMATION SYSTEMS

Skills

▮ Critical thinking	▮ Creative	▮ Product development	▮ Computer
▮ Analytical	▮ Project management	▮ Coding/programming	▮ Training
▮ System integration	▮ Technical	▮ Technology evaluation	▮ Documentation
▮ Mathematical	▮ Application analysis	▮ Solutions identification	▮ Consulting

Personal Traits

▮ Innovative	▮ Ingenious	▮ Methodical	▮ Resourceful
▮ Analytical	▮ Technical	▮ Tenacious	▮ Meticulous
▮ Logical	▮ Accuracy-driven	▮ Inquisitive	▮ Proficient
▮ Mission-focused	▮ Systematic	▮ Process-oriented	▮ Synergistic

Phrases That Describe These Skills and Traits

- Innovator of customized technology solutions that ensure efficient and top-quality computing functions.
- Display in-depth process-control management background combined with outstanding technical acuity.
- Offer broad experience incorporating diverse platforms, including mainframe, distributed processor, SUN, UNIX, C, client-server, and Web technology, using structured and object-oriented programming methods.
- Astute project planning and coordination skills, as well as an undisputed ability to maximize resources.
- Highly evolved ability to detect technical problems and create effective organizational solutions.
- Exhibit an unusual degree of talent in communicating highly technical information to nontechnical staff.
- Proven software programming expertise with a high degree of applicable technical abilities.
- Capable of successfully revising existing code and writing multifaceted programs in team settings.
- Display effective problem analysis techniques combined with responsive system troubleshooting skills.
- Exhibit proven acumen in efficiently maintaining and managing complex, integrated computer systems.

LEGAL / PARALEGAL

Skills

▮ Case management	▮ Information management	▮ Organizational	▮ Interpretation
▮ Client development	▮ Tracking	▮ Decision making	▮ Communication
▮ Research	▮ Documentation	▮ Analytical	▮ Record-keeping
▮ Follow-up	▮ Mediation	▮ Writing	▮ Negotiation

Personal Traits

▮ Ethical	▮ Accuracy-driven	▮ Conscientious	▮ Detail-oriented
▮ Objective	▮ Thorough	▮ Logical	▮ Judicious
▮ Self-directed	▮ Focused	▮ Articulate	▮ Tenacious

Phrases That Describe These Skills and Traits

- Exhibit strong writing, research, and investigation techniques essential to case development.
- Persuasive and persistent individual demonstrating distinctive communication and writing skills.
- Proven entrepreneur with critical analytical, problem-solving, and practice management abilities.
- Self-directed, focused, and ambitious professional who interfaces well with diverse individuals.

- Personally manage cases from initial receipt of file with sole case management responsibility.
- Skilled in discovery process, selection of experts, conducting depositions, preparing pleadings, trial preparation, evaluating cases, and settlement negotiations of high-profile, large-asset cases.
- Highly skilled drafting, analytical, and interpretive abilities critical to legal counsel.
- Proven litigation track record with in-depth trial experience in both jury and nonjury formats.
- Strong case management skills exemplified through commercial and personal injury litigation.
- Demonstrated ability to excel in all aspects of new client development and practice management.
- Experienced in marketing and promoting legal expertise within a highly competitive market.

MANAGEMENT

Skills

Decision making	Organization	Team-building	Listening
Mentoring	Negotiation	Cost control	Training
Leadership	Supervisory	Staff development	Coaching
Problem solving	Strategic planning	Financial	Recruiting

Personal Traits

Responsive	Self-directed	Tenacious	Focused
Bottomline-oriented	Deadline-driven	Multitasking	Proactive
Diplomatic	Hard working	Multifaceted	Resourceful
Profit-minded	Political	Strategic	Visionary

Phrases That Describe These Skills and Traits

- Critical insight into maximizing business profitability through proactive management techniques.
- Illustrate dynamic team-building skills while directing extremely diverse cross-discipline personnel.
- Demonstrate strong staff selection, supervisory, cost control, and decision-making skills.
- Self-directed, results-oriented leader with key experience in managing departmental start-ups.
- Highly strategic, multitasking individual with excellent mission management and prioritization skills.
- Proven leadership techniques with an outstanding talent for training, developing, and mentoring staff.
- Talented in all aspects of business development, acquisition planning, and merger management.
- Possess critical strengths in rallying key political support that positions company for expansion.
- Dramatically improved organizational efficiency and profits during complex mergers and rapid growth.
- Profit-minded professional who is a visionary that leverages proactive financial management tactics.

MARKETING / ADVERTISING

Skills

Campaign development	Market planning	Public relations	Promotion
Program concepting	Alliance-building	Client management	Copywriting
Communications	Event execution	Idea manufacturing	Design
Production coordination	Strategic advertising	Proofreading/editing	Presentation

Personal Traits

- Creative
- Strategic
- Convincing
- Analytical

- Original
- Clever
- Multitasking
- Visionary

- Imaginative
- Mission-focused
- Insightful
- Nonconforming

- Verbal
- Resourceful
- Observant
- Bright

Phrases That Describe These Skills and Traits

• Resourceful and dynamic event manager possessing a strong media relations and promotions background.

• Offer a keen insight into using visual materials to market and promote a concept, product, or service.

• Original in establishing creative images and in conceptualizing advertising and marketing concepts.

• Over 10 years of design experience in ad agencies as well as in communication and graphic design firms.

• Highly creative with a proven ability to conceptualize design projects with tremendous originality.

• Skillfully identify product marketability and apply knowledge of quickly changing, competitive markets.

• Recorded a weekly public relations message and actively publicized a multidimensional creative effort.

• Historical success in building award-winning marketing campaigns targeting consumer and trade markets.

• Vast marketing expertise encompassing the design of packaging, collaterals (media kits, sales videos, multimedia presentations), customer hospitality events, advertiser cross-promotions, and trade events.

• Talented in strategic brand positioning and brand management with tangible and intangible products.

MEDICAL / NURSING

Skills

- Treatment planning
- Medical procedure
- Case management
- Medication administration

- Crisis management
- Emergency response
- Patient relations
- Condition evaluation

- Decision making
- Prioritization
- Quality assurance
- Organization

- Problem solving
- Charting
- Tracking
- Documentation

Personal Traits

- Empathic
- Team-spirited
- Consultative
- Selfless

- Caring
- Supportive
- Intuitive
- Consistent

- Compassionate
- Encouraging
- Regimented
- Communicative

- Responsive
- Conscientious
- Precise
- Devoted

Phrases That Describe These Skills and Traits

• Demonstrate a critical commitment to providing quality care in the rapidly changing healthcare field.

• Proficient charting and general nursing skills, including implementing needs-specific medical plans.

• Utilized critical thinking and active listening skills to ensure highest-quality patient care.

• Skilled in analyzing and interpreting data to generate detailed, accurate, and timely reports.

• Proven ability to manage multiple tasks simultaneously utilizing sharp decision-making skills.

• Extensive experience working as a patient advocate with an emphasis on supporting, educating, and counseling clients on a wide range of health issues, including disease, aging, and prevention.

• Vast experience in charge, telemetry, float, and staff nursing with diverse hospital departments.

• Proven case management expertise emphasizing care coordination and discharge planning.

• Possess in-depth knowledge of managed care, workers' compensation, and utilization review.

• Skilled in educating medical personnel on insurance-related issues, including Medicare.

SALES

Skills

- Cold calling
- Negotiation
- Territory planning
- Business development
- Relationship building
- Account management
- Market identification
- Closing
- Consultative selling
- Customer training
- Account acquisition
- Expense control
- Needs analysis
- Client relations
- Presentation
- Solutions selling

Personal Traits

- Persistent
- Professional
- Service-oriented
- Relentless
- Success-driven
- Persuasive
- Articulate
- Observant
- Aggressive
- Competitive
- Mission-focused
- Innovative
- Self-motivated
- Independent
- Goal-directed
- Outgoing

Phrases That Describe These Skills and Traits

- Adept at conceptualizing and implementing sales strategies to develop ground zero revenue centers.
- Launched divisions into national and international markets utilizing astute conceptual selling skills.
- Proven track record in all the phases of sales and marketing within technology-driven industries.
- Skilled in relationship selling, proposal development, price negotiations, and product introductions.
- Continuously attain company initiatives and objectives, producing award-winning sales results.
- Persistent prospecting and cold-calling skills, resulting in relentless success in account development.
- Innovative and proactive professional demonstrating extensive consultative selling experience.
- Possess proven needs-identification skills and systems-based solutions selling expertise.
- Excel in highly competitive sales arenas utilizing exceptional account management techniques.
- Fundamental commitment to continuously top achievement, resulting in verifiable sales results.
- Highly motivated, articulate individual with superior presentation and intangible selling skills.
- Exhibit proven prospecting/business development techniques and persuasive selling strategies.

TEACHING / TRAINING

Skills

- Lesson planning
- Test evaluation
- Delegation
- Instruction
- Curriculum development
- Portfolio assessment
- Manual writing
- Performance analysis
- Classroom management
- Parent communications
- Rapport building
- Program implementation
- Presentation
- Scheduling
- Administrative
- Coaching

Personal Traits

- Patient
- Diplomatic
- Resourceful
- Poised
- Articulate
- Expressive
- Creative
- Concise
- Proactive
- Responsive
- Inspirational
- Forward-thinking
- Open-minded
- Detail-oriented
- Nurturing
- Innovative

Phrases That Describe These Skills and Traits

• Collectively evaluate human resource training requirements and design needs-based curriculum.

• Aggressively source, screen, and select ideally suited soft-skills development materials.

• Experienced in utilizing vast multimedia training tools, including video, audio, and print resources.

• Served as an adjunct professor at a four-year college, instructing multifaceted business classes.

• Skilled in all aspects of lesson planning, curriculum modification, and large-group facilitation.

• Conceptualized and implemented eight-week modules for a series of courses covering diverse subject matter.

• Demonstrated effectiveness in program research and analysis as well as writing and reporting skills.

• Developed and coordinated annual study tours abroad, ultimately increasing student enrollment by 300%.

• Spearheaded forerunning training to minimize legal liabilities and ensure safe, high-quality patient care.

• Exceptional trainer/educator possessing strong presentation, communication, and interpersonal skills.

• Highly skilled in delivering interactive training programs that incorporate high-impact group participation and learning activities combined with traditional and multimedia training resources.

WRITING

Skills

▌ Creative	▌ Research	▌ Composition	▌ Investigative
▌ Copywriting	▌ Editorial	▌ Story development	▌ Production
▌ Language management	▌ Conceptualization	▌ Journalistic	▌ Word mapping
▌ Deadline management	▌ Project management	▌ Idea manufacturing	▌ Communication

Personal Traits

▌ Introspective	▌ Analytical	▌ Observant	▌ Insightful
▌ Expressive	▌ Communicative	▌ Meticulous	▌ Original
▌ Open-minded	▌ Intellectual	▌ Sharp	▌ Inquisitive

Phrases That Describe Skills and Traits

• Capable of transforming highly complex, technical information into comprehensible text.

• Published author possessing an innate talent to conceive, develop, and compose diverse written materials.

• Noted for extremely effective writing skills with an acute ability to convey messages concisely.

• Proficiently manage numerous projects simultaneously while working within strict deadlines.

• Uniquely equipped to flourish in creative, unstructured environments as well as in corporate arenas.

• Exceptionally professional demeanor and unobtrusive interview style resulting in quality work.

• Wrote articles for and edited a newsletter that educated membership in a variety of topics.

• Conceptualized, wrote, and hosted radio show with live and prerecorded segments for two years.

• Coordinate stringent and critical editorial deadlines, frequently involving software releases.

• Skilled in publication editing, emphasizing consistency and ensuring style guidelines.

• Manage the production of up to three to five books simultaneously which ranged from 250 to 1,600 pages.

NOTES

Write down the following sentence as many times as you wish; we suggest at least 9.

I am talented, valuable, confident, and prosperous.

STEP 2
CHOOSING YOUR RESUME FORMAT

Strategic planning is crucial to creating a resume that works. This is true for two major reasons. First, you have a very short time—usually no more than 15 to 30 seconds—and limited space—only one to two pages—to let the person reading your resume know your qualifications. Frequently a resume won't get an employer's attention unless it is properly organized. This means it must be strategically planned so that it emphasizes your strengths while minimizing your weaknesses.

There are three widely accepted formats for preparing a resume: the **chronological resume**, the **functional resume**, and the **combination resume**. It is important to choose a resume format that will best suit your individual background.

You will probably want to use a **chronological resume** if you have a steady work history with a proven track record in a particular field or industry. In that case, much or all of your work experience probably is extremely relevant to the positions you are pursuing. Although this is the least creative format, it is an excellent choice if you wish to highlight your current and previous employment endeavors. An example of a chronological resume is shown on page 15.

You will probably want to use a **functional resume** if you're ready to change industries or make other significant transitions in your career. Perhaps you are looking for employment in an industry in which you've never worked. With this format, you can downplay your job history and emphasize your diverse range of abilities or transferable skills. For example, you may have acquired skills in prior jobs or in volunteer, community, or nonjob-related activities to help you move into another field of interest.

This format gives you maximum flexibility and maximum creativity because you can vary the categories of skills and abilities you choose to highlight. This format directs the reader's focus to relevant skills required to excel in the specific positions you are pursuing. An example of a functional resume is shown on page 16.

Finally, you might prefer a **combination resume**. This format is particularly useful if you want to increase your responsibilities or to pursue a higher-level position in your current field. For example, you might not have a proven track record as a sales manager but have a proven track record in sales and have the transferable skills necessary to excel in a leadership role. The combination resume provides an opportunity to highlight relevant skills, like the functional resume, without minimizing your job history and your proven industry-related track record. An example of a combination resume is shown on pages 17-18.

Before you can select the best format for you, it's important to understand the pros and cons of each format. The table on page 14 summarizes the benefits and weaknesses of each.

PROS AND CONS OF EACH RESUME FORMAT

Chronological Resume

PRO: Emphasizes a strong, steady employment history and proven professional track record

PRO: Valuable if your skills parallel the skills required in the job you're pursuing

CON: Least creative, most restrictive format

Functional Resume

PRO: Emphasizes your general skills set, rather than your job history and related accomplishments

PRO: Emphasizes abilities acquired through employment but also through other experiences

PRO: Allows for creativity in design and targeting of skills toward a particular position

CON: Dramatically downplays your job history and eliminates job-related details

Combination Resume

PRO: More flexible than a chronological resume

PRO: Highlights transferable skills as well as your job history and related accomplishments

CON: Requires careful prioritization of which skills and which aspects of your job history you will include based on space limitations

---

Take a moment to decide which of the three formats—chronological, functional, or combination—is best suited to presenting your background based on your career goals. Once you've selected your resume format, turn to pages 117-126 and tear out the corresponding worksheet, either Worksheet Three (A), (B), or (C). **DO NOT FILL IN THE WORKSHEET.** Then turn to page 19 and begin Step 3.

SPECIAL NOTE: Recent graduates should use Worksheet Three (D) on pages 127-129.

SARAH J. SEARCH

123 Job Hunting Lane
Big Time, USA 10101
(444) 567-8910

Confidentiality Requested

OBJECTIVE

To secure a sales position within the hotel industry where I may utilize my superior sales strategies as well as my demonstrated abilities to solicit new business and dramatically increase revenues.

EXPERIENCE

HOTEL USA - Anytown, USA   (9/93-Present)
Sales Manager
Perform a vast array of sales functions for this four-star hotel in order to increase both individual and group patronage. Conduct in-depth sales analyses, budget development, revenue projections, and volume forecasting. Solicit new business primarily through continuous prospecting and account management activities. Travel throughout a 4-state region to cultivate national account relationships.

- Successfully developed a revenue base of $1M+ from a base of $300K.
- Produced over 100 new accounts through the utilization of effective relationship selling techniques; negotiate room contracts as well as value-added services.
- Secured various key accounts (i.e., Big Phone Company, Insurance USA, Software Specialists, Major Communications, Temporaries Now, and Electric Company).
- Facilitated an increase in the average daily rate from $118 to $140 per night.
- Achieved #2 ranking for revenue production within the Boston facility as well as a national ranking in the top 5 company-wide.
- Establish loyal relationships with travelers as well as corporate decision makers.
- Provide top-notch service by communicating closely with various hotel departments in order to fully and satisfactorily accommodate guests' needs.
- Received numerous commendation letters from clients and upper-level management team.

SUITE HOTELS AMERICA - Anytown, USA   (9/89-9/93)
Sales Manager
Conducted numerous activities aimed toward increasing the existing customer base while maintaining a focus on both individual and group sales. Primarily called on meeting planners and corporate travel departments. Coordinated room accommodations and marketed meeting space, which included negotiating contract agreements.

- Targeted major accounts and developed a $1M local territory from ground zero.
- Successfully sold a product that had four-star competition in an already dense market.
- Planned and implemented various client appreciation events to promote customer loyalty.
- Consistently exceeded predetermined corporate goals and objectives.

AMERICA'S BEST HOTELS - Anytown, USA   (9/88-9/89)
Sales Assistant
Provided comprehensive support to the Senior Catering Manager and Senior Sales Manager. Handled numerous administrative-based functions, conducted sales follow-up, and provided troubleshooting skills. Gained highly diverse industry training.

EDUCATION

SUCCESS COLLEGE - Sometown, USA
Elementary Education Major

AFFILIATIONS

- Meeting Planners International, Member; Annual fundraiser, *Committee Chair*, Accountable for securing corporate sponsorships.
- Camp Happytown, *Committee Chair*, key contributor in implementing a charitable event.

COMPUTER

- Highly proficient in the utilization of WordPerfect and Landmark applications.

REFERENCES AVAILABLE UPON REQUEST

JOHN J. SEEKER

123 Looking Hard Avenue
Top Dog, USA 20202
(555) 678-9101

CAREER OBJECTIVE	To pursue a career with an organization that values strong financial, management, customer service, and interpersonal skills.

EDUCATION	**BACHELOR OF SCIENCE DEGREE IN MANAGEMENT**, 1989 <u>USA INSTITUTE OF TECHNOLOGY</u> - Anytown, USA - Self-financed 100% through full-time employment. - Former member of Sigma Nu Fraternity.

COMPUTER	• Lotus 1-2-3 • WordPerfect • Pro-Write • Wordstar

QUALIFICATIONS

Management
- Oversee the daily operations of a large parking organization, including staff selection and management, ensuring procedural compliance and providing key on-site troubleshooting.
- Effectively directed statewide sales, service, and distribution functions for a national supplier.
- Demonstrated effectiveness in managing a multimillion-dollar property in the Rich City area.
- Efficiently coordinated product distribution for an international manufacturer/distributor.
- Successfully monitored up to $90K in product inventory, utilizing proven recordkeeping skills.
- Talented in all aspects of recruiting, screening, interviewing, and supervising staff.

Customer Service
- Exceptional troubleshooting skills with a keen ability to resolve financial disputes expediently.
- Possess an outstanding track record in all aspects of inside sales and customer service.
- Demonstrate excellent organizational, time management, and decision-making skills.

Training
- Resourceful and creative individual who develops effective instructional programs.
- Exceptional instructor with effective presentation, communication, and counseling skills.

Accounting
- Restructured accounting procedures and improved financial efficiency for a newspaper operation.
- Experienced in processing payroll, preparing billing, generating monthly financial statements, and managing accounts receivables of up to $200K/month.

Professional Profile
- Poised individual who upholds the highest standards of excellence in all endeavors.
- Consistently display a diverse range of talents and overall professional integrity.

EMPLOYMENT HISTORY	**CITY MANAGER** AMERICAN PARKING SYSTEMS - Anytown, USA	1996-Present
	TERRITORY REPRESENTATIVE USA CINEMA SUPPLY - Anytown, USA	1994-96
	ESTATE MANAGER SMITH - Anytown, USA	1992-93
	ACCOUNTING MANAGER THE DAILY NEWSPAPERS - Anothertown, USA	1991-92
	SHIPPING DIRECTOR ADVANCED HEALTH PRODUCTS - Anytown, USA	1988-90

REFERENCES AVAILABLE UPON REQUEST

JOHN J. SEEKER

123 Looking Hard Avenue
Top Dog, USA 20202
(555) 678-9101

CAREER SUMMARY

A multitalented professional demonstrating a proven track record in the areas of sales and management combined with a vast understanding of information technology and telecommunications.

SIGNIFICANT QUALIFICATIONS

- Extremely innovative and proactive professional demonstrating extensive consultative selling experience.
- Adept in needs analysis, product development, and complex solutions implementation at an international level.
- Strong understanding of manufacturing combined with award-winning TQM and ISO 9000 expertise.
- Excel in highly competitive sales arenas utilizing exceptional account development and closing techniques.
- Effective strategic planning, market positioning, objective identification, and goal management skills.
- Demonstrate a fundamental commitment to continued top achievement, resulting in verifiable success.
- Recognized as a resourceful and results-oriented individual capable of instituting nontraditional business strategies despite constraints of traditional business philosophies characteristic of conglomerate corporations.

EXPERIENCE   <u>USA TELEPHONE COMPANY</u> - Anytown, USA; Anothertown, USA   (6/88-Present)

INTERNATIONAL ACCOUNT MANAGER - (1/96-Present)
Collectively manage a base of 33 national and international Fortune 500 accounts producing company revenues of $22.3M. Market network and consulting services internationally. Consult accounts on overcoming foreign communication challenges, ultimately establishing international communication networks. Demonstrate a keen ability to analyze and interpret clients' needs and utilize technologically driven applications to create critical business solutions. Work closely with cross-functional teams in launching new products.

- Understand causes and effects of market change and the business opportunities created.
- Serve as the international expert, participating in joint presentations with domestic sales teams.
- Successfully pioneer new markets and leading-edge applications for this industry leader.
- Overcome broad cultural barriers to cultivate key relationships with senior-level management.
- Coordinate diverse product development teams in formulating complex customized products.
- Assist in establishment of specific industry groups for international product and service offers.

ACCOUNT EXECUTIVE, HOTEL USA GLOBAL ACCOUNT - (2/95-12/95)
Sold and managed value-added network services to 400 franchised hotels throughout a 20-state Eastern region affiliated with this key corporate account. Identified decision makers, developed proposals, conducted executive presentations, and devised custom telecommunications solutions for major properties. Provided technical support to end users and supplied in-depth account service.

- Selected for the V.P. Leadership Council and co-chaired this prestigious 13-member committee, serving as liaison between 477 national account sales people and the Southern Regional V.P.
- Excelled in a competitive selling environment which incorporated dual contracted vendors.
- Managed revenues of $21.2M and achieved 130% of key account goal.
- Instituted standardized processes for account management teams, which improved service quality.
- Chosen to expand the sales effort into the international market, which required introducing the company at the corporate and director levels.

High-Tech Business Unit
QUALITY SPECIALIST - (6/93-1/95)
Promoted into a staff role reporting to the Business Unit Leader accountable for $160M in Power Systems product revenues. Assisted in developing quality-control strategies, conducting route cause analyses, checking and managing points, establishing countermeasures, and implementing solutions that maximized productivity, efficiency, and quality. Implemented statistical controls utilizing control charts and other tools to assess performance and evaluate impact of new processes.

**EXPERIENCE
continued...**

- Worked with Labs USA project managers, research and development engineers, and production staff, assisting with development of new products and improving time to market.
- Played a key role as a member of first U.S. manufacturing company to receive the Deming Award.
- Completed cultural training in order to interface with Deming Award Examiners; acted as a lead contact, which required responding to examiners' challenging questions during the final evaluation.
- Assisted in the achievement of ISO 9000 Certification and strategic international positioning.
- Created, developed, and implemented business processes impacting a staff of 4,000.
- Utilized sales and negotiation skills to create acceptance within diverse tiers of management.

Consumer Sales Division
ACCOUNT EXECUTIVE - (11/90-5/93)
Promoted calling cards and collect calling services to a 3-state government market. Conceptualized and implemented successful marketing strategies. Oversaw sales support and administrative staff.

- Pursued and penetrated a new market, which resulted in the first sale nationwide.
- Successfully generated $17M in corporate revenues, representing a $2M sales increase.
- Conducted market analyses and identified vertical market opportunities in state-run facilities.
- Developed a team that incorporated external vendors and provided a turn-key solution for the State of Eagles; incepted an innovative strategy that guaranteed significant returns to the State.
- Acted as leader of an industry-specific project team, which lobbied support for the $188M four-year Inmate Calling Proposal.
- Assisted in the critical dissolution of previously competitive barriers with key players.

Commercial Markets
ACCOUNT EXECUTIVE - (1/90-10/90)
Managed an assigned geographic territory, primarily cold-calling corporations, with an emphasis in win-back business. Key contributor to the opening of the Dallas sales office; assisted in the development of policies, procedures, and sales strategies. Ranked #33 out of 2,700 reps nationally.

Primary Markets
ACCOUNT EXECUTIVE - (6/88-12/89)
As one of a 12-member pilot sales program, aggressively sold telecommunication services to small businesses. Assisted in developing the Telemarketing Sales Representative Certification Package, which was utilized throughout the Southern Region.

ABC TECHNICAL - Anytown, USA   (10/87-4/88)
ACCOUNT EXECUTIVE
Gained initial experience in the sale of telecommunication products and services to corporate markets.

EDUCATION

UNIVERSITY OF SUCCESS - Anywhere, USA
M.B.A. Candidate, GPA: 3.75/4.00

SUCCESS UNIVERSITY - Smalltown, USA
B.S. Degree - 1986
* *Member of the Varsity Football Team*

**AWARDS/
RECOGNITION**

- General Manager Awards for Sales Production - 1991, 1992
- Spot Award for Sales Production - 1992
- Achievers Club - 1991, 1992, 1993
- Eagle Award of Excellence - 1988
- Telematic Achievers Club, Intercompany Award - *1st Recipient as an External Provider*

COMPUTER

- MS Word   • MS Excel   • MS PowerPoint   • Internet/Intranet

---

REFERENCES AVAILABLE UPON REQUEST

STEP 3
WRITING YOUR OBJECTIVE, MISSION, OR CAREER SUMMARY

Many people include a statement at the beginning of their resume that summarizes their background or specifies their career objective/mission. Many other people do not include such a statement. Those who don't typically believe it narrows the jobs for which they'll be considered. Those in favor usually believe that an objective, mission, or career summary quickly identifies their areas of expertise or assists an employer in understanding their goals.

We strongly encourage you to include an objective, mission, or career summary at the beginning of your resume. It can be written in a way that is targeted to a specific position, or it can be more general, and therefore appropriate for pursuing a broad range of jobs. The trick is to make sure that the statement is carefully constructed. If it's well written, an employer will be able to quickly classify your credentials and overall background. This is extremely important as more companies categorize resumes in a computerized database. At the same time, you'll be considered for a wide variety of jobs. Below are two examples of objectives.

Targeted Objective: To pursue a position as a meeting planner in which I may employ my related training and practical experience for the benefit of your company.

Generalized Objective: To secure a position in publishing in which I may fully utilize my proven writing, proofreading, and research abilities as well as my creativity, computer skills, and awareness of cultural diversity.

Notice that the first objective is very targeted, and the type of position the person is seeking is clearly and specifically stated. By contrast, the second objective highlights only the types of skills or industry experience the person has. Nonetheless, an employer could quickly classify the job seeker's credentials into several key categories, such as writing, proofreading, and research.

Some people prefer to call an objective a mission statement. A mission statement is just another way to describe the direction you would like your career to take.

Still another option is to include a career summary. A career summary is similar to a generalized objective statement, like the second objective statement above. A career summary highlights your background and provides a brief overview of your most important qualifications. Including a career summary does not have to limit your job search in any way. Below are two examples of career summaries.

■ Multitalented professional with a unique set of training, consulting, staff development, and counseling qualifications that includes a long-term career with a Fortune 500 organization.

■ Dynamic, multifaceted executive with a proven financial planning and consulting background consisting of in-depth expertise in accounting, finance, asset management, and strategic planning.

As more and more companies store resumes in databases for future reference, it is becoming increasingly important to include some type of statement in your resume that enables an employer to classify and catalog it easily based on key words used in the opening sentence. Without such a statement, your resume may be put aside, misfiled, or dismissed altogether.

Now that you better understand your options and the importance of including an objective, mission, or career summary in your resume, turn to Worksheet Four on page 130. Answering the four questions on the worksheet will help you decide which kind of statement to include—a targeted objective/mission, a broad objective/mission, or a career summary—based on your individual preferences and career goals.

Take a moment to imagine your ideal job. Picture yourself in that job and experiencing great success. Create a clear visual image of how happy you are in this position. Allow yourself to feel excited and enthusiastic about having attained your career goal. Once you've experienced a deep sense of satisfaction, ask yourself these questions. "What steps do I need to take to get my ideal job? What can I do today to begin making that happen?" Write down your answers.

SAMPLE OBJECTIVES / MISSIONS / CAREER SUMMARIES

(The information below is grouped in 16 major professional categories.)

ADMINISTRATION

OBJECTIVE   To utilize my proven analytical and organizational abilities, combined with my extensive administrative experience, toward a successful career in office administration.

MISSION   An executive-level support/office management position that utilizes my proven administrative skills, strong interpersonal abilities, and demonstrated competence in a multitask environment.

SUMMARY   Over 16 years of proven experience in international business that includes a comprehensive administrative, support, and office management background.

CONSULTING

OBJECTIVE   To apply a multifaceted professional background and graduate degree in business administration toward a consulting position where demonstrated success in project management, strategic planning, financial analysis, marketing, and operations supervision would be highly valued and fully applied.

MISSION   A consulting position that capitalizes on 15 years of project management and technical design experience combined with vast expertise in the telecommunications industry.

SUMMARY   Proven consulting, marketing, customer service, training, financial, and management skills.

COUNSELING / SOCIAL WORK

OBJECTIVE   A career opportunity using an in-depth social services and clinical supervision background combined with proven case management, program development, counseling, and staffing skills.

MISSION   A counseling position where I may apply my education and experience in the psychology field in order to provide therapy that utilizes artistic and creative processes.

SUMMARY   A seasoned professional with 16 years' practical experience in the field of social work.

CREATIVE

OBJECTIVE A position requiring proven creativity and effective client management skills as well as diverse corporate communications experience in the graphics, marketing, and advertising arenas.

MISSION A career in interior design where I may fully leverage my proven creativity and visual expertise.

SUMMARY A highly creative individual who has demonstrated outstanding communication and project management skills, specifically in the areas of design, layout, writing, editing, and proofing,

CUSTOMER SERVICE

OBJECTIVE Immediate goal: Position in Customer Service with a focus on outperforming the competition through exceptional service. Long-term goal: Position in Sales.

MISSION A challenging position where I utilize my extensive background in customer service, management, and administration to provide critical organizational support.

SUMMARY Top-notch professional with over 10 years of customer service experience combined with efficient problem-solving and effective account management skills.

ENGINEERING

OBJECTIVE An engineering position that demands a strong environmental and design background combined with proven analytical, problem-solving, and team management skills.

MISSION To utilize a wealth of manufacturing, engineering, and technical knowledge combined with a strong understanding of diverse business applications in an engineering role.

SUMMARY A skilled professional demonstrating success in all aspects of the mechanical engineering field with extensive experience working on commercial and industrial projects.

FINANCE / ACCOUNTING

OBJECTIVE To pursue a Trust Specialist position with a financial institution that is able to fully capitalize on my aggressive selling skills, financial acumen, and industry-related background.

MISSION A senior-level position utilizing proven accounting, finance, and business administration experience combined with astute budgeting, cost-control, and financial management expertise.

SUMMARY Historical success in accounting and finance, demonstrating excellent financial abilities, proven project management skills, and outstanding customer relations strategies that impact profits.

HUMAN RESOURCES

OBJECTIVE   To pursue a career in Human Resources where I may fully utilize my solid track record in the areas of training and management toward a myriad of future contributions.

MISSION   A generalist position that capitalizes on my proven staffing, employee relations, benefits, compensation, training, and legal/compliance experience to foster peak performance.

SUMMARY   Results-focused human resources executive with over 17 years of generalist experience in high-growth, technology-based organizations requiring acute strategy-building and human resource management skills.

INFORMATION SYSTEMS

OBJECTIVE   To continue a successful career in the software engineering field where I may fully utilize my demonstrated expertise in all phases of software development.

MISSION   To obtain a position in computer operations where I may utilize my related education combined with my proven skills and demonstrated computer technology experience.

SUMMARY   Experienced professional demonstrating a proven track record in systems integration, network engineering, and technical support combined with strong leadership skills.

LEGAL / PARALEGAL

OBJECTIVE   To excel as a Paralegal by utilizing my in-depth legal training as well as my research and insurance background combined with my acute interview and writing skills.

MISSION   An attorney position in a small law firm where I may leverage my strong project management, research, and writing skills combined with public speaking abilities toward future success.

SUMMARY   Accomplished corporate paralegal with a proven track record in demanding legal support roles.

MANAGEMENT

OBJECTIVE   To obtain a challenging position where my related experience and proven abilities will be rewarded with advancement within the residential property management field.

MISSION   To fully utilize my outstanding sales management skills, astute selling abilities, and talent development expertise for the ultimate enhancement of company growth and profitability.

SUMMARY   Talented, multilingual professional demonstrating 18 years of proven experience as a pharmacist in upper-level management and scientific research endeavors.

MARKETING / ADVERTISING

OBJECTIVE To continue a highly successful career as an Art Director with an advertising agency that values over 15 years of industry expertise and an exceptional level of creativity.

MISSION A senior executive role that capitalizes on my 10-year proven track record and competitive edge in marketing, advertising, operations management, and strategic business planning.

SUMMARY An accomplished and multitalented professional possessing strong international business knowledge combined with a vast background in all aspects of marketing and business development.

MEDICAL / NURSING

OBJECTIVE To continue a successful nursing career where I may further utilize my proven management abilities, diverse medical background, and six years of intensive care experience to provide skilled patient care and achieve professional advancement.

MISSION A Nurse Practitioner role using an extensive background in nursing and clinical psychology.

SUMMARY Experienced physician demonstrating a proven track record in all aspects of internal medicine for two highly respected medical facilities and private medical practices.

SALES

OBJECTIVE To secure a pharmaceutical sales position that capitalizes on my superior marketing, product introduction, presentation, and business development skills to increase profits.

MISSION To obtain a position in industrial products sales where I may apply my diverse array of training, presentation, relationship-building, and management skills.

SUMMARY A multitalented revenue-producer possessing significant experience and proven success in sales and marketing combined with an impressive career in the hospitality industry.

TEACHING / TRAINING

OBJECTIVE An instructor position that draws on outstanding leadership and training techniques, effective facilitation abilities, and creative curriculum development skills.

MISSION To utilize my 23 years of experience in the field of Physical Education, which includes 11 years of hands-on teaching expertise at all levels combined with a Master of Science in Athletic Training.

SUMMARY   Mission-focused, multitalented professional with a proven leadership background in all facets of curriculum design, training and development, staff recruitment, and operations management.

WRITING

OBJECTIVE   Accomplished professional pursuing a career opportunity that utilizes 10 years of successful writing and publication management experience in both corporate and freelance environments.

MISSION   Multitalented individual seeking an editor position that capitalizes on my professional expertise in writing, editing, production management, and public relations.

SUMMARY   A uniquely talented, multilingual professional with an extensive journalism and field reporting background combining a vast knowledge of international social, political, and cultural differences. Possess knowledge of various writing styles, including AP, *Chicago Manual*, and custom formats.

GENERAL / ALL PURPOSE

OBJECTIVE   A personally and professionally rewarding position in which I can utilize my diverse talents, valuable skills set, and multifaceted experiences to impact an organization positively.

OBJECTIVE   To utilize my political experience, international exposure, and strong interpersonal skills to pursue a career that will reward professional dedication and top performance.

SUMMARY   Multitalented professional demonstrating a diverse background in all phases of operations management, staff supervision, and sales, including over 13 years of successful experience in the agricultural and landscape industries.

CAREER SUMMARY   A vastly talented professional with more than 19 years of successful employment, coupled with outstanding skills in the areas of cost management, marketing, sales, and client relations.

CAREER SUMMARY   A multilingual professional demonstrating a proven track record in sales and management within international markets.

CAREER MISSION   A senior executive position where I can leverage my 10-year proven track record in all facets of sports marketing, brand management, promotions, special events, and sales.

CAREER SUMMARY   Successful professional demonstrating a background in medical- and insurance-related positions that require strong analytical, computer, and troubleshooting skills.

CAREER SUMMARY   Multitalented professional who demonstrates a broad range of professional abilities and a proven track record in generating revenues and facilitating company profits.

CAREER SUMMARY A talented executive with vast experience in driving entrepreneurial growth, launching new business opportunities, developing and introducing products, and structuring sales organizations.

CAREER SUMMARY A multitalented executive possessing 20+ years of proven core strengths in the areas of operations and resource management coupled with expertise in strategic planning, leadership, and training.

> **NOTE: A Summary and a Career Summary are the same—either term is appropriate. Similarly, a Mission and a Career Mission are the same—either term is appropriate.**

Think You Can or Think You Can't — Either Way You'll Be Correct

HENRY FORD

STEP 4
CHOOSING KEY PHRASES FOR YOUR JOB DESCRIPTIONS

The content or words you use throughout your resume are as important as the resume format you choose. This is particularly true in today's technologically advanced world, where many companies looking to fill positions retrieve resumes from large computer databases or Internet resume-posting sites weeks or even months after receiving a resume. Using what's known as a word search, computers search through resume databases for resumes of candidates with the specific set of qualifications required for a particular job. Searching for resumes containing certain key words, the computer selects only those that fit the desired specifications. To "get noticed" or chosen by the computer, your resume must make a strong case that you are the right candidate to fill a particular position. To do this, the resume must include well-thought-out, clearly stated job descriptions that contain key words, skills, or industry-related terminology the computer will be searching for.

This section will prepare you to write job descriptions that incorporate key words. Including these key words in your resume will help ensure that it gets the attention it deserves.

To get started, turn to pages 28-41 to review key phrases used to describe a variety of professions. Although many terms are included, not all the popular terms used in any one profession are covered. However, they should still assist you when you begin developing your own job descriptions. Be sure to review some of the phrases for jobs outside your profession. They may give you good ideas of ways to describe your specific job history.

Now tear out Worksheet Five on pages 131-133. Complete the exercise by writing down five key phrases that describe each position you've held. Begin with your current or most recent position and go as far back in your job history as you feel comfortable. Refer to the key phrases as necessary.

Remember, completing this exercise will make writing your job descriptions far easier than you ever imagined.

KEY PHRASES FOR JOB DESCRIPTIONS

(More than 100 positions are listed below in alphabetical order.)

Account Executive (Production)

Manage diverse projects ranging from postcard layouts to 64-page four-color catalogs • provide art direction for photography shoots, including background and lighting selection • coordinate all project and production management functions • utilize creative expertise to maximize exposure and marketability of advertised products • act as key liaison between design teams and clients • manage four to five client accounts, each producing revenues of $30K to $80K • negotiate fees with outside vendors

Account Manager

Promoted to a national account team with assignment to a multistate subsidiary company • strategically coordinated account coverage of 32 customer facilities • directed the efforts of 12 tactical sales representatives • successfully nurtured the growth of a $12M revenue base

Account Manager (Telecommunications)

Extensive experience in all areas of new account development • skilled in lead generation, proposal preparation, and sales presentations • interface with all levels from administration to senior management tiers • successfully cultivate and expand an existing customer base • utilized dynamic closing techniques and customer service training • award-winning track record for increasing corporate profits • consistently surpass quotas by up to 75%

Accountant (Corporate)

Manage a diverse range of accounting functions including general ledger, client write-ups, payroll, and bank reconciliations • prepare monthly and quarterly financial statements as well as quarterly and annual tax returns • work with individual and corporate clientele

Accountant (Manufacturing)

Personally revised annual budget and formulated projected budget • established standard materials costs and inventory management strategies • ensure achievement of cost objectives and budget guidelines • manage a $2M inventory and schedule production • prepare income statement, balance sheet, yield loss analysis, payroll, A/P, and bank reconciliations

Accounting Manager

Key contributor in implementing an automated accounting system • collaborate with programmers to customize accounting packages • manage diverse range of accounting functions for a $2M company • manage automated payroll and administer payroll deductions for 75 employees • handle G/L, A/P, A/R, invoicing, bank reconciliations, fund transfers, and collections

Archivist (TV Network)

Conducted in-depth client meetings to assess project parameters • creatively apply project requirements to resources available in a broadcast library with over 200,000 films • utilized consultative approach to assist clients in achieving positive on-air impact • performed high-quality project research for producers using state-of-the-art computers

Assistant Manager (Health Club)

Revitalize sales programs for underperforming operations • conceived effective promotions and incentives to improve staff performance • resolve customer problems expeditiously • strengthen membership loyalty • motivated sales team • promoted into management based on excellent leadership skills

Benefits Administrator

During numerous acquisitions, introduced benefits programs to new employees and performed enrollment • sole administrator of COBRA medical/dental coverage • instituted custom-designed voice response benefits system • reconciled HMO billings for active and former employees • adept in benefits planning, development, and implementation

Broker (Real Estate)

Represent lenders, investors, and developers in acquisition, disposition, management, and leasing of residential assets • conduct market analyses, property valuations, and marketing plans • direct contract negotiations, title searches, and closings • develop effective marketing and advertising strategies • achieve target selling prices within 90 to 120 days of list date

Business Systems Analyst

Analyzed diverse business processes and recommended technology and automation strategies • directed ground-floor automation project from manual system • conducted new employee orientations related to computing technology and LAN access • created and produced user-friendly system orientation package • provided technical training to PC support specialists

Case Manager (Insurance)

Manage rehabilitation services for complex workers' compensation cases • arrange medical rehabilitation care • coordinate expert witness testimony • provide care management and labor market assessments • ensure top-quality delivery of case management services

Catering Manager

Experienced in food preparation, food presentation, purchasing, inventory control, and menu development • manage corporate and social catering business • direct full-service catering and event management ranging from theme development and logistical planning to client selection and on-site supervision

Chef

Prepare, serve, and operate pantry, fryer, saute, and inside expeditor for an open kitchen • prepared buffets for private parties of 60-600 • create menu, recipes, and plate sets • experienced in ordering, inventory control, and cost control • hands-on culinary training under the auspices of highly visible, well-known chefs

Chemist

Conducted assay analyses and documented sampling • adept in the use of diverse instrumentation • performed complex environmental and contaminated water testing • identified concentrations of active ingredients

Chief Executive Officer (Hospital)

Oversee management of all operations for specialized 14-bed medical facility • provide leading treatment to disabled patients with chronic pain and spinal diseases • ensure proper business administration and quality control of care • direct feasibility studies • facilitate marketing and public relations efforts • serve as healthcare spokesperson • maintain broad civic and professional visibility • participate in cutting-edge research • key contributor to generation of $1.1M in gross revenues

Chief Financial Officer (Distributor)

Serve as driving force behind finance and administration of newly acquired distributorship • revise business strategies • manage A/R, A/P, and collections • handle corporate reporting, banking, and cash management • act as key company contact with supplier/manufacturer • instrumental in initial revenue increase of 150% • institute financial planning programs

Claims Adjuster

Negotiated cost-effective insurance settlements and managed a case load of 200+ active files • conducted in-depth claims investigations and expedited claimants' return to the workforce • interpreted law in determining compensability of medical conditions • researched in-depth medical histories, reviewed treatment plans, and authorized medical expenditures

Clothing Designer

Design apparel in seasonal segments for national distribution • determine market trends, colors, and fabrics • establish exclusive design prints, special trims, and garment styling • develop line from concept board to completion • manage domestic contractors and international vendors

Commercial Developer

Effectively orchestrate design teams • establish and disseminate project specifications • secure design/construction approvals with governing authorities • direct lot clearing, grading, and excavation activities • conceptualized and implemented design/construction report as a tracking tool • launch marketing efforts

Commercial Property Manager

Manage 1 million sq. ft. of retail space, office buildings, and commercial properties • handle financial duties such as CAM billings, taxes, insurance, tenant statement reviews, and collections • negotiate vendor contracts, conduct building inspections, and ensure contract compliance • determined strategies related to tax assessment appeals and reduced tax bill by $50K+

Communications Manager (New Technology)

Spearheaded a marketing approach that increased productivity by 45% through the use of applied technology • developed promotional slogan and publicized products through national newsletter • fostered increase in E-mail usage from 500 to 3,000 users by expanding from one user post office to 20-city post office network • strategically promoted new communications venues

Computer Project Coordinator

Formulate and write high-tech sales proposals • utilize strong understanding of cutting-edge technology applications • identify customer requirements and specifications • work closely with engineers and sales staff • coordinate account surveys to ensure customer satisfaction

Computer Training and Support Associate

Provided in-depth knowledge of Windows and Microsoft business applications • possess strong hardware expertise related to IBM, Toshiba, and Compaq computers • ensured end-user software access by resolving connectivity issues with IBM mainframes • selected as one of two computer specialists supporting 1,200 users in multiple departments • develop strong client rapport • provided effective PC training to 6,000+ company employees • designated as one of the top three trainers companywide

Concierge

Personally handled VIP and celebrity requests • demonstrated poise in interfacing with a broad international clientele • serve as a critical resource to guests • exhibit strong public relations and responsive troubleshooting skills

Consul (Embassy)

Develop key marketing programs to recruit companies in target vertical industries • utilize intense public relations strategies • create critical organizational alliances • educate trade-related associations on international business opportunities • serve as a key representative at receptions and special events • promote commercial and economic development through international trade

Contract Administrator

Analyze corporate contracts • review pricing, terms, schedules, maintenance, depreciation, and specifications • generate benefit sheets which outline profit margins • complete various research projects for senior management • analyze overhead structures and profitability

Contractor

Proven track record in business development, construction management, and operations supervision • respond to RFPs, develop bids, and negotiate commercial contracts • manage labor budget of $240K and a staff of up to 40 • strictly control labor and material costs • ensure timely completion of retail commercial structures according to contract specifications

Convention Planner

Comprehensively managed hotel convention services from inception for an upscale property • efficiently planned and implemented events for a 40,000 sq. ft. banquet space with capacity for up to 3,000 guests • coordinated accommodations and transportation • ensured operational efficiency and served as a key client contact during event execution

Cost Management Consultant

Direct project roll-outs • design customer-specific medical/hospital bill reviews and pharmaceutical service partnerships • actively market and implement a workers' compensation service network • develop critical healthcare alliances • maintain ongoing physician relationships • ensure program compliance • provide training to more than 100 regional staff

Customer Service Representative Supervisor (Medical Records)

Researched billing discrepancies and resolved accounting disputes • interacted with probate and bankruptcy courts during resolution process • updated medical records and altered coding information • conducted extensive account research • supervised customer service staff of 6 • member of quality control team committee • earned authorized access to highly confidential diagnosis information

Designer/Project Manager (Interior Design)

Co-chaired high-profile corporate hospitality design project • create presentation boards • handle purchasing, distribution, fabrication, and installation • interface with builders on color schemes, wall coverings, and carpet selection • serve as merchandise buyer for showroom and high-end clients • reorganized office procedures to maximize operational efficiency

Detective

Display keen insight into investigation management and securing confessions, resulting in numerous convictions • compile cases exemplifying thoroughness and effectiveness • successfully recovered up to $20K in stolen merchandise • exceptional investigative, analytical, and decision-making skills with ultimate authority to assign fault • develop in-depth accident reconstruction reports in fatality investigations

Documentation Specialist

Participated in writing end-user documentation • created and produced training materials for nationwide presentations • handle system-quality assurance and testing to ensure application functionality • evaluated help-desk software packages • acted as on-line troubleshooter

Editorial Assistant (Trade Publications)

Perform wide array of writing and editorial duties for monthly trade publications targeting specific industries • write feature and profile articles • handle all aspects of story conceptualization and development • conduct interviews, select photography, and assist in proofreading • organized and supervised preproduction functions

Engineer (Computer)

Managed high-profile application development projects • conducted operations analysis prior to creating a GUI application • performed configuration and installation • extensive knowledge of communications protocols • vast background in system integration and LAN administration • adept in OS/2, NT, and Novell

Flight Attendant

Utilized a highly successful approach to providing top-quality, proactive client service • handle all emergency and nonemergency decision-making • acted as direct liaison between aircraft captain and service crew • accurately documented and reported in-flight incidences • expediently resolve critical passenger problems

Finance Director

Handle diverse business planning functions • manage a $9.3M operations budget • streamlined operations and increased bottom-line profits by 150% • instituted new reporting procedures • improved cash-flow management • conceived and implemented financial controls • develop corporate guidelines for capital expenditures • negotiated a $2.5M capital infusion • strengthened banking relationships

Government Affairs Director

Serve as corporate lobbyist and public affairs manager • cultivate key relationships with state legislators in order to leverage corporate business opportunities with multinational industrial companies • developed politically favorable relationships that positioned company for significant growth • implemented a strategic approach to using influential contacts to impact business development

Hardware Specialist

Installed operating systems, motherboards, and power supplies for over 100 systems nationwide • adeptly format hard drives, assemble hardware, automate printers, and connect modems • perform system testing and administration for clients • efficiently resolve user problems

Hotel Manager (Guest Services)

Full P&L accountability for a 650-room resort hotel • direct a staff of 45 with total accountability for 70 employees • increased daily revenues by $14/guest for corporate stays and by $25/guest for walk-ins • conceive and develop staff incentives and value-added marketing programs • initiated a critical customer transportation support service • improved client service ratings by 40% within one year by fostering a staff empowerment philosophy

Inventory Manager

Managed an inventory of $4M+ in manufactured goods and $2M in raw goods • increased number of annual inventory turns • reduced inventory variance from 23.5% to 3% within eight months

Inventor/Developer (Healthcare Software)

Invented, developed, and copyrighted software that eliminates physician dictations in regional anesthesia for medical records production, documentation of medical necessity, and insurance billing purposes • handled all aspects of product development • marketed niche product to the medical community • formally presented product to numerous medical societies and scientific meetings

Legal Secretary

Assisted attorneys with documentation work for corporate cases • performed diverse support and legal administration functions • acted as a client liaison • improved efficiency of the switchboard • scheduled and prepared conference rooms

Manufacturers' Representative

Promote 10 manufacturers' product lines • establish relationships with major multilocation wholesalers • facilitate significant revenue growth by expanding manufacturers' marketshare • maintain cooperative manufacturer relations • cultivate long-lasting client relations with dominant wholesalers • comprehensive experience in warehousing and distributing products for key manufacturers

Marketing Director

Tripled branch market penetration • launched 3 major initiatives • ranked in top 10% for performance in commercial markets • achieved benchmark in customer satisfaction standards • implemented marketing strategy for target distribution channel • managed annual budget of $15M • exceeded campaign quotas for all business units

Medical Representative

Actively sell orthopedic soft goods, surgicals, and disposables tailored primarily to operating room procedures • cultivate key relationships with O.R. directors, hospital administrators, and clinical coordinators • integrally involved in production forecasting and inventory/production control • conduct cross-functional account analyses • manage an existing revenue base of $3.6M • selected to manage one of the company's largest accounts • ranked #1 out of a national sales force • admitted to President's Club for $1M in sales production volume • increased product line penetration from 47% to 600%

Merchandiser

Develop and evaluate merchandising plans for 62 stores • achieve optimal inventory levels due to accurate planning and critical decision-making • coordinate variable architectural and space variances • conceive visual strategies • create themes that ensure continuity in imaging

Multimedia Producer

Strong background in digital multimedia production, and project management • directed teams of experts in graphic arts, audio/video, hardware/software engineering, and programming • perform creative and technical functions, including concept development, editing, and testing

Network Engineer

As a member of 10-person project team, designed, coded, and tested a Windows application • developed a user interface and database for an elaborate PC-based voice mail system • maintained Novell and LAN networks • resolved network problems for major clients

New Business Development Assistant (Radio)

Conceptualize and strategically create promotional partnerships with third-party clients • structure lucrative trade opportunities to achieve profit objectives • coordinate effective couponing/redemption programs fundamentally important to driving ad sales and solidifying contracts • plan and execute all facets of event planning and management including sponsorship sales • enhance future revenue streams in collaboration with national and local sales team

Nurse

Performed all aspects of pre- and post-elective surgery patient care as a Shift Charge Nurse • handled post-anesthesia care of surgical patients • assisted physicians in emergency operations • facilitated emergency patient treatment in second busiest emergency room in the state • provided pre- and post-angioplasty care • cared for patients with advanced cardiac disease awaiting heart transplants

Office Manager

Increased quality of service by introducing higher standards of operational procedures • transformed employee morale, enhanced employee skills, and facilitated improved staff performance • reversed declining front-desk operations • orchestrated management meetings

Paralegal

Utilize keen analytical and problem-solving techniques • Demonstrate meticulous proofreading, concise writing, and exceptional editing skills • drafted, reviewed, and filed legal documents • conducted in-depth legal research • managed litigation matters and pretrial discovery

Patrol Officer

Served as a member of a tactical anti-crime unit • selected for a team accountable for developing a stake-out unit • diplomatically address public concerns and resolve a variety of citizen complaints • assisted in investigations regarding internal affairs cases • possess a law enforcement background that ranges from undercover narcotic investigations to traffic control assignments

Personal Shopper

Conduct retail and on-site presentations of products and services • handle extensive cold calling to generate leads • attend shows to scout for new vendors • negotiate with vendors to coordinate delivery of products within strict time frames • pioneered diverse marketing efforts to pursue corporate clientele • research prospective customers to compile a comprehensive marketing database • consistently surpassed quotas with sales of $670K+ annually • participated in regular promotional events

Preservation Planner

Performed resource surveys • conducted in-depth site analyses • formulated planning tools • developed design policies • completed a detailed site nominations process • conducted historic research • directed growth management of preservation projects • participated in environmental assessment projects

President (International Business)

Manage the start-up of a Latin American operation from ground zero • direct all marketing and sales functions throughout Latin America and Mexico • maintain full accountability for financial and operational effectiveness with bottom-line authority • initiated and developed strategic alliances with Mexican companies • established a profitable $2M revenue center in less than one year

President/Owner (Manufacturer)

Conceptualized and brought to fruition a start-up customized insulated glass and wholesale distribution corporation • developed and implemented initial business plan • instituted production and distribution procedures • created a successful forerunning product • purchased raw materials • directed fabricating and insulating procedures • managed sales efforts targeting mill workshops and commercial installers • generated key outside vendor relationships • developed company compensation and benefits package • managed 42,000 sq. ft. facility • achieved sales of $2M in less than 2 years

Principal

Comprehensively manage a private educational institution • key contributor in creating organizational missions, strategic plans, and detailed program outlines • conceived and instituted crucial and far-reaching policy revisions • managed complex classroom, teaching, and conference scheduling

Production Coordinator

Directed all aspects of prepress and print production utilizing one-, two-, and four-color processes • exhibit acute planning and deadline management skills • managed outside vendor services, including purchasing, estimating, scheduling, and press checks

Production Planner (Manufacturing)

Comprehensively managed production planning and scheduling for an apparel manufacturer • developed critical reports to establish optimal production time lines • reduced average production turn around time from 16 to 8 weeks

Programmer

Contributed to the programming of successful projects, ultimately marketed publicly • researched and customized programs from inception to implementation • instituted a version control system to strengthen programming, tracking, and maintenance processes • created an automated back-up process to avoid catastrophic data losses

Programs Assistant (History Museum)

Contribute to development of effective programs that complement museum's exhibits • participate in program-development brainstorming sessions • conduct research regarding exhibit formats and contents • assisted in implementing and managing a newly established interactive educational program targeting young children • recruit, train, and schedule volunteer docents

Project Leader (Fuel Management Systems)

Key representative and consultant to utility accounts • provide critical analysis, strategic planning, and solutions development in the areas of accounting and fuel procurement/storage • possess in-depth application-related data modeling experience • manage 2,700-hour system implementation projects • personally salvaged two hostile accounts • identify core product enhancements • produced over $100K in incremental income by cross-selling full management services

Project Manager (Market Research)

Evaluated and authorized market research in assigned geographic areas • ensured quality of procedural standards and project results • provided key input into research interpretation • negotiated joint projects and ensured sponsorship compliance • managed packaging, market sizing, consumer attitudes, and psychographics studies

Property Manager (Residential)

Comprehensively manage a townhome community with full supervision of leasing, maintenance, and office administration • prepared a rent and market analysis that resulted in increased rental rates • increased declining occupancy level from 82% to 98% • originate marketing plans and prepare operating budgets • decreased overdue receivables from 14% to 5%

Purchasing Agent

Negotiate pricing for up to 1,500 SKUs and arrange shipping terms with seven major vendors • maintain total purchasing authority for $40M in merchandise • strengthened forecasting methods and formulated customized spreadsheets • decreased inventory shortages by trending sales cycles

Purchasing Supervisor

Experienced in vehicle disposal and warranty negotiations • manage all aspects of purchasing including price negotiation, inventory control, and vendor selection • implemented field sales support programs • recommended customized product specifications • organize training programs • aggressively pursue vendor relationships to ensure competitive purchasing • coordinate new product testing

Quality-Control Specialist

Demonstrated in-depth knowledge of strict regulatory guidelines • ensured ongoing compliance with GMP and FDA standards • improved testing methodology and restructured standard operating procedures • provided quality control related to new product approvals

Real Estate Agent (Residential)

Represented purchasers and sellers in diverse transactions (i.e., commercial sites, retail, government projects, land tracts, and single-family residences) • demonstrated acumen in negotiating difficult transactions • possess a broad base of tax knowledge • offer undisputed strength in market identification and product sourcing

Real Estate Appraiser

Performed over 200 appraisal assignments for properties throughout the U.S. • experienced in use-feasibility and market studies, tenant mix evaluations, demographics analyses, operating expense cost reviews, and tax assessment parity investigations • provide expert witness testimony • managed all types of retail appraisal projects, such as anchor, freestanding, and regional malls in suburban, urban, and rural trade areas • skillfully defend appraisal report findings

Recruiter

Handle all preliminary testing and employee screening functions • work closely with corporate clients to identify the scope of available positions • conduct salary surveys to determine optimal labor costs • establish and negotiate compensation rates • experienced in attracting qualified talent and ongoing succession planning

Renovations Manager

Planned and implemented an extensive historical renovation project • researched government guidelines and completed all historic records • worked closely with a draftsman and an engineer in developing plans to restore a 3,410 sq. ft. home • negotiated pricing with construction company • identified investor tax advantage and achieved a yield of 18% annually

Research Analyst

Extrapolate and analyze complex and highly detailed data • direct research efforts of consulting teams • produce status reports • prepare supply and demand analyses

Research Designer

Identified goals and project specifications • conceptualized an instrument for business plan development in the field • wrote market research guides that provided methodology for evaluating corporate positioning • created multifaceted studies integrating multiple variables

Restaurant Manager

Consistently achieved targeted food, labor, and other controllable costs • established and instituted restaurant procedures from ground zero • manage operations with annual sales of $5.5M • motivated a team of up to 45 personnel • facilitated the highest levels of customer service

Safety Director

Experienced in securing workers' compensation claims rebates and uncovering fraudulent cases • minimized medical bills, lost wages, and attorneys' fees by strictly monitoring claims • conceived innovative safety programs and security guidelines • exceeded industry standard related to injury index with averages of 3.5

Sales Associate (Interior Design)

Cultivate strong client relationships with broad base of regional designers • utilize creativity to assist and coordinate fabric, furniture, and accessory selections • develop price quotes • act as a liaison between designers and manufacturers • increase sales by cross-selling products • provide top-notch customer service • contribute to showroom merchandising

Sales Automation Director (Medical Billing)

Designed a streamlined automation plan that reduced operational costs by $60K per year • selected to assume a primary role in providing turn-key technical solutions for highly visible automation project • identified user requirements and proposed cost-effective technology remedies • conducted a critical high-tech presentation to a 200+ national sales force • launched a major project in 8 weeks involving notebook computing and E-mail connectivity to the field

Sales Manager (Engineering)

Direct a 10-person sales operation • develop marketing plans • implement strategic tactics • cultivate critical partnering relationships • manage and mentor staff • negotiate contracts and increase market share • exceed sales goals • initiate vertical marketing efforts • upheld employee morale during corporate buyout • refocused organization and directed a reengineering effort

Sales Representative (Cable Company)

Instigated programs to salvage disconnected customers • increased customer account base by thousands of new clients • created and implemented strategies to reduce corporate debt from 5% to 1% • recognized as most awarded telemarketer in the company by winning 75% of all contests • grew department revenues to $500K • achieved #1 sales statistics

Sales Representative (Computer Dealer)

Performed aggressive selling and account management functions for a major computer dealer supplying commercial buyers • accumulated extensive knowledge of 150 product lines through close contact with manufacturers • handled all lead generation, proposal development, sales presentations, and client negotiations • coordinated delivery, installation, and follow-up • secured and managed national accounts through tenacious sales efforts

Sales Representative (Distributor)

Marketed consumer products to major and independent retailers • conducted sales presentations to corporate buyers • instituted promotions and secured product approvals in key accounts • improved revenues by providing effective merchandising support and superior customer service

Sales Representative (Furniture)

Stimulated sales through persistent cold calling and relationship development among designers, architects, and specifiers • handled preparation of bids and negotiated final pricing • sold 9 upscale furniture, lighting, and leather lines to a wholesale client base • utilized design background to assist in customizing products

Sales Representative (Giftware/Accessories)

Implement successful promotions and merchandising strategies • coordinate trade show participation • strategically pursue new business within existing accounts and actively develop new account base through targeted cold calling • handle all phases of sales process including territory planning, product presentations, display development, inventory control, and troubleshooting • manage a customer base of 180+ accounts in a 2-state region • initiated and established 20 new accounts in one year and facilitated a 20% increase in sales

Sales Representative (Hotel)

Conduct in-depth sales analyses • solicit new business through continuous prospecting and account management functions • cultivate long-term account relationships • negotiate room contracts and value-added services • increase group and individual patronage

Sales Representative (Office Equipment)

Originate a structured call schedule • mapped out target geographical zones • instituted computerized method of tracking account activity • conduct cold calls and developed direct mail program campaigns • performed persuasive product demonstrations and sales presentations

Sales Representative (Software)

Aggressively sold UNIX-based client/server computing equipment • expanded an unexplored territory targeting end-user and reseller accounts • marketed turn-key solutions within 2 vertical markets regionally • generated a $2.1M sale with an annual run rate of $500K • secured previously unavailable and highly profitable key accounts

Sales Representative (Telecommunications)

Marketed data and voice applications • created and implemented an aggressive call strategy • sold services targeted at high-volume users • achieved top ranking out of 350 sales representatives • earned corporate incentives • consistently surpassed sales goals • awarded District Representative of the Month five times

School Founder/Manager (Vocational Trade)

Facilitated the progressive development of a post-secondary trade and vocational school from ground zero • formulated and structured entire curriculum • conceptualized and developed the institution's regionally focused marketing plan • secured highly sought-after temporary licensure by state Department of Education and Professional Board of Massage • ensured compliance with stringent state department regulations

Security Manager

Exceptional abilities in the risk-control field with expertise in program development to minimize loss and liability • vast knowledge of cutting-edge security/loss prevention strategies • managed security administration for theft, embezzlement, and inventory control for $500M in assets • developed new drug-testing policy

Social Worker

Manage heavy caseloads of up to 30 cases • implement action plans involving educational systems, parents, hospitals, religious groups, and healthcare services • exercise excellent problem-solving and troubleshooting skills in situations involving severe resistance and complex relational dynamics • establish trust and credibility while working with dysfunctional families • institute goals for improvement of severe behavioral issues • conduct investigations to evaluate family situations

Special Events/Promotions Coordinator

Organized a citywide promotional campaign • secured extensive media coverage • coordinated 17 events during corporate grand opening for major retailer • authored feature article in niche publication • planned and facilitated corporate-sponsored workshops • negotiated lower-cost entertainment contracts • nurtured strong relationships with key media personnel, celebrities, and designers • developed innovative marketing events to increase sales volume

Systems Analyst

Analyzed and prioritized all system maintenance and enhancement revisions • automated procedures and ensured accuracy of coding • prepared cost estimates and obtained application specifications • performed program design and executed system testing • documented all phases of development projects

Teacher

Developed pilot program introducing portfolio assessment techniques • fostered parental acceptance of innovative teaching methods • created curriculum for an interdisciplinary thematic unit • demonstrated initiative in spearheading an after-school environmental club • applied Bloom's Taxonomy in lesson planning

Technology Manager

Planned and implemented equipment, power, and space requirements • Solely managed venue budget of $1M • designed video, voice, and data equipment for major sports broadcast • directed telecommunications, radio communications, document services, and information systems

Television Production Coordinator

Manage all aspects of production for promotional shoots • arrange talent scheduling, location scouting, and final editing • coordinate post-production details • interface with sales, marketing, and promotions departments • conduct preliminary research for product launch • rewrote voice-over scripts for international programs • conceptualize program content

Training Coordinator

Conduct training programs ranging from one-day to two-week courses • facilitated highly visible synergy workshop program for management personnel • receive excellent instructor performance ratings • talented in formatting training curriculum and educating diverse student populations • conduct computer-based training modules utilizing leading technology

Travel Agent

Handle all phases of corporate travel • arrange airfare, hotel accommodations, car rentals, ticketing, and delivery • coordinate group tickets, leisure vacation packages, and small-scale cruises • successfully interface with preferred client base • negotiate profitable tour packages with clients • develop strong relationships with tour wholesalers • background includes leisure and corporate travel destinations

Underwriting Manager (Insurance)

Total accountability for a $2.5M underwriting portfolio • facilitated company's lowest branch loss ratio • supervised a team of technical assistants, loss-control specialists, and underwriters • originated cooperative relationships with agents and brokers throughout an 11-state Southeast region • negotiated favorable reinsurance commissions • consistently attained net profit goals

Venue Manager

Managed the production and implementation of 100+ events annually with budgets up to $800K • Developed special events with accountability for market research, event design, stage production, logistics planning, promotions, and on-site event supervision • comprehensively produced a four-day consumer venue • contracted concessionaires and coordinated press conferences • planned venue security

Vice President/General Manager (Office Equipment)

Directed the efforts of 11 managers • maintained full P&L responsibility for a $12.5M budget • managed a region consisting of three branches with a total of 115 personnel • reduced operational expenditures by 6% while continuing to achieve goals • increased bottom-line profits by 60% and consumable supply sales by 25% • negotiated favorable lease agreements and vendor contracts • implemented paperwork and procedural changes • achieved President's Club based on achievement

Vice President/Managing Director (Environmental Services)

Promote complex environmental and engineering services including regulatory and remediation services, hazardous waste management, and air-process engineering projects • devise and implement marketing strategies to sell diverse industrial services, including production process consulting and design, traditional engineering, construction management/consulting, and laboratory testing services • generate projects that involve contaminants and noncontaminants • provide internal support to 100+ engineers • handle program marketing, budgeting, strategic planning, and advertising

Vice President of Sales (Waste Management)

Successfully negotiated massive landfill expansion • participated in in-depth legal and government negotiation resulting in expansion plan approval rulings • generated dramatic growth in annual revenues • identified optimal pricing structures and developed customized contracts • aggressively market landfill services • pursue and establish lucrative disposal contracts

Warehouse/Distribution Manager

Effectively control warehouse inventory of 5,000 items • facilitate the efficient distribution of up to 50 orders daily • employ strong decision-making skills in prioritizing shipments for delivery • coordinate and schedule incoming/outgoing product shipments • manage invoicing and dispute resolutions • prepare and analyze sales reports

Writer

Possess superior proofreading skills • demonstrate effective editorial abilities and proven creativity • verify accuracy of critical content • capable of researching, managing, and interpreting complex, detailed information

The Past
Does Not Equal
the Future

UNKNOWN

Make a list of all the things you like about yourself. Then read this list every day of your job search.

Watch out, though, it may become habit-forming!

I am...

IDENTIFYING YOUR RESPONSIBILITIES AND ACCOMPLISHMENTS

To ensure that your resume stands out in the stack, your job descriptions must include not only key phrases that apply to your profession, but also your responsibilities and accomplishments. Worksheet Six on pages 134-139, called *Your Work History Questionnaire*, will help you recall your specific responsibilities and quantify your accomplishments. Once you have completed this worksheet, you will be able to describe your work history more powerfully and persuasively. The exercise will also help you define many personal attributes and marketable qualifications that you will want to mention in job interviews.

Take your time in completing the worksheet. The more time you spend on this exercise, the more prepared you will be to describe your skills and credentials effectively in your resume. This effort will help you to succeed in an interview and possibly help you better sell yourself during salary negotiations as well. Do your homework now—it will definitely pay off.

After completing the work history questionnaire, put it aside. You will refer to it later when you write your job descriptions.

Now turn to Worksheet Six on pages 134-139, tear out the questionnaire, and answer all the questions.

Close your eyes, take three deep breaths, and think of 5 things you're grateful for about your current

or most recent job. Write these down.

Remember: Having a positive mental attitude is a critical component of a successful job search.

_____

_____

_____

_____

_____

_____

_____

_____

_____

_____

_____

_____

_____

_____

_____

_____

_____

_____

STEP 6

PUTTING POWER IN YOUR WORDS

One of the most overlooked but most effective ways to get your resume noticed is to use powerful words and phrases. By using what we call "power words," it is possible to evoke a vivid image in a reader's mind, which creates greater interest and more clarity about the message you're trying to convey. Consequently, you are more likely to influence a prospective employer to select you for an interview if you can grab his or her attention.

There are three types of words in a resume that can create high impact—verbs, adverbs, and adjectives. Typically, verbs are loaded with action and give a sentence movement and "life." Similarly, adjectives can give color and vitality to otherwise mundane nouns. Finally, adverbs often add clarity to an action being taken or make the action of a verb more specific. Notice the vivid pictures created by the verbs, adjectives, and adverbs in the following examples:

Verb	**Reversed** an underperforming business operation.
Adjective	Possess **results-oriented** sales skills.
Adverb	Remedied severe client problems **expeditiously**.

If you're like many people, you may be afraid to overstate your qualifications or believe you need to come across as humble in your resume. Wrong, wrong, wrong. Humility is necessary and attractive in some situations, but not during the job search. If you don't describe your qualifications powerfully and favorably— even brag about them—you are not marketing your professional skills and capabilities as effectively as you could. Furthermore, not describing yourself in as positive a light as possible can hurt your chances of landing the job you want. After all, an employer will not assume you have specific skills or talents unless you let the employer know you have them. The burden of successfully promoting your skills and experience is your responsibility. One way to do this is by using power words.

Pages 46-51 contain a list of power words that will be helpful in completing the next exercise. Spend a few minutes reviewing the list.

Now turn to page 140 and tear out Worksheet Seven, the *Power Words Worksheet*. If you use the worksheet while writing your job descriptions, it should help prevent you from getting writer's block. Ultimately, power words give your resume impact and evoke interest from prospective employers.

POWER WORDS

- Accept
- Acclaim
- Accommodate
- Accomplish
- Accredit
- Accumulate
- Achieve
- Acknowledge
- Acquire
- Act
- Activate
- Adapt
- Address
- Adopt
- Advance
- Advertise
- Advise
- Affirm
- Align
- Amount
- Analyze
- Announce
- Anticipate
- Appeal
- Appear
- Applaud
- Apply
- Appoint
- Appraise
- Appreciate
- Approach
- Appropriate
- Approve
- Approximate
- Archive
- Arise
- Arrange
- Array
- Articulate
- Ascend
- Ascertain

- Ask
- Aspire
- Assemble
- Assign
- Assimilate
- Assist
- Associate
- Assume
- Assure
- Astonish
- Attach
- Attend
- Attract
- Audit
- Augment
- Author
- Authorize
- Automate
- Award
- Balance
- Beat
- Believe
- Blend
- Blitz
- Bonus
- Book
- Brand
- Broaden
- Budget
- Build
- Buy
- Calculate
- Cancel
- Capsulize
- Cause
- Centralize
- Champion
- Change
- Characterize
- Charter
- Circulate

- Clarify
- Classify
- Close
- Code
- Coincide
- Collect
- Combine
- Commiserate
- Commission
- Commit
- Communicate
- Compensate
- Compete
- Compile
- Complete
- Comply
- Compose
- Compound
- Comprehend
- Comprise
- Conceive
- Conceptualize
- Conclude
- Concur
- Conduct
- Conjoin
- Connect
- Consider
- Consolidate
- Construct
- Consult
- Contact
- Contain
- Contribute
- Control
- Convene
- Convert
- Convey
- Cooperate
- Coordinate
- Copy

- Correspond
- Counsel
- Cover
- Create
- Credit
- Critique
- Cultivate
- Customize
- Decentralize
- Decide
- Declare
- Decline
- Defend
- Define
- Delegate
- Delete
- Deliver
- Demand
- Demonstrate
- Deny
- Deposit
- Depreciate
- Derail
- Derive
- Descend
- Describe
- Design
- Designate
- Desist
- Detail
- Detect
- Deter
- Determine
- Develop
- Diagnose
- Dialog
- Dictate
- Differentiate
- Diffuse
- Diminish
- Direct

- Disclose
- Discover
- Discuss
- Dispose
- Dispute
- Dissolve
- Distinguish
- Distribute
- Divert
- Divide
- Document
- Draft
- Drive
- Duplicate
- Earn
- Edit
- Effect
- Elevate
- Eliminate
- Embellish
- Embrace
- Emerge
- Empathize
- Emphasize
- Employ
- Empower
- Enclose
- Encompass
- Encounter
- Encourage
- Endorse
- Enforce
- Engage
- Engender
- Enhance
- Enlarge
- Enlighten
- Ensue
- Ensure
- Enter
- Entertain
- Entrust
- Envision
- Equip
- Escalate
- Establish

- Estimate
- Evacuate
- Examine
- Exceed
- Excel
- Exclude
- Execute
- Exemplify
- Exhaust
- Exhibit
- Expand
- Expect
- Expedite
- Expense
- Experiment
- Explain
- Explode
- Explore
- Expound
- Express
- Extend
- Extract
- Exude
- Fabricate
- Facilitate
- Fashion
- Feature
- Feel
- Field
- Fight
- Finalize
- Finance
- Finish
- Finesse
- Focus
- Follow
- Force
- Forecast
- Forfeit
- Forge
- Form
- Format
- Formulate
- Foster
- Found
- Fragment

- Frame
- Franchise
- Frequent
- Fuel
- Fulfill
- Furnish
- Gain
- Garner
- Garnish
- Gather
- Generalize
- Generate
- Give
- Globalize
- Glorify
- Graduate
- Grasp
- Group
- Grow
- Guide
- Handle
- Harbor
- Heal
- Heighten
- Help
- Highlight
- Hire
- Hold
- Honor
- Identify
- Illustrate
- Imagine
- Imitate
- Implement
- Imply
- Import
- Improve
- Incept
- Incite
- Include
- Increase
- Indicate
- Infer
- Influence
- Inform
- Infuse

- Initialize
- Initiate
- Inject
- Inspire
- Install
- Instigate
- Institute
- Integrate
- Intend
- Intensify
- Interact
- Intercede
- Interface
- Interfere
- Interpret
- Intertwine
- Intervene
- Interview
- Introduce
- Invent
- Inventory
- Invert
- Invest
- Investigate
- Invoice
- Involve
- Isolate
- Itemize
- Join
- Judge
- Justify
- Know
- Label
- Launch
- Lead
- Lease
- Liaise
- List
- Loan
- Look
- Magnify
- Maintain
- Manage
- Mandate
- Market
- Master

- Mature
- Maximize
- Measure
- Mechanize
- Mediate
- Meet
- Merge
- Mobilize
- Moderate
- Modify
- Monitor
- Motivate
- Move
- Multiply
- Negate
- Negotiate
- Network
- Neutralize
- Normalize
- Note
- Nurture
- Object
- Observe
- Obtain
- Occupy
- Offer
- Open
- Operate
- Oppose
- Optimize
- Orchestrate
- Organize
- Orient
- Originate
- Outline
- Outpace
- Outsell
- Overcome
- Oversee
- Overtake
- Paginate
- Parallel
- Participate
- Partner
- Pave
- Pay

- Penalize
- Penetrate
- Perform
- Permeate
- Permit
- Personalize
- Persuade
- Phase
- Pinpoint
- Pioneer
- Place
- Plan
- Portray
- Possess
- Prearrange
- Predict
- Precipitate
- Predetermine
- Prefer
- Prepare
- Present
- Prescribe
- Preserve
- Prevail
- Preview
- Print
- Prioritize
- Proclaim
- Proceed
- Procure
- Produce
- Program
- Progress
- Project
- Pronounce
- Proofread
- Propose
- Prorate
- Prospect
- Protect
- Protest
- Provide
- Publicize
- Publish
- Punctuate
- Purchase

- Pursue
- Qualify
- Quantify
- Question
- Radiate
- Rank
- Rate
- Rationalize
- Reach
- Read
- Reason
- Rebuild
- Receive
- Reciprocate
- Recognize
- Recommend
- Reconcile
- Reconsider
- Record
- Recreate
- Recruit
- Rectify
- Recycle
- Reduce
- Reflect
- Reform
- Refund
- Refurbish
- Regenerate
- Regionalize
- Register
- Regulate
- Reinforce
- Reinvent
- Reject
- Rejuvenate
- Release
- Relocate
- Remediate
- Remind
- Remit
- Remodel
- Remove
- Renew
- Render
- Renovate

- Repair
- Repeat
- Report
- Replace
- Reply
- Represent
- Reproduce
- Request
- Require
- Research
- Reserve
- Resist
- Resolve
- Resort
- Restore
- Restrain
- Restrict
- Retain
- Retire
- Retrieve
- Return
- Reveal
- Reverse
- Review
- Revise
- Revitalize
- Revive
- Revolutionize
- Reward
- Rewrite
- Ride
- Rise
- Roll out
- Rotate
- Run
- Salvage
- Sanction
- Satisfy
- Saturate
- Save
- Scan
- Schedule
- Score
- Screen
- Script
- Search

- Secure
- Seek
- Segment
- Seize
- Select
- Sell
- Send
- Serve
- Set
- Settle
- Set up
- Sever
- Share
- Sharpen
- Shelter
- Shepherd
- Shift
- Show
- Shrink
- Sign
- Signify
- Simplify
- Simulate
- Size
- Solicit
- Solidify
- Solve

- Speak
- Spearhead
- Specialize
- Specify
- Standardize
- Start
- Start up
- State
- Station
- Steer
- Stimulate
- Stock
- Straighten
- Streamline
- Strengthen
- Structure
- Struggle
- Study
- Subject
- Succeed
- Suggest
- Summarize
- Supersede
- Support
- Surge
- Surmount
- Surpass

- Surrender
- Survey
- Survive
- Suspend
- Sympathize
- Synthesize
- Systemize
- Target
- Teach
- Team
- Test
- Testify
- Thrive
- Track
- Trade
- Train
- Transcend
- Transfer
- Transform
- Transition
- Translate
- Transmit
- Transport
- Travel
- Treat
- Trend
- Triple

- Troubleshoot
- Turn
- Uncover
- Understand
- Undertake
- Underwrite
- Unify
- Unleash
- Update
- Use
- Utilize
- Validate
- Vary
- View
- Violate
- Visualize
- Vitalize
- Voice
- Vote
- Wage
- Warrant
- Withdraw
- Witness
- Work
- Worthy
- Write
- Yield

ADJECTIVES

- Able
- Accomplished
- Accountable
- Active
- Acute
- Adaptable
- Adept
- Adjunct
- Advanced
- Ambitious
- Analytical
- Annual
- Approximate
- Assertive
- Astute

- Basic
- Brilliant
- Broad-minded
- Capable
- Certain
- Challenging
- Charming
- Cheerful
- Committed
- Comparable
- Compelling
- Competent
- Complex
- Comprehensive
- Concise

- Confidential
- Confident
- Conscientious
- Considerable
- Considerate
- Consultative
- Continuous
- Convincing
- Creative
- Credible
- Critical
- Crucial
- Decision-making
- Decisive
- Dedicated

- Demanding
- Demonstrated
- Dependable
- Descriptive
- Detail-oriented
- Detailed
- Determined
- Differential
- Disciplined
- Distinguishable
- Distinguished
- Diverse
- Dynamic
- Effective
- Efficient

- Enormous
- Enthusiastic
- Entire
- Essential
- Ethical
- Eventual
- Exalted
- Excellent
- Exceptional
- Excessive
- Exciting
- Exclusive
- Existing
- Expected
- Experienced
- Expert
- Explicit
- Express
- Expressive
- Extensive
- Extraordinary
- Extreme
- Favorable
- Feasible
- Flexible
- Floundering
- Focused
- Forceful
- Former
- Forthright
- Frequent
- Fundamental
- Futuristic
- Global
- Goal-oriented
- Governmental
- Greater
- Gross
- Growth-oriented
- Hands-on
- Hard-working
- Imaginative
- Impending
- Important
- In-depth
- Incredible

- Independent
- Individual
- Informed
- Inquisitive
- Inside
- Insightful
- Intelligent
- Interior
- Internal
- Interpersonal
- Inventive
- Involved
- Itemized
- Keen
- Kind
- Knowledgeable
- Large
- Level
- Long-term
- Loyal
- Magnificent
- Major
- Maximum
- Measurable
- Meticulous
- Minimum
- Multifaceted
- Multilingual
- Multitalented
- Nationally
- Necessary
- New
- Noteworthy
- Noticeable
- Numerous
- Ongoing
- Open-minded
- Optimal
- Outside
- Outstanding
- Patient
- Persevering
- Persistent
- Persuasive
- Pilot
- Poised

- Political
- Positive
- Possible
- Powerful
- Precious
- Precise
- Preferable
- Prestigious
- Proactive
- Problem-solving
- Productive
- Professional
- Proficient
- Profit-minded
- Profitable
- Progressive
- Proven
- Punctual
- Qualified
- Qualifying
- Qualitative
- Quantitative
- Quick
- Rapid
- Rare
- Record-breaking
- Regional
- Relevant
- Reliable
- Remarkable
- Resourceful
- Responsible
- Responsive
- Results-oriented
- Rewarding
- Rigid
- Selective
- Self-assured
- Self-determined
- Self-motivated
- Separate
- Several
- Short-term
- Significant
- Simple
- Sizable

- Smooth
- Sophisticated
- Sound
- Stable
- Straightforward
- Strategic
- Stringent
- Strong
- Success-driven
- Successful
- Superior
- Swift
- Talented
- Team-oriented
- Technological
- Thorough
- Tireless
- Top
- Top-notch
- Trustworthy
- Turn-key
- Underperforming
- Underlying
- Undisputed
- Unequaled
- Unique
- Unknown
- Unlimited
- Unmatched
- Unparalleled
- Unusual
- Unwavering
- Upper
- Utmost
- Valuable
- Value-added
- Variable
- Various
- Vast
- Versatile
- Visible
- Visionary
- Well-rounded
- Widespread
- Worthwhile

ADVERBS

- Aboveboard
- Absolutely
- Accurately
- Additionally
- Adequately
- Aggressively
- Altogether
- Annually
- Assertively
- Astutely
- Capably
- Certainly
- Clearly
- Compellingly
- Competently
- Completely
- Comprehensively
- Concentratedly
- Concisely
- Confidentially
- Confidently
- Consequently
- Considerably
- Consistently
- Continuously
- Decidedly
- Direct
- Directly
- Discretely
- Dutifully
- Easily
- Effectively
- Efficiently
- Effortlessly
- Enormously
- Entirely
- Environmentally
- Essentially
- Eventually
- Exactly
- Exceptionally
- Excessively
- Expeditiously
- Expertly
- Expressly
- Extensively
- Extremely
- Finally
- Forcefully
- Formerly
- Frequently
- Fully
- Furthermore
- Highly
- However
- Ideally
- Increasingly
- Indirectly
- Indiscriminately
- Initially
- Instead
- Integrally
- Mindfully
- Newly
- Obviously
- Personally
- Positively
- Possibly
- Precisely
- Previously
- Primarily
- Prudently
- Quickly
- Rapidly
- Rarely
- Repeatedly
- Respectfully
- Selectively
- Simply
- Simultaneously
- Sincerely
- Singularly
- Skillfully
- Solely
- Specifically
- Strictly
- Strongly
- Subsequently
- Successfully
- Swiftly
- Throughout
- Timely
- Totally
- Truly
- Ultimately
- Unusually
- Well
- Wholly
- Widely

Write down the following statement at least 9 times.

I am energized, excited, and effective in my job search.

CHOOSING YOUR JOB DESCRIPTION FORMAT

There are several possible formats for writing job descriptions. For instance, some people use a paragraph format to describe their job responsibilities and accomplishments. Other people use a bullet format so that each sentence of their job description is highlighted as a separate statement. The job description format we most often recommend, assuming space permits, is to use both paragraphs and bullet points. To best apply this format, we suggest you briefly describe the *scope of your responsibilities* in paragraph form. We suggest you then use bullets to highlight specific text that you don't want overlooked. These bullets should provide *specific quantifiable information* about your accomplishments or contributions.

There are three advantages to using this format.

1. Using a paragraph to describe your job responsibilities gives the reader a clear idea of the job functions you are capable of performing.
2. Using bullet points to highlight your accomplishments enables the reader to review quickly those points you feel are most important.
3. Using bullet points also enables you to create a vivid picture in the reader's mind of how well you have performed throughout each period of employment without requiring the person to read every word of your resume.

Although it may be hard to believe, people usually spend only 15 to 30 seconds reviewing a resume. That means your resume must have instant appeal.

Bullets are best used to highlight activities that led to positive results. For example, perhaps you improved systems, reduced costs, strengthened client relations, improved morale, increased efficiency, helped improve quality, or boosted revenues.

Bullets can also be an effective way to demonstrate that you were valued as an employee. For example, you might include awards you earned, promotions you secured, or recognition you received from peers. Highlighting your accomplishments with bullets, in addition to using concise and powerful paragraphs to describe your job history, is an effective way to reach an employer quickly and to demonstrate why the employer should interview you.

To bolster the content of your job descriptions, it is imperative that you use verifiable facts and figures whenever possible. Not only do facts and figures build credibility, but they also provide a great deal of valuable information an employer can use to assess your skills and performance.

> Notice in the following job description that the size of the company ($65M) is quantified and the type of business (distribution of software) is qualified.

National Sales Manager

Hired initially as a Sales Trainee for this $65M company specializing in distribution of software. Rapidly promoted to increased accountability as a Manager for four years during tenure.

Subsequently promoted into a Sales position. Successfully pioneered a new sales market throughout a national territory. Additional responsibilities included purchasing, bid development, corporate presentations, product testing, specifications compliance, extensive follow-up, and troubleshooting. Aggressively cold called, pursuing key accounts.

- Ranked as one of the top three Sales Representatives 6 out of 11 years.
- Generated annual sales volume of up to $2.5M and negotiated 40% profit margins.
- Achieved recognized status on top supplier lists for 10 out of 12 major accounts.
- Ranked in the top 1% out of 10,000 vendors and as one of the top 5 out of 2,000 suppliers.
- Demonstrated account management skills negotiating product purchases of $500K annually.
- Developed a sales forecasting method that better identified profitable corporate strategies.
- Managed over $3M in inventory with crucial product traceability.

Similarly, in the following job description the size of the territory (five states) is quantified and its location (Southeastern region) is qualified.

Account Executive

Aggressively pioneer a start-up territory with primary focus on selling WAN and LAN networking products for a Fortune 50 company throughout a five-state Southeastern territory. Plan and implement multifaceted sales strategy involving cold calling on Fortune 100 accounts, third-party distribution channels, trade shows, and industry conferences. Experienced in training reseller sales teams in product knowledge and accompanying sales reps during the sales process. Adept at managing long sales cycles.

- Increased revenue by 65% in FY-95 over FY-94; currently accountable for a $2M quota.
- Qualified and developed a profitable VAR channel that generated end-user leads.
- Penetrated Internet Service Provider market and established relationships with key providers in Southeast by executing a sales plan that mar-

keted Asynchronous and ISDN routers.
- Launched a co-marketing program with Apple to pursue key reseller and end-user markets.
- Assisted in establishing key contacts to develop an OEM relationship with IBM.
- Promoted from Sales Representative to Account Executive based on outstanding performance.

Well-written job descriptions also communicate many implied messages. For instance, an employer might assume from the above example that because the account executive services a five-state region, she is willing to travel. The employer might also assume that the account executive is efficient and able to prioritize multiple responsibilities.

Essentially, by including these kinds of details, an employer can more concretely evaluate your experience as it relates to the position the employer is attempting to fill. Details also give the employer enough information to determine whether to invest more time in meeting with you.

Remember, every resume is a unique document. For this reason, there are no hard and fast rules for writing resumes. For example, functional resumes don't usually lend themselves to the use of bullet points in the job description section. Concrete details are usually incorporated into the qualifications section. In this case, to deemphasize the job history, brief paragraphs or simply listing job titles is a much better strategy. What is important is that you understand the reason we are recommending certain strategies over others. Then, it's simply a matter of deciding what will work best for you in highlighting your background.

At this juncture, we suggest you turn to page 55, the beginning of the Job Description Library. This section provides numerous examples of job descriptions that have helped many job seekers market themselves successfully. After reviewing as many of these sample job descriptions as possible, take a moment to write down on your resume worksheet the specific page numbers of the job descriptions you would like to use as guides when writing your own job descriptions.

JOB DESCRIPTION LIBRARY

(The information below is categorized into 16 major professions.)

ADMINISTRATION

<u>MAJOR BANK</u> - Moneytown, USA   (8/93-Present)
ADMINISTRATIVE ASSISTANT
In a vital support role for the General Counsel/Secretary and Senior Attorney within the legal department, effectively serve as coordinator for several boards of directors and related committee meetings. Administrative functions involve crucial organizational, writing, and management skills. Capably interact with executive officers and upper-level managers. Efficiently perform technical support and essential troubleshooting functions. Revise legal documents and serve as liaison with other company departments. Maintain litigation files for General Counsel while acquiring valuable knowledge and experience regarding a variety of pleadings.

<u>GLOBAL TECHNOLOGY COMPANY</u> - Big City, USA   (8/89-1/96)
EXECUTIVE ASSISTANT
Provided executive and administrative support to the Director of Government Affairs, an advocate in various branches of government, who managed federal, legislative, and regulatory matters. Operated as the key communications link between the Director and four direct reports throughout a four-state Southern region, addressing a variety of administrative and personnel issues.

Selected Highlights:
- Served as region coordinator for a 50-member 1996 Olympic Committee; established procedures to address the transportation barriers during the Olympic games.
- Assisted in controlling project deadlines and validating proper administration of benefits programs and affirmative action annual reviews, which impacted a team of 30.
- Scrutinized and audited travel expenses to ensure compliance with company guidelines.
- Analyzed budget reports to assist in expense management and budget monitoring.
- Reviewed and managed documentation to verify appropriate allocation of lobbying funds.
- Comprehensively coordinated attendance of the lead executive at government functions, which required heavy travel planning and calendar management skills.

<u>RECRUITERS INTERNATIONAL</u> - Staffing, USA   (7/88-10/94)
ADMINISTRATIVE MANAGER
Supervised office support staff in addition to managing bookkeeping functions that included invoicing, billing, A/R, A/P, collections, and payroll for salaried and commissioned personnel. Tracked and created weekly, monthly, and annual sales, cash, and production reports. Provided critical assistance to the branch manager in expense control and budgeting.

<u>BIG TELEPHONE COMPANY</u> - Hello, USA   (1/96-12/96)
LEGAL SECRETARY
Provided primary management support to the senior attorney, Chief Regulatory Counsel, and secondary support to a team of in-house general attorneys. Acted as a primary liaison with internal/external counsel involved in retrieving information, fielding questions, and responding to file-related inquiries. Managed, updated, and tracked information for pleadings in addition to preparing testimony and auditing external attorney fees.

• Effectively organized, produced, and controlled time-sensitive, critical information/correspondence.
• Key player in providing support required to file the Joint Venture Interconnection Agreement.
• Swiftly responded to regulatory complaints, interfacing with customers and the Public Service
  Commission; conducted internal investigations and resolved issues to the PSC's satisfaction.
• Chosen to serve as a departmental representative on a 1996 Olympic Games Committee.
• Selected for position requiring immense trust based on exposure to highly confidential information.

VIDEO SUPPLY DISTRIBUTOR - Visual City, USA   (8/93-Present)
EXECUTIVE ASSISTANT/OFFICE MANAGER
Expertly arrange all business travel for headquarters office and 5 affiliate offices.
Effectively oversee all payroll administration and distribution for a staff of 250+
employees. Provide program updates and troubleshooting expertise for sophisticated
telecommunications systems and software programs. Manage and evaluate support staff.
Perform essential administrative functions for the General Manager and Assistant
General Manager, which include addressing human resources and legal issues. Additional
functions frequently include collections, database management, account reconciliation,
billing research, order processing, and multiline reception.

• Provide key administrative support to President, using strong scheduling,
  meeting planning, correspondence, and troubleshooting abilities.
• Produce accurate and timely labor and sales reports for 15 in-house properties.
• Contribute excellent formatting and editing skills in preparing a quarterly newsletter.
• Awarded Employee of the Month, which honors outstanding job performance.
• Utilize strong relationship-building skills during extensive customer contact.
• Hired initially in a contract position; based on qualifications progressed rapidly to
  full-time status with a continually increasing set of responsibilities.

JOHN U. CUREME, M.D. - Healthy Village, USA   (1991-1994)
MEDICAL INSURANCE CODER
Reviewed office and operation records of patients for this private-practice surgeon
specializing in plastic, reconstructive, and hand surgery. Accurately encoded medical
data, calculated billing charges, and prepared insurance forms for processing. Utilized
strong data-entry and clerical skills. Assisted in various office support functions,
including reception, scheduling, and filing.

• Intensive utilization of ICD-9 and CPT coding combined with a strong
  knowledge of medical terminology.
• Experienced in preparing workers' comp, Medicare, and Medicaid forms.
• Assisted in compiling medical data during a major computer conversion.

<u>ABC INSURANCE COMPANIES</u> - Beachville, USA   (9/85-Present)
COST MANAGEMENT CONSULTANT

Perform a variety of network development/maintenance as well as project roll-out functions. Actively market and implement a workers' compensation service network called *Workers' Network*, serving as both a leader and a team player in all aspects of a group-selling process. Develop critical healthcare alliances, ultimately building, creating, and expanding an approved provider network. Additionally, maintain an ongoing relationship with physicians to ensure quality of care and program compliance.

- Conduct new program sales presentations to risk-management teams targeting existing customers.
- Direct project roll-outs ranging up to 6 weeks, working with internal claims staff and customers.
- Develop MCOs and PPOs from ground zero; approve existing networks, negotiate vendor fees and provider services, draft service contracts, supervise customer roll-outs, and manage progress.
- Market and implement customized cost-management programs to reduce customer medical costs.
- Design customer programs, which include medical/hospital bill reviews, peer reviews, durable equipment provider analyses, and pharmaceutical service partnerships.

<u>ENVIRONMENTAL COMPANY, INC.</u> - Cleanup, USA   (1993-1996)
PROJECT MANAGER

One of 25 managers in a 200-person office with full financial and project accountability for multimillion-dollar construction, remediation, litigation support, and consulting assignments. Manage all resources, logistics, and time lines to deliver technical quality. Report directly to clients, managing diverse projects and consistently achieving all deadlines and budgets.

Project Highlights:
- Managed construction projects, including facility development and upgrade/expansions, i.e., $2M project that involved 35 cross-functional staff on a fuel system upgrade.
- Designed and directed $2.9M environmental remediation project; reduced operation costs 60%.
- Spearheaded a regulatory compliance and testing program that impacted 1,500 tanks throughout Asia; conceived corrective strategies that incorporated multinational environmental standards.
- Contributed to client's successful pretrial settlement of $380K on a $15M litigation claim.
- Managed an environmental contamination cost-recovery project; provided defensible data against costly remediation based on technical/cost reviews and technology assessments.
- Developed, created, and installed a $320K bioremediation system for a multi-well site.

<u>COMMERCIAL DEVELOPER</u> - Builders, USA   (1/95-Present)
PROJECT MANAGER

During a long-term association with this internationally recognized real estate developer and consultant, performed a wide array of management functions related to shopping center development, leasing, management, and marketing. Diverse present and previous responsibilities are outlined below:

Construction Coordination
- Coordinate all aspects of development construction including scheduling, deadline management, and extensive troubleshooting.
- Establish and disseminate specifications information as well as review construction documents to ensure compliance with all of the developer's criteria.
- Serve as a key liaison between the developer, general contractors, architects, tenants, and tenants' contractors.
- Successfully ensured a timely grand opening of 25 retail stores within 4 months.

| **Expansion/** | • Talented in the areas of project management and owner representation involving |
| **Renovation** | major retail stores from design planning to construction phases. |

• Talented in the areas of project management and owner representation involving major retail stores from design planning to construction phases.
• Effectively orchestrate design teams, including architects, engineers, and consultants.
• Experienced in securing design/construction approvals with governing authorities.
• Coordinated expansion projects from design/construction to grand opening, including managing all architectural, engineering, and construction contracts.

COUNSELING / SOCIAL WORK

HOSPITAL COUNSELING CENTER - Support City, USA   (10/97-11/98)
COUNSELOR
Provided individual and group counseling, with an emphasis on addressing life-threatening and chronic illnesses, for both a hospitalized and an outpatient clientele. Comprehensively managed an assigned caseload, handling initial intake, formulating treatment plans, documenting sessions, evaluating progress, and directing therapeutic processes.

• Initiated a strong clinical presence on the High Risk Pregnancy Unit, demonstrating the need and benefit of health psychology services, which included individual assessments and counseling.
• Participated in the Perinatal Loss Program, which involved planning and implementing both individual and group support grief counseling sessions for patients.
• Conducted ongoing evaluations and counseling for a diverse array of medical patients.
• Key contributor in developing the psychological aspect of the new Stem Cell Transplant program through the Oncology Department.

STATE AGENCY - Helping Hand, USA   (1972-1995)
CASEWORKER PRINCIPAL
Investigated allegations of neglect, abuse, and exploitation of aged and disabled persons. Assessed disabilities and determined eligibility for various services. Extensive field work was required. Developed case plans and coordinated rehabilitation services. Caseload consisted of 30 clients and included legal guardianship and representative payee case management duties. Filed, organized, and presented guardianship petitions in probate court; represented the state agency in a variety of matters as acting guardian. Provided individual counseling and client follow-up.

LOCAL MIDDLE SCHOOL - Teaching, USA   (1997-Present)
SCHOOL COUNSELOR INTERN
Assist in utilizing developmental, preventive, and crisis intervention techniques to advance social, emotional, and cognitive development in students. Specifically, conduct small-group guidance sessions on topics such as self-esteem building and improving study skills. Provide classroom guidance regarding conflict resolution and stress management. Counsel individuals regarding scheduling and other important issues affecting a student's physical, mental, and intellectual well-being.

• Received extremely high performance ratings from supervising counselor and noted for interacting exceptionally well with faculty members.
• Experienced in reading and interpreting aptitude and achievement tests.
• Gaining considerable exposure to community referral programs.
• Successfully contributed to the coordination and implementation of Career Day.

BIG AGENCY - Creative, USA   (1978-Present)
SENIOR ART DIRECTOR
Progressed through the corporate structure from a Production Artist position.
As Senior Art Director, comprehensively manage a diverse range of assignments
on the agency's primary account ($50M). Demonstrated success in originating
diverse forms of advertising on a national scale for this account, including
four-color newspaper and magazine, television, billboards, brochures, and
collateral materials. Assignments require close interaction with account
managers, copywriters, production staff, and printers. Hire and supervise
photographers and talent for on-location shoots.

- Conceptualized and implemented a 20-city outdoor campaign; developed
  billboards from both 30-sheet posters and paint.
- Create and produce 30-second television ad spots from point of inception
  to final production, including story board development and filming.
- Singularly developed brochures as well as color magazine and television ads.
- Consistently complete projects within budget and according to deadlines.

NICHE TELEVISION CHANNEL - Teletown, USA   (5/95-Present)
PRODUCTION COORDINATOR
Manage all aspects of production for promotional shoots, ranging from talent scheduling and
location scouting to invoice tracking and final editing. Manage all on-site production
details as well as coordinate post-production. Interface with multiple departments, including
sales, marketing, and promotions. Conduct presentations to upper-level management.

- Utilize a great deal of diplomacy and finesse to cultivate strong intercompany relations.
- Created and designed a marketing piece targeting prospective and existing customers.
- Conducted preliminary research for an international product launch.
- Developed a comparison report to clearly define and justify budget objectives.
- Rewrote voice-over scripts of international programs into an Americanized format.

INTERIORS USA - Interiorville, USA   (1996-Present)
DESIGN ASSISTANT
Work extremely closely with the company owner and serve as a direct client liaison for a
designer specializing in high-end residential interiors. Research products according to
customer specifications and contribute to the selection of furniture, fabrics, wall covering,
art, and accessories. Additionally, utilize strong drafting, space planning, and client-
directed conceptual selling skills.

- Demonstrated success in conceptualizing interior schemes, developing design proposals,
  producing presentation boards, and formulating product pricing.
- Utilize effective project management skills in handling product ordering, scheduling,
  implementation coordination, and supervision of installation teams.
- Act as the primary vendor contact, which includes sourcing new product lines and
  suppliers as well as contributing to vendor-produced product development activities.
- Ensure top-notch customer service by expeditiously resolving problems related to
  product deliveries, back orders, billing, and deadlines.

<u>DESIGNS OF AMERICA</u> - Creativetown, USA
DESIGN DIRECTOR
Personally developed a full-service design firm from inception.
Conceptualized and managed projects with full accountability for creative
and production functions. Directed outside personnel in copywriting,
photography, and illustration. Managed all print buying and project
budgeting. Acted as the sole client contact throughout the design process.

CUSTOMER SERVICE

<u>GRAPHICS & INTERIORS, INC.</u> - Design City, USA   (3/96-Present)
CUSTOMER SERVICE REPRESENTATIVE
Manage all customer service functions related to office furniture catalog telephone sales for an
organization with two major wholesale suppliers. Research and gather industry comparison data to
prepare revenue-generating customer proposals. Perform key support functions including purchasing
supplies, handling communication system and return authorizations, and scheduling service/deliveries.

• Established effective client-relationships with 200+ vendors as a result of outstanding service.
• Maintain current knowledge of product information available with 300+ manufacturers.

<u>SETTLEMENT SERVICES USA</u> - Technology, USA   (1992-Present)
ACCOUNT SERVICES MANAGER
Rapidly progressed from customer service, to sales, to corporate account services
manager. As the sole point of contact for 900 accounts, manage an income stream of $7.8M
for this data communications network services provider. Support sales and EDI processes
to ensure fulfillment of highly complex data-exchange services. Cold call accounts
and identify clients' needs, along with recommending adjunct services and customized
data-exchange solutions. Work closely with senior-level staff, managing customer
and account relationships in national, international, and entrepreneurial markets.

• Identified cost-reduction opportunity and devised cost controls to optimize returns.
• Comprehensively researched and acquired encripting technology to enhance service offering,
  which resulted in impacting profitability through vastly increased internal efficiency.
• Skilled in account management, including resolving data errors and network problems.
• Function as trainer for customer service staff, involving teaching up to 18 applications
  combined with communicating knowledge regarding various account histories.
• Consistently exceeded sales goals and singularly increased grow rate by 35%.

<u>PETROLEUM USA</u> - Gastown, USA   (1/91-8/92)
CUSTOMER SERVICE REPRESENTATIVE
Performed a variety of customer-oriented and management support functions with competence and
professionalism. Reviewed and monitored tank levels and managed cash flow positions utilizing
strong financial planning skills. Reconciled daily cash receipts, balanced transactions, and produced
detailed credit card reports. Handled stock receiving, merchandising, and retail display development.

• Demonstrated excellent customer service, troubleshooting, and public relations skills.
• Entrusted as key holder accountable for managing the daily facility and cash-closing functions.

<u>MANUFACTURERS OF AMERICA</u> - Makers, USA   (1996-Present)
DIRECTOR OF CUSTOMER SERVICE
Launched an efficient and centralized customer service center from ground zero
serving 5,000+ equipment dealers nationwide with full accountability for a capital and expense
budget in excess of $1M. Merged finance, credit, sales, service, and technical support functions
into a central call center operation. Hired, trained, and directed a management staff of 3
and 45 customer support specialists. Leveraged focus group-based research to raise performance.

• Met or exceeded $25M variable monthly revenue goals by astute start-up operations management.
• Installed an advanced telephone switch functionality to accomplish a quick service philosophy.
• Achieved business-business and business-consumer service-level agreement goals relative to
  the quantity and quality of calls answered and efficiency of customer handling time.

ENGINEERING

<u>METAL CORPORATION OF AMERICA</u> - Steeltown, USA   (1996-1998)
PROJECT ENGINEER
Developed an in-house mechanical and instrumentation control group from ground zero that
produced project revenues of $10M. Skillfully hired personnel and captured expertise required
to revert projects from external to internal. Maintained full project management accountability
with a heavy emphasis on equipment and subassembly procurement, quality assurance, and
labor-related cost control from project inception to equipment erection in the field.

Highlights:
• Controlled project-specific budgets for multiple projects ranging from $250K up to $10M.
• Coordinated project teams and scheduling to achieve critical project deadlines.
• Completed programming and system integration of first-generation PLCs introduced to market.
• Designed digital mini vax system production control and information management architecture.
• Key liaison interfacing with automotive and construction equipment manufacturer accounts.
• Hired engineering and contracting teams that included union-organized personnel.

<u>USA CONSTRUCTION COMPANY</u> - Building Town, USA   (1987-Present)
SUPERINTENDENT/ENGINEER
Comprehensively manage mechanical, electrical, and plumbing engineering from inception
to completion. Review all shop drawings. Schedule and track equipment delivery.
Contribute to the subcontractor selection and contract negotiations. Conduct coordination
meetings to assure equipment is compatible with space requirements. Supervise and
monitor subcontractors' performance. Indirectly accountable for 100+ staff. Promoted
into a leadership position from an initial engineering role.

• Current Project: $48 million nine-story new structure as part of a local hospital expansion;
  personally control a $12 million budget, currently within budget and ahead of schedule.
• Project: $45 million 450-room upscale hotel, 20-month project in Resort Island;
  managed a $12 million budget, completed assignment within budget and on time.
• Project: $40 million Credit Card Company Computer Center, 12-month project in
  Creditville; $10 million budget, completed assignment within budget and on time.

SMITH CONSULTING FIRM - Advice Land, USA   (1/96-12/98)
LEAD ELECTRICAL ENGINEER
Designed complex electrical systems involving lighting, power distribution, signaling,
and computer networks utilized within office buildings and institutional facilities.
Intimately involved in structural, mechanical, and architectural designs.

Highlights: • Earned architectural and engineering award for a $12.5M detention facility project.

FINANCE / ACCOUNTING

INTERNATIONAL SOFTWARE COMPANY - Moneytown, USA   (1996-Present)
CHIEF FINANCIAL OFFICER
Comprehensively manage the financial growth and profitability of a foreign-owned, rapidly
emerging international software development and marketing company that specializes in
the production and distribution of IBM mainframe software throughout North America and
Mexico. Report directly to the Board of Directors in Europe and serve as an
integral member of the U.S. Board of Directors.

Accountabilities   • Maintain full P&L accountability for a $5M subsidiary, which requires strict control
Overview: of diverse accounting, finance, and bookkeeping functions for 3 distinct entities.
                        • Utilize savvy strategic management, financial analysis, and decision-making skills to
                          overcome the operational challenges evolving as a result of a highly restrictive cash flow.
                        • Remain critically involved in quarterly consolidations/reviews, auditing, and budgeting.
                        • One of 2 professionals empowered to negotiate and authorize sales and expense contracts.
                        • Collectively direct all business administration, accounting, and human resource operations.
                        • Serve as the primary liaison with Overseas Headquarters, legal counsel, and auditors.

Contribution   • Recognized as one of 2 key executive leaders who spearheaded growth from a 10-person
Highlights: team to a 50-employee company during a highly visible start-up of the U.S. operation.
                        • Defined and implemented all internal accounting/office procedures, internal controls,
                          reporting structures, and business administration operations from ground zero.
                        • Completed detailed, time-sensitive regulatory reports during a 1997 public offering.
                        • Key contributor to the successful acquisition of a U.S. software company with critical
                          influence over the review and evaluation of the balance sheet, assets, and sales.
                        • Initiated and instituted expanded reporting protocols incorporating both domestic
                          and internationally accepted accounting principles.
                        • Researched, selected, and integrated a new accounting software company-wide, which
                          required logistical coordination and reinterpretation of in-depth financial data.
                        • Implemented a human resource management software and formulated a 401(k) program.
                        • Authored the employee handbook, which included devising governing personnel policies.

NATIONAL DEVELOPMENT CORPORATION - Builders, USA   (1984-1989)
CFO/EXECUTIVE VICE PRESIDENT OF MARKETING
Maintained a highly visible role during NDC's leveraged buyout for $100M, which
involved a capital investment of $30M by two Fortune 500 pensions funds with
Smith Investment Company acting as a fiduciary and a $70M debt financed by Parent
National Corporation. Negotiated complex joint-venture real estate transactions,
including purchase/disposition, capital improvement, refinancing, leasing, and full-
scale asset management for a diversified real estate company with a $700M portfolio
consisting of over 3.5 million sq. ft. in office space, 1.7 million sq. ft. in retail

space, 4,000+ rooms in hotel property, 1,300+ units in apartment property, 500K sq. ft. of industrial holdings, and 535 acres of raw land throughout a 26-state region.

- Successfully repaid $35M of $70M debt within one year through aggressive sale of assets, retiring the entire $70M debt within 4 rather than the projected 5 years.
- Consistently exceeded portfolio proformas during the disposition of assets.
- Reduced portfolio from 85 assets to 10 assets, liquidating commercial properties in 4 years despite the 1986 Tax Reform Act, which eliminated the tax incentives for real estate investors.
- Structured complex real estate sales transactions, which required interfacing with multiple partners of both the development company and diverse investor entities throughout the transaction.
- Assisted property managers in developing marketing packages/proformas during disposition.
- Performed asset disposition through to closing, working closely with brokerage community and independent counsel; also retained critical control over accounting and auditing functions.

SOFTWARE COMPANY - Automatetown, USA   (1988-Present)
DIRECTOR OF FINANCE
Comprehensively manage all finance and accounting functions for this $13.5M software company that targets two niche markets and employs 152 staff. Manage a $9.3M operations budget and purchase $7M in equipment and supplies annually. Handle diverse business planning, forecasting, purchasing, month-end and year-end reporting, tax preparation, financial statements, payroll, A/R, A/P, and benefits administration. Other functions include staff management and sales management. Develop alliances with value-added resellers. Personally manage all banking relations. Hired initially as Assistant Corporate Controller.

- Streamlined operations and successfully increased bottom-line profits by 150%.
- Initiated and directed a business strategy that boosted revenues by $4.5M.
- Instituted new reporting procedures and implemented strengthened internal controls.
- Negotiated a $2.5M capital infusion and improved the cash-flow management system.
- Automated accounting functions to maximize operational efficiency.
- Authored an industry-specific paper on how to maximize profits through automation.
- Conceived initial corporate policies, including human resources regulations.
- Personally advise the company President on a variety of highly confidential matters.

BIG SIX FIRM - Tax City, USA   (1989-1991)
SUPERVISING TAX SENIOR
Promoted from Tax Senior to Supervising Tax Senior within 8 months. Managed 55 state and local tax projects, including sales and use and property tax research, audit defense, refund procurement, merger and acquisition research, transaction support, and state income tax research. Supervised multioffice project teams of up to 5 staff members. Handled extensive negotiations with Tax Departments of various states pertaining to clients' tax audits.

- Designated as first State and Local Tax Specialist for the Western region who was selected to handle all phases of a new practice area start-up for this major corporation.
- Wrote client-specific sales and use tax procedure manuals; consulted clients on reducing state and local tax liabilities and assisted in multistate tax planning.
- Key participant in sales presentations, assisting in new client development and management.
- Established strong professional rapport with states' tax, audit, and legal personnel.
- Continually earned top evaluations based on outstanding management and technical knowledge.
- Co-authored an article on sales tax published in an industrial trade journal.

SOMEBODY & ASSOCIATES - Careful Calculators, USA   (1/95-11/98)
FINANCIAL ANALYST
Conducted lease analysis, project development analysis, and real estate valuation to assess
project feasibility. Researched market demands and validated income projections. Prepared
financial reports, which required transactional analysis. Prepared strategic planning, risk
management, cash-flow, performance, and financing reports. Also prepared ad hoc reports
for management at its request. Reported directly to the group Vice President.

- Key contributor in facilitating increased asset performance, which was record-breaking.
- Performed analyses for real estate acquisition/disposition and joint venture administration
  projects for a company with a diversified $550M commercial real estate portfolio.
- Selected to assist in the start-up of dedicated asset management department, which
  involved in-depth staff training and development of initial internal reporting systems.

STOCKBROKER USA - Money Manager, USA   (4/90-Present)
FINANCIAL PLANNING ASSOCIATE
Prepare partial financial plans with emphasis on estate planning or retirement planning.
Analyze diverse client profiles and outline most favorable investment options. Develop
financial plans in a timely manner. Proficient in computer-based college and retirement
planning, tax calculation, and capital-needs analysis. Other responsibilities involve
researching tax questions and preparing spreadsheet solutions. Perform recordkeeping,
including logging annual planning activity within the division, updating tax services,
and maintaining employee attendance reports.

- Initiated and designed three retirement planning computer programs that have been
  implemented company-wide in order to better identify client needs.
- Communicate with financial consultants in clarifying client information to be analyzed.
- Monitor efficiency of department hardware and software; recommend automation updates.
- Develop collateral materials for ad campaigns in conjunction with marketing personnel.
- Lecture in training seminars for new financial consultants regarding financial planning.
- Conduct branch meetings to discuss product information and maintain relations.
- Educate interns regarding the company's financial planning department.

COMPUTER USA CORPORATION - Compuville, USA   (1990-1991)
SENIOR FINANCIAL ANALYST
Employed by Financial Service Center of America with sole responsibility for handling
2 corporate divisions totalling $40 million in sales, the City Sales District and the
Mid Region Engineering District.

- Solely forecasted operating results and predicted corporate cash flow for 2 divisions.
- Personally responsible for planning budgets of $17M and $30M for respective divisions.
- Reviewed and approved advanced commission reports for 15 sales representatives and analyzed sales
  productivity; generated summary reports by salesperson to reflect monthly and YTD figures.
- Selected as the sole Financial Analyst on a special assignment involving a major account generating
  $1M in sales; worked in a team of 22 company representatives to assess client needs.
- Recognized for extreme professionalism and diplomacy in a project that involved securing highly
  sensitive and confidential financial materials; analyzed financial ratios, performance, and projections.

ELECTRONICS USA - Lightening, USA   (10/97-Present)
ACCOUNTING MANAGER
Maintain a full range of controller accountabilities for an international $38M electronics
company. Prepare all financial statements for 5 Electronics USA subsidiaries with combined
revenues of $55M. Consolidate the financials of 12 subsidiaries in order to produce
quarterly reports for the international headquarters.

Selected Highlights:
- Reorganized the department by restructuring job accountabilities, streamlining reporting processes, and reducing staff while maintaining equal productivity levels.
- Handle cash forecasting and cash management for 4 entities with $55M in revenues.
- Perform all bank-related record-keeping, which includes managing lending disbursements and intercompany fund transfers involving multiple international subsidiaries.
- Manage the accounting department, supervising a team in all general accounting functions, i.e., G/L, A/P, A/R, payroll, sales tax reporting, and bank reconciliations.
- Prepare year-end reports and respond to external auditors' inquiries.
- Serve as the company's sole contact accountable for providing first-level MIS support.

SMITH, JONES & ASSOCIATES, CPA - Calculations, USA   (1985-1989)
SENIOR ACCOUNTANT/COMPUTER CONSULTANT
Performed a wide array of accounting functions for this small accounting firm, including generating
monthly and year-end financial statements, quarterly payroll reports, monthly bank
reconciliations, and corporate and partnership tax returns. Managed a client base of 20 companies,
primarily in construction, retail, and service industries. Consulted clients on all phases of their
computer operations. Assisted in software/hardware selection, conducted end-user training, and
provided technical support. Trained junior accounting staff.

HUMAN RESOURCES

TECHNOLOGY USA - Technology, USA   (5/96-Present)
HUMAN RESOURCES GENERALIST
Comprehensively coordinate staffing efforts and deliver high-quality HR support to a 500-member
organization with key decision-making authority related to hiring and employee relations.

Accountability Highlights:
- Skillfully manage staffing during rapid growth, including multiple mergers/acquisitions.
- Develop and implement annual Affirmative Action plans for 5 locations.
- Coordinate a major outplacement effort, serving as a key resource during job search process.
- Conduct industry salary surveys to ensure competitiveness of staff recruitment efforts.
- Display keen insight and leadership in managing intern selection and supervisor assignments.
- Contribute to producing a weekly newsletter; key contact during employee relocations.

Contribution Highlights:
- Personally recruited and hired 400+ high-tech employees within a 2-year period.
- Re-engineered hiring process and reduced staffing cycle time from 30+ days to 7-10 days.
- Rolled out a referral program that raised candidate quality and reduced recruiting costs.
- Initiated and launched a Job Fair, partnering with other affiliated companies, to encourage transitioning of employees during downsizing, ultimately eliminating unemployment costs.
- Created a start-up employee filing system that produced first-time records compliance.
- Developed and implemented a forerunning, full-day employee orientation program.
- Formulated employee satisfaction survey that became the basis of a union-avoidance strategy.
- Conceived and devised management reporting and tracking tools to improve HR services.
- Earned 3 performance awards in acknowledgment of key corporate contributions.

<u>DEPARTMENT OF GOVERNMENT</u> - Secret City, USA   (1/90-Present)
BENEFITS MANAGER/ANALYST
Managed all benefits administration for a 13-state region. Skillfully determined government benefits of employees and their beneficiaries according to strict guidelines. Carefully reviewed all medical, state, and military records. Interpreted eligibility related to Government Title ABC regarding education, compensation/pension, and disability benefits. Comprehensively managed all correspondence to employees and case-related parties, (i.e., dependents, beneficiaries, powers of attorney), of crucial program changes and claims-related actions. Demonstrate excellent records management and documentation skills.

• Successfully managed up to 15,000 employee cases each month.
• Maintained total and complete decision-making authority for approving benefits.
• Expertly interpreted laws regarding guidelines specified in interagency manuals
  and remained abreast of all rapidly changing laws affecting benefits.
• Attain all production standards related to accuracy and timeliness.
• Consistently received outstanding employment ratings based on superior performance.

<u>THEME PARK USA</u> - Fun City, USA   (6/91-Present)
Good State Park (1987-1991, Part-time)
HUMAN RESOURCES GENERALIST
Comprehensively direct all recruiting efforts for seasonal personnel. Supervise a team of up to 4 Recruiters. Organize all employee relations programs as well as all recognition and incentive programs for the 4,225 seasonal and full-time staff. Experienced in all phases of staffing including interviewing, screening, hiring, and training. Plan and coordinate widely publicized company-sponsored job fairs involving on-site interviews of over 1,000 applicants. Experienced in handling all media promotions for recruiting events. Previously performed office administration functions while in a part-time position.

Accountability Highlights:
• Directed all aspects of the international program involving 212 participants, including housing/international transportation issues, itinerary development, and event planning.
• Gained extensive experience in developing a recruiting program from ground zero, i.e., creating application, hiring, and evaluation procedures as well as job descriptions.
• Facilitated the submission of 12,000+ applicants through strong recruitment strategies in 1995.
• Personally manage a $30K annual media budget related to employment opportunities.
• Possess extensive knowledge of ADA and EEOC governing regulations as well as strict employment guidelines related to the employment of minors.

Contribution Highlights:
• Conceptualized and implemented a highly successful international recruitment program that provided needed personnel resources during a critical time of low staff availability.
• Incepted an internship program through college campuses which effectively impacted the maturity level of employees based on an increase in the average age of the staff.
• Developed the 1994 Employee Handbook, which included significant department revisions.
• Established creative incentive programs to improve job performance and productivity, i.e., Quality Invitation Growth, Service Superstar, Funny Money, Mystery Guest.
• Initiated an innovative screening tool to expedite the hiring process and maximize the efficiency of the hiring process for a high-traffic department.
• Instituted a new training format which improved staff performance and productivity.

CONSUMER GOODS CONGLOMERATE, INC. - Good Food, USA   (1990-Present)
NETWORK DESIGNER/PROJECT LEAD

Perform a broad range of project management functions related to voice systems and network services for this global corporation with $12M annual telecommunication costs. Analyze facility requirements for new, expanded, and updated systems. Work with purveyors to manage the planning and design of telecommunications systems and networks.

Accountability Highlights:
- Direct hardware, software, and cabling design; submit system proposals and manage bidding.
- Develop project implementation plans including resource management and project tracking.
- Utilize acute logistical coordination and problem-solving skills to achieve project objectives.
- Analyze 200 domestic and 30 international facility networks in order to devise methods of minimizing voice and data telecommunications expenditures.
- Consistently attain rigid deadlines and budget restraints while ensuring user satisfaction.

Contribution Highlights:
- Key contributor in compiling financial analyses, preparing cost comparison reports, and negotiating a $5M telecommunications contract which ultimately reduced costs by 48%.
- Successfully designed and implemented 60 systems involving as many as 500 stations each.
- Identified voice and data solutions that decreased telecommunications costs in 1996 by $600K.
- Contributed to the research and planning of a centralized telecommunications environment.
- Developed standardized methodology for conducting telecommunications network inventories which strengthened internal control over communications expenses.

COMPUTERVILLE - Technoland, USA   (1997-Present)
Formerly Computer Information Systems
PROJECT MANAGER

Manage multiple projects which involve software installation, data import/conversion, system reconciliation, end-user training, and post-conversion testing to ensure accuracy, efficiency, and internal application acceptance of new billing software utilized by the cable industry worldwide. Collaborate with programming experts in devising technical solutions to complex problems. Formerly held a training role which required strong presentation and facilitation skills.

Management Highlights:
- Astutely manage projects which range in length from 6 to 8 weeks, requiring 90% travel nationwide.
- Expertly coordinate the efforts of up to 15 project consultants, succinctly managing all training logistics and quality control, including scheduling, agenda development, and session auditing.
- Lead weekly status meetings and evaluate projects to ensure achievement of goals and deadlines.
- Demonstrate strong consulting skills in managing projects for major clients, i.e., Big Communications, Major Movie Producer, Multimedia USA, ABC Communications, and XYZ.
- Interface well with up to 5 different project managers and up to 40 software consultants.

Training and Support Highlights:
- Facilitated application training classes for groups of up to 35, providing account-specific recommendations to maximize clients' software usage based on situational challenges or issues.
- Extend ongoing post-implementation account support to remedy problems during system roll-out, closely consulting the project team in resolving escalated technical difficulties.
- Team with in-house developers by communicating customers' requests for product enhancements.
- Display an in-depth knowledge of financial software; also completed telephony training.

Performance Highlights:
- Consistently earn the highest possible project evaluations and performance reports.
- Promoted to leadership position in less than 2 years, surpassing more experienced peers.

TELEPHONE SERVICE PROVIDERS USA - Talkie, USA   (1/95-5/97)
MANAGER, ORDER ENTRY SYSTEMS DEVELOPMENT
Directed a staff of 6 analysts serving as liaisons between branch sales offices
and system development to determine end-user requirements and develop applications.
Managed $1M budget and all phases of project design, testing, and implementation.

• Developed a GUI application as replacement for legacy order entry system, which
  significantly minimized order-entry time and system downtime.
• Successfully coordinated User Groups and JAD sessions during project development.
• Expansive knowledge of OS/2 LAN utilizing Netbios and TCP/IP protocols with
  troubleshooting expertise related to a LAN/WAN architecture.

LEGAL / PARALEGAL

Litigation Attorneys, Inc. - Fighter, USA   (11/92-Present)
ASSOCIATE
As a member of this 85-attorney firm which handles all areas of insurance defense, personal
practice emphasizes workers' compensation defense. Manage cases from initial receipt of file,
including sole responsibility for all aspects of investigation, discovery process, selection of
experts, conducting depositions, preparing pleadings, trial preparation, evaluating cases, and
settlement negotiations. Handled high-profile, large-asset, and complex cases. Train and
supervise Junior Associates.

• Possess extensive trial and appellate experience from over 75 court appearances as Sole
  Counsel within all levels of the state courts, including the Court of Appeals of Happy State.
• Successfully established a number of new revenue-producing clients through both
  formal and informal presentations.

STATE EMPLOYEES UNION - Employed, USA   (5/92-8/95)
DIRECTOR OF LEGAL AFFAIRS
Demonstrated strong litigation experience as sole representative for a labor
membership of 6,000. Managed all aspects of the case emphasizing employment issues
with full accountability for preliminary investigation, legal research, depositions,
trial preparation, drafting documents, and negotiating settlements. Represented clients
in Administrative Hearings, Superior Court, and Court of Appeals. Efficiently
managed multiple cases per month. Position requires extensive client contact.

• Successfully managed 180+ cases during tenure, including highly visible
  cases resulting in national publicity; displayed outstanding negotiation skills.
• Acquired an in-depth knowledge of employment law.

ATTORNEYS, LLP - Legaltown, USA   (1998-Present)
Commercial Real Estate Department
REAL ESTATE PARALEGAL
Provide critical legal support in facilitating commercial real estate closings which requires
interfacing closely with clients. Assemble documentation, including exhibits, sales contracts,
title information, surveys, and inspection reports. Prepare and distribute closing binders
as well as secure and submit earnest money to escrow agents. Develop outlines of critical
dates and create weekly client status reports throughout the closing process.

- Skilled in conducting detailed lease, survey, and title reviews as well as writing legal descriptions, preparing estoppel letters, drafting tenant notification letters, and reviewing warranties/service contracts.
- Utilize strong document management and organizational skills in preparing closing documents for developed and undeveloped properties with multiple tenants.
- Ensure documentation and closing procedures comply with variable state regulations.

MANAGEMENT

STEEL PRODUCTS COMPANY - Tube Town, USA (2/73-Present)
PLANT MANAGER, 6/90-Present
Comprehensively manage plant operations for a $75M stainless-steel and high-alloy pipe/tubing manufacturer with global distribution in a highly competitive worldwide industry. Direct cost management, quality control, safety program development, customer service, production, inventory control, and shipping with full P/L accountability for gross revenues of $25M. Oversee and evaluate management team of 6 that supervise 100 plant personnel. Handle interviewing, hiring, staff training, and major labor disputes. Report directly to corporate President.

Strategic Overview:
- Identify critical commodity cost-reduction areas and monitor customer delivery efficiencies.
- Examine key factors to determine pricing parameters that generate maximum revenues.
- Negotiate optimum value-added vendor/city utility contracts as a production cost-control measure.
- Review and track expenditures and A/P data to ensure operation at appropriate manpower levels.
- Analyze weekly quality reports to identify/investigate problems and initiate corrective strategies.
- Design industry-specific products based on extensive client needs analyses that boost revenues.
- Chief representative at bi-annual trade shows to initiate prospective business relationships.

Critical Contributions:
- Key contributor to securing the $1.5M+ Beer Brewer contract, the largest one-year vendor contract in company's history, which broke a 10-year volume shipping record.
- Maintain integral involvement in massive 12-month due diligence efforts for potential acquisition.
- Reduced production costs of several lines 50% by streamlining manufacturing processes.
- Successfully negotiated two 4-year union labor contracts under difficult circumstances.
- Created smooth materials/work flow during $1M renovations due to restructuring expertise.
- Achieved best safety record corporate-wide with no lost time claims for 16 consecutive months.
- Key player in final pre-arbitration phase of grievances by applying exceptional communication skills.
- Greatly improve all aspects of plant operations through effective personnel training programs.

TELECOMMUNICATIONS, INC. - Chattersville, USA (3/89-Present)
MANAGER, SMALL BUSINESS ORDER PROCESSING
Comprehensively manage 3 teams which include development, program/project management, and LAN/network administration related to Small Business segment's processing and sales support. Direct projects which impact high-volume telemarketing environment with transactions of up to 1.53M during 1994. Manage large capital budgets, $1.8M in 1994. Experienced in major system revisions utilizing strong exception management and analysis skills. Handle all staffing, strategic planning, and quality assurance functions.

- Redesigned the order processing system from a batch to a client/server environment; replacing legacy systems resulted in enhanced functionality and efficiency.
- System enhancements improved work-flow efficiencies from 80% to 99.75% and order installation from 4 days to 2 hours, resulting in net profits of $1.5M.
- Conceived and implemented a process which increased division's revenue by $2.2M/month.

<u>WORK-OUT CLUB AMERICA</u> - Fitnessway, USA   (6/95-Present)
ATHLETIC DIRECTOR

Comprehensively manage all facets of a 900-member private athletic facility. Ensure effectiveness of the front-desk operations, housekeeping, aerobics program, spa services, personal training, and tennis department. Formulate and manage a $200K budget, closely controlling all payroll, expenses, and revenues. Also, manage facility improvements.

Accountability Highlights:
- Direct a team of up to 40, handling all hiring, training, and staff development.
- Manage all athletic programming and special events, i.e., tournaments, fitness challenges.
- Assign departmental objectives and calculate performance-based bonuses/incentives.
- Creatively develop and efficiently execute off-site member development programs.
- Serve as Chair of 15-person Athletic Committee, which includes club members.

Contribution Highlights:
- Initiated and implemented major changes which doubled participation in the Aerobics program, including revising scheduling, reformatting classes, and restaffing.
- Introduced and developed a new revenue-generating Spinning/Indoor Cycling Program which required procuring equipment, creating schedules, recruiting instructors, and marketing services.
- Dramatically turned around and expanded a formerly limited pro shop to include club identity items, sports apparel, and equipment, ultimately reversing losses and achieving profitability.
- Improved operating margin by reducing variable costs such as payroll while simultaneously increasing revenues in personal training and spa services programs.

<u>LANDSCAPE ENTERPRISES, INC.</u> - Lawncare, USA   (1986-1987)
LANDSCAPE MANAGER

Directed various responsibilities related to landscape design, installation, irrigation, lighting, and maintenance for 9 commercial properties. Handled all negotiations and purchasing of plant supplies and landscape materials.

- Coordinated all staffing functions, including hiring, training, and supervising.
- Interfaced closely with property management teams to ensure operational efficiency.
- Maximized profit margins by maintaining target cost controls and budgets.

<u>INTERNATIONAL CLAIMS</u> - Investigators, USA   (1993-Present)
CLAIMS MANAGER

Supervise the investigation of potentially fraudulent insurance claims throughout a 3-state area. Manage all phases of formal investigations, including interviewing claimants and related professionals, as well as extensive records review. Interface closely with medical, legal, and law enforcement professionals. Prepare both status reports and final recommendation reports. Selected and trained as a Claims Manager. Personally analyze, price, delegate, and supervise claims cases. Oversee the efforts of 6 Claims Consultants. Report directly to the V.P. of the Eastern Region.

- Negotiate case budgets and ensure the achievement of investigation deadlines.
- Consistently exceed production quotas by up to 50% based on efficiency.
- Successfully manage up to 25 cases simultaneously with claims of up to $2M.
- Correspond effectively with 100+ insurance companies nationwide.
- Acquiring extensive knowledge of life, health, and property/casualty insurance policy guidelines and state regulations.

ABC WAREHOUSE USA, INC. - Export City, USA   (1990-Present)
OFFICE MANAGER
Perform a wide array of critical operations support functions for this international
freight forwarder which manages import/export transactions, frequently involving
high-priced, fragile merchandise. Direct a team of administrative personnel.
Coordinate international oceanic and domestic inland transportation. Perform other
internal duties including approving payables for payment, handling customer billing,
purchasing office supplies, and overseeing equipment maintenance.

• Successfully negotiate profitable transportation fees with steamship lines.
• Effectively prepare in-depth documentation according to regulations compliance.
• Secure powers of attorney and prepare extensive written correspondence.
• Interface with agents and customs brokers to ensure completion of smooth transactions.
• Contribute to business development through relationship-building with prospective clients.
• Calculate and establish customer rates, communicating regularly with international accounts.

SHIPPING INTERNATIONAL - Overseas, Europe   (1992-Present)
SUPERVISOR
Manage a wide array of operational functions for this leading commercial
shipping agency. Act as the primary liaison between operations and crew.
Interface directly with the vessel's Captain, providing ongoing management
support and strengthening agency relations. Coordinate the arrival of
cargo for multiple vessels. Also experienced with planning the discharging
and embarking of passengers. Handle aspects of billing and invoicing.

• Translate between English and Italian as well as German and Italian.
• Possess extensive knowledge of exporting and harbor operations.
• Utilize a computer in the preparation of in-depth cargo documentation.
• Demonstrate strong planning, financial, and troubleshooting skills.

HAPPY PET RETAILER - Ruff Ruff, USA   (1984-Present)
VICE PRESIDENT/GENERAL MANAGER
Comprehensively supervise a 2,000 sq. ft. retail facility with full P&L
accountability. Direct all operational and sales activities, including managing
a staff of 10 and supervising crucial animal maintenance. Affect
bottom-line profitability through highly controlled inventory and expenses
as well as creative merchandising and promotions strategies. Directed the
design and construction of a new facility from ground zero. Developed store
layout, oversaw contractors, handled all licensing, established purchasing and
merchandising plans, created grand opening promotions, and retrained staff.

• Increased total revenues by 20% with annual sales volume of up to $700K.
• Achieved a ranking of 8th out of 200 corporate locations.
• Earned an award for operating the "Best All Around" store corporate-wide.
• Received recognition for producing the highest sales volume of dog units.
• Instituted employee incentives and strategic selling/team-building techniques.
• Established excellent vendor relations with animal and dry goods suppliers.
• Possess extensive knowledge of industry-specific health and legal regulations.

<u>HAIR SALON</u> - Hairy, USA   (1993-1994)
MANAGER
Comprehensively managed a service operation which employed up to 25 staff.
Directed all daily activities including sales, customer service, purchasing,
inventory control, record-keeping, bookkeeping, cash management, reporting,
and staff supervision. Demonstrated excellent phone techniques,
troubleshooting abilities, client relations, and time management skills.

• Conducted an in-depth market analysis to assess the feasibility of
  a facility expansion subsequent to new ownership.
• Key contributor in the coordination of a major facility expansion.
• Conceived and implemented effective marketing and advertising strategies.
• Automated operations to improve efficiency with full accountability for
  selecting, installing, and managing a computer system.
• Facilitated an increase in sales and client base by 300% within one year.
• Produced an increase in bottom-line profits of 200% during first year.

<u>PRODUCT SUPPLY DISTRIBUTOR</u> - Products Village, USA   (1/93-Present)
DISTRIBUTION MANAGER
Comprehensively manage the distribution of wholesale merchandise to retailers,
end-users, and independent distributors for this supplier which generates $250K
in annual revenues. Coordinate and schedule incoming/outgoing product shipments,
manage invoicing functions, prepare and analyze sales reports. Work closely with
sales and customer service personnel. Report directly to the CFO.
Hired initially as a key staff member in the start-up of the Big City operation.

• Manage the successful and efficient distribution of up to 50 orders per day.
• Effectively control warehouse inventory consisting of 5,000 different items.
• Employ strong decision-making skills in prioritizing shipments for delivery.
• Designed and distributed advertising and promotional materials to increase sales.
• Solely responsible for negotiating delivery contracts and contracting carriers.
• Successfully planned and implemented start-up distribution operations, including staffing.

<u>TELECOMMUNICATIONS DOMINATOR</u>   (2/94-Present)
GLOBAL SERVICES PROJECT MANAGER
Serve as the lead professional coordinating the complexities of in-bound and out-bound
network services initialization for multinational accounts with a vast number of service
locations. Comprehensively plan and manage service installation, including the on-line
order issuance process, simultaneously managing multiple voice service projects.

Accountability Highlights:

• Act as a critical liaison between equipment providers and global customers'
  Project Managers and Telecommunications Specialists.
• Oversee implementation teams, monitoring engineering and operations activities.
• Effectively facilitate customer meetings to clarify project expectations, assisting
  in network designs and determining critical schedules.
• Work closely with Account Executives in order to communicate project status.

**Contribution
Highlights:**

- Consistently achieve on-time project roll-outs and above-target customer satisfaction
  ratings while ensuring project-specific quality control and contract compliance.
- Directed a successful implementation of a $3.5M 53-location voice network
  involving conversion and start-up services for a major hotel chain within 6 months.
- Managed a $2M project for XYZ, Inc. and a 3-year network contract for Broadcasters, Inc.
- Exhibit strong consulting techniques in advising clients on equipment specifications
  and advanced applications, consequently maximizing clients' existing resources.

MARKETING / ADVERTISING

<u>TELECOMMUNICATIONS, INC.</u> - Talktown, USA   (1986-1991)
DIRECTOR OF MARKETING COMMUNICATIONS
Promoted from a position as Manager of Advertising and Public Relations. Comprehensively
developed and managed international marketing, advertising, promotions, and public relations
programs targeted at third-party sales channel for this telecommunications company.
Managed a $3.5M budget and supervised a creative staff of 12.

- Developed a value-added dealer support program to foster dealer loyalty and long-term growth.
- Introduced integrated advertising, sales support, direct mail, and public relations programs.
- Spearheaded company's first marketing communications program in line with corporate goals.

<u>EXECUTIVE RECRUITERS, INC.</u> - Placement Valley, USA   (1985-1986)
DIRECTOR OF CORPORATE COMMUNICATIONS
Reorganized the corporate communications strategy toward targeted audiences for this
executive placement firm. Handled the development and planning of all events, meetings,
and trade shows. Managed press relations. Directed in-house planning/production staff.

**Selected
Highlights:**

- Created the company's first consistent corporate image.
- Instituted an employee communications program to foster company cohesiveness.
- Implemented a direct-response marketing program and lead distribution/tracking system.
- Increased the efficiency of the production operation and reduced overhead.

<u>CONSUMER PRODUCTS COMPANY</u> - Products, USA   (2/87-Present)
DIRECTOR OF CONSUMER PRODUCTS
Comprehensively manage a team of 3 Product Managers, directing all product management
functions for 30 nationally distributed product lines grossing $160M in sales. Maintain full
accountability for increasing product line profitability and proactively instituting
marketing initiatives which strategically support the sales process.

**Accountability
Highlights:**

- Identify highest profit distribution solutions based on product cost versus sales margin analyses.
- Conduct market research and acquire customer feedback which influences product enhancements.
- Create POS/in-package marketing and consumer awareness programs which accelerate sales.
- Determine slow-growth or declining products, recommending strategic solutions or modifications.
- Orchestrate preparation for the 1999 product introduction, i.e., define product offering, analyze
  consumer/marketing media research, evaluate industry trends, and plan distribution/promotions.
- Generate and manage 12 relationships for licensed products; source new licenses, negotiate
  contracts, monitor financials, prepare quarterly forecasts, and submit annual marketing plans.

Strategic Initiatives:

- Accelerated $160M revenues with a 1% annual growth rate by increasing per-order revenues and altering the product mix to incorporate higher-profit product lines.
- Created and implemented new customer ordering processes which control cost of sales.
- Formulated revenue-generating programs by defining/packaging customer partnering strategies.
- Developed an integrated product sales initiative which supports mergers and acquisitions.
- Instituted targeted marketing campaigns encompassing personalized marketing literature.
- Identified customer segmentations, enabling the cross-promotion of select product lines.
- Launched a preproposal sales process that ensures profitability of custom products using operating minimums and thresholds; delivered to sales force and track program success.

SMITH ADVERTISING - Advertisers, USA   (11/85-1/87)
ASSISTANT ART DIRECTOR
Assisted in the management of two primary accounts and performed extensive design and art direction responsibilities for client advertisements and collateral materials. Oversaw the design work of other creative staff.

- Hired initially as a Graphic Artist and promoted to the highly visible Assistant Art Director position within one year.

CABLE INTERNATIONAL - Connections, USA   (1981-1986)
MARKETING & ADVERTISING MANAGER
Reported directly to the V.P. of Marketing with full accountability for development and implementation of marketing and advertising plans. Maintained strong public relations and advertiser communications. Liaisoned with ad agencies, program suppliers, and cable company management.

- Coordinated multimedia ad campaigns which included TV, radio, outdoor, and direct mail.
- Developed media budgets as well as negotiated and purchased airtime and print ads.
- Conceived and instituted regional campaigns involving cooperative funding.

FOODS COMPANY INTERNATIONAL - Good Food, USA   (5/90-Present)
DIRECTOR, PUBLIC RELATIONS
Hired as a Manager of Public Relations and was promoted within 6 months to Director with comprehensive program responsibility and management of a $2.5 M budget. Solely authorized to act as a national spokesperson and media contact. Manage in-house staff and two public relations agencies.

- Within one year, organized and implemented the launching of 9 new product lines; scheduled press conferences, 20-city radio promos, sampling programs, and trade show events.
- Extended brand awareness by expanding celebrity testimonials through publicity campaign.
- As Supervisor of *Foods Magazine*, contributed significantly to the development of a national, corporate magazine with a $1.3M budget; manage production of premier and quarterly issues; approve all articles and direct photo shoots to ensure compliance with company philosophy.
- Coordinate event marketing and sponsorships. i.e., National Sponsor of Sports Leagues, International Sports Tournament, National Racing Teams.
- Arrange charitable events, including a sports auction, to project a favorable image.
- Acted as spokesperson and coordinated with legal department and FDA to draft communication in product recall situation.
- Developed a publicity program as a part of an integrated marketing campaign that increased units sold by 15% in 1991.
- Personally quoted in national publications, gaining widespread corporate publicity.

INTERNATIONAL CONSULATE GENERAL OFFICE - Diplomacy Village, USA   (1991-Present)
VICE CONSULATE
Create programs to entice international companies to export, relocate, or expand to U.S. markets.
Develop key marketing programs to recruit companies within target vertical industries. Utilize
intense public relations strategies to create critical organizational alliances, particularly with
the targeted American Business Groups. Educate companies abroad as well as trade-related
associations on prospective opportunities of mutual benefit to the interests of the nations.
Serve as a representative at numerous receptions and special events in order to promote
commercial and economic development through international trade.

• Travel throughout a 6-state region creating opportunities to source new products.
• Work closely with the Chambers of Commerce as a facilitator of joint presentations overseas.
• Attend trade shows to efficiently research prospective industries and companies receptive
  to benefiting from consultation and support of future international business efforts.
• In a consultative role for companies interested in expansion, identify business objectives, conduct
  market research, develop and implement multifaceted marketing strategies and programs.
• Lobby for continuous economic support of foreign companies during market penetration process.

MEDICAL / NURSING

STATE HOSPITAL - Goodtown, USA   (1992-1996)
STAFF NURSE
Provided medical care to 4-5 patients in an 18-bed adult oncology unit. Handled patient
admissions, charting, and discharging. Established rapport with patients' families and worked
cooperatively with all medical professionals providing patient care.

HELPING HAND HOSPITAL - Comfortable Care, USA   (3/92-Present)
RN Coordinator for Admissions
Consult with diverse medical personnel to organize the proper patient assignments and
utilization of beds for maximum inpatient services. Maintain all established policies and
procedures with 24-hour accountability. Supervise staff of 5. Strategically plan
facility utilization with Nursing Administration, Admissions Department, and hospital
physicians. Demonstrate excellent operations and financial decision-making skills.
Also exhibit crucial troubleshooting and problem-solving abilities.

Accountabilities: • Practiced holistic treatment approach with patients to accurately assess and address their
emotional, physical, psychological, and medical needs.
• Provided vital input during patient status meetings with cross-functioning medical professionals.
• Received excellent evaluations from both supervisors based on nursing skill levels.

MEDICAL CENTER OF AMERICA - Healthy, USA   (1998-1999)
HOUSE SUPERVISOR & RN CHARGE NURSE
Provided on-site management expertise for this acute care community hospital. Supervised
all hospital administrative duties. Provided excellent response to staff and hospital needs in
a supervisory role while managing a staff of 150 to 300. Ensured that schedules were followed
and staffing requirements were met. Rotated among the areas of OR, ER, CCU, and recovery
room PRN. Effectively managed all administrative and medical crisis situations. Maintained
direct communication with patients and families regarding terminal illnesses and accompanying
details. Served critical need as Charge Nurse on the Surgical Unit. Demonstrated vast
experience in preoperative and postoperative care.

HOSPITALS OF AMERICA - Well Wishers, USA   (1988-Present)
EMERGENCY CENTER STAFF NURSE
Provide emergency nursing care to children with a wide array of illnesses, injuries, and traumas.
Diverse duties include acute and trauma care and emergency triage. As a team leader, prioritize
care and oversee staff with a patient load of 30-50 per shift. Utilize a high level of technical
and nursing skills.

Committee Highlights:
- Home Care Education–Develop preprinted instructional materials on
  child health care and injury prevention.
- Trauma Committee–Liaison between Trauma Committee and Safe Kids program.
- Nursing Standards Committee–Developed standardized nursing careplans;
  chaired the committee in 1988.

HEALERS INC. - Feel Better, USA   (1986-1988)
CHARGE NURSE/STAFF NURSE
Reported to the Nurse Manager in this middle-management position. Worked on the
Chronic Medical Floor and supervised a staff of 15. Managed all aspects of staff
development and precepting, evaluating, and scheduling. Directed the care of children
with chronic and infectious illnesses. Promoted from a position as Staff Nurse.
Gained supervisory experience as a Team Leader.

SALES / SALES MANAGEMENT

CAR DEALER COMPANIES - Autoland, USA   (1976-1994)
COMMERCIAL SALES MANAGER
Managed all automotive product lines involving major domestic and foreign manufacturers, such
as Hot Cars, Fast Cars, and Luxury Cars, for 4 dealerships, with full accountability for commercial
fleet sales to large corporations and leasing companies. Directed, supervised, and motivated
a team of 7 sales representatives. Demonstrated strong account management and follow-up skills,
i.e., coordinating deliveries, organizing tag/title information, processing time-sensitive
paperwork, and ensuring timely customer payments. Collaboratively worked with other company
management staff regarding advertising, finance, and retail sales. Established sales quotas
and assisted sales representatives in negotiating large fleet contracts.

- Nurtured the company into becoming the largest fleet dealer in the Northeast; consistently earned
  the annual Best of the Best award for being one of the top 10 national producers.
- Developed commercial car and truck fleet business from ground zero through the utilization
  of effective cold-calling skills and critical relationship-building abilities.
- Significantly grew sales division, ultimately producing $36M in annual revenues.
- Demonstrated business acumen in inventory management, forecasting, and ordering.
- Drove revenues by establishing a unique buyer service program with major corporations.
- Conceptualized and initiated a $2M cooperative marketing program which involved
  negotiating with other dealers to market cars at fleet rates directly to corporations.

OFFICE PRODUCTS - Office City, USA   (1986-Present)
Records Management Solutions Division
SALES MANAGER
Dynamic sales achiever in the highly competitive electronic document imaging market
whose preliminary sales methods and aggressive closing techniques have repeatedly ensured
annual quotas and company objectives are exceeded. Successfully manage a Midwest

territory and direct the efforts of up to 8 Sales Representatives. Represent 12 hardware/ software manufacturers as a systems integrator with full accountability for marketing equipment, applications, and software. Report directly to the General Manager. Promoted to management from a Sales Representative position.

- Pioneered document imaging solutions, developing the company into a market leader.
- Developed an impressive client base consisting of numerous Fortune 1000 companies.
- Achieved up to 150% of sales quota with annual revenues totaling $2.7M.
- Consistently attain 100% of profit goals despite complex, in-depth sales process.
- Recognized for top sales performance by Copier USA, earning 3 Inner Circle Awards.
- Facilitated a national sales ranking in the top 5 out of over 70 dealers.
- Won 9 consecutive annual awards known as the Office Products Pleasureland Club.
- Cultivated valuable product knowledge related to microfilm and optical disk equipment.
- Judiciously review customer service strategies to ensure long-term client retention.
- Initiated creative selling solutions unique to the digital technology field.
- Successfully plan and execute sales presentations, product demonstrations, seminars, and trade shows which target senior-level executives; conduct ongoing sales training.

PREMIER HOTEL COMPANY - Luxury, USA   (10/93-4/97)
553-Room 5 Diamond Property
NATIONAL SALES MANAGER
Developed strategic sales efforts to drive revenue growth by developing the association market as well as corporate accounts nationwide. Key contributor in the collaborative formulation of competitive analyses, marketing plans, and sales budgets. Also, designated as Property Trainer for new sales managers, instructing on revenue management, internal processes, and industry-related sales strategies.

Contribution Highlights:

- Consistently ranked in company's overall top 1% of 200+ sales managers based on revenues.
- Recognized as top producer out of 5 national sales managers based on annual sales.
- Repeatedly ranked in the top 10 out of 350 sales people for cross-selling other properties.
- Managed rooms and catering revenues of $5.7M and surpassed revenue goals by 20% annually.
- Key contributor in increasing Average Daily Rate by 24%, exceeding the industry growth rate.
- Utilized strong account relationship-building skills to increase repeat customer revenues by 43%.
- One of 4 selected to implement a revenue optimization program which required the in-depth analysis of 18 properties, then recommending corrective, revenue-building strategies.
- Served as Quality Improvement Team Leader for team of 50 personnel at an assigned location.
- Developed a quality control process which resulted in improved customer satisfaction ratings by J.D. Powers and Associates from very good to excellent.
- Utilized innovative sales strategy which resulted in 49% revenue increase in a major account.

EYE CARE PRODUCTS, INC. - Eyeway, USA   (3/92-5/96)
SENIOR TERRITORY MANAGER
Managed sales of 30+ pharmaceutical products servicing a base of over 350 medical professional clients in the metro Big City, USA, area for a company with $1B+ in annual revenues. As Territory Manager, participated in ongoing Preceptorships which included observing physicians in-office, attending optometric classes, and writing product reports. Completed formal staff training at Eye Care Learningtown in industry-specific issues to achieve corporate objectives and earn Senior Territory promotion.

Key Contributions:
- Generated annual sales of $2M by aggressively pursuing current product line market shares.
- Achieved #1 product category ranking and increased market share from 27% to 52%.
- Realized 130% of product-specific sales objectives by account needs identification and service.
- Generated $200K+ in incremental revenues selling physicians 2/3 of all data service systems sold.
- Optimized corporate resources and cultivated strong relationships to expand market share.
- Developed innovative product training tools that facilitated continuous territory growth.
- Demonstrated perseverance in attaining formulary listings with 3 separate hospital accounts.

ABC SECURITIES, LP - Financial City, USA (10/95-10/96)
Previously Securities USA Corporation
INSTITUTIONAL ACCOUNT EXECUTIVE

Generated new accounts and initiated key institutional relationships for a $40M company recognized as the city's largest regional institutional bond firm. Demonstrated astute sales abilities in marketing mortgage-backed, SBA loans/pools and municipal securities to financial institutions for the nation's forerunner in the SBA market. Proven experience also includes selling distressed securities to money managers.

- Succeeded within the State of Pastureville territory, marketing to both rural and metro areas.
- Excelled in the highly competitive securities market, calling on senior management and bank officials in order to introduce a wide range of financial products and services.

RESIDENTIAL HOMES - Homey, USA (1995-1996)
SALES AGENT

Selected as one of the key on-site sales staff to promote and sell an under-construction residential development for a widely recognized real estate developer. Contributed to a variety of advertising functions, including establishing community signage. Participated in new business development activities, including handling follow-up on prospective customer leads, presenting properties, and employment feature/benefit selling strategies. Exhibited strong troubleshooting skills required to develop long-term satisfied customer relationships.

- Involved in the development of the entire marketing plan for new high-end property.
- Monitored progress during construction phase, ensuring deadlines and quality of performance.
- Successfully negotiated sales contracts, demonstrating strong client relations skills.
- Assisted in decision-making regarding proposed design of speculative homes.

STOCK BROKERS INTERNATIONAL - Moneymakers, USA (6/92-Present)
REGISTERED REPRESENTATIVE

Market a wide array of stocks, corporate/municipal/treasury bonds, mutual funds, and unit investment trusts for this full-service discount firm. Aggressively cold call and cultivate referrals through strategic marketing and client acquisition activities. Simultaneously accountable for performing all client management, sales support, and back-office administration functions.

- Developed customer base of 200+ from ground zero, producing $19.5M in assets under management, earning $150K in average gross commissions for the past 3 years.
- During tenure achieved top 1/3 ranking out a national sales force of 900.
- Establish one-on-one consultative relationships with high net-worth individuals, frequently arranging in-person customer meetings which strengthen client loyalty.
- Conduct training, extend mentoring, and effectively manage an assistant while providing leadership and support in developing a strong sales performer.

<u>CELLULAR COMPANY</u> - Talktime, USA (1/91-2/95)
DIRECT SALES REPRESENTATIVE
Established a high volume of business marketing cellular service throughout the metro
Big City area. Developed an effective lead-generation strategy targeting both individuals
and businesses. Displayed proven presentation, product demonstration, and closing techniques.
Consistently exceeded quotas related to revenues and number of new accounts.

• Generated $24K+ per month in total sales volume.
• Achieved 119% of quota in 1993 and 129% of quota during 1994.
• Earned recognition as a member of the President's Club in 1993 and 1994.
• Recognized for top performance through the 110% Club, Q1-95, Q2-94, Q3-94,
  Q4-94, Q1-93, Q3-93, Q4-93, Q3-92, Q4-92.
• Recipient of the Director's Award based on a wide range of criteria involving
  sales performance and team-player qualities, 1991.
• Awarded Sales Representative of the Month numerous times during 1991, 1992, 1993.
• Served as a member of the Employment Satisfaction Survey Team, Mailout
  Improvement Team, and PhonePac Bucks Quality Action Team.

<u>INDUSTRIAL SOUTHEAST</u> - Metalsville, USA (12/94-12/95)
Beach City Territory
SALES REPRESENTATIVE
Selected as the first sales representative to spearhead the Central Beachville sales effort.
As a territory forerunner, implemented extensive marketing and product introduction activities
including group seminars and trade show participation. Managed product/equipment inventory
and coordinated the receipt of internationally distributed products.

• Experienced in analyzing clients' needs, developing quotes, and consistently closing sales.
• Conducted extensive account education which included training on proper product usage.
• Successfully cultivated and maintained key relationships to establish a loyal customer base.
• Demonstrated strong creative abilities related to development of marketing materials.
• Grew company revenues from ground zero by excelling in a relationship-driven sales role.
• Planned and managed aggressive sales efforts at local and regional trade shows.
• Chosen to open and develop another highly visible metropolitan area due to prior success.

TEACHING / TRAINING

<u>AGENCY-OWNED HOSPITAL</u> - Helpers, USA (1/97-Present)
DIRECTOR OF STAFF DEVELOPMENT & TRAINING
Maintain a high-level management position in a 62-bed private nonprofit residential treatment
facility serving an exceptionally high-risk population, ages 9-17.

Primary
Accountabilities:
• Direct staff development, including training requirement evaluation and program development as
  well as curriculum planning, approval, and implementation of on-campus education services.
• Manage all staffing functions such as hiring of Activity Therapists/Behavioral Specialists/Trainers,
  developing multi-shift schedules for 85 direct-care staff, and authorizing/processing payroll.
• Co-facilitate new Patient Advisory Committee to enhance communication and protect rights.
• Create preventive safety programs as part of risk and behavior management staff training; also,
  as Safety Committee member, review staff/patient injury reports and define corrective actions.

- Developed and integrated special medical conditioning training for foster care programs.
- Created an education day entailing risk and behavior management, crisis debriefing, team-building, cultural diversity, psychotropic medications, and case-specific training.
- Spearheaded as well as facilitate sex education curricula designed for different age populations.
- Instituted forerunning risk management training, i.e., Prevention & Management of Aggressive Behavior (PMAB), focusing on effective crisis management using least restrictive measures.
- Mobilized staff into securing certification in the Ropes Course and the area of Lifesaving.
- Revitalized Quality Assurance Department to closely track delivery of services and quality of care.

TELEPHONE BOOK PUBLISHERS - Look Up, USA   (10/91-9/93)
COURSE DEVELOPER/TRAINING MANAGER
Managed a wide array of duties related to the development and implementation of corporately sponsored managerial training programs. Handled all aspects of training from extensive research to vendor selection to actual instruction.

- Formulated and implemented a computerized coaching guide, Corporate Observation Summary.
- Gained valuable experience in the procurement and development of software, management of field trials, and all phases of installation related to a PC network.
- Developed and integrated cornerstone post-training measurement procedures to ensure training program effectiveness.
- Initiated various management training courses on the following topics: Situational Leadership, Customer-Focused Selling, and Manager-as-Developer Coaching.
- Conducted a needs analysis assessment regarding training for Major Account Representatives.
- Conducted training for 225 Managers during 1992.

HARD COUNTY USA - Teaching City, USA   (9/79-6/87)
Simpletown High School
DIVISION HEAD/SPECIAL EDUCATION TEACHER
Created, launched, and oversaw all operational aspects of first RVI and self-contained behavior disorders programs for 150 high school-level special education students. Supervised and instructed 15 special education teachers and coordinated efforts of 5 ancillary agencies, ensuring compliance with federal, state, and local guidelines. Coordinated complex teacher-student schedules. Structured, developed, and oversaw implementation of IEPs with student-specific goals based on current functioning and testing information for a caseload of 24. Managed general budget of $25K.

- Developed and implemented strategies and behavior management plans for special needs students.
- Instructed 12-35 students, 9th-12th graders, via self-contained, resource, team-teaching delivery models.
- Coordinated staff development and licensing activities for up to 8 Special Education paraprofessionals.
- Planned and managed all aspects of staff facility, i.e., purchasing, deliveries, space design/layout.
- Created, executed, and supervised school-to-work programs.
- Initially worked in a pilot special needs regional teacher training program, 8/77-8/78.

WRITING

BIG DOG PUBLISHING - Printstown, USA   (5/94-Present)
PROJECT EDITOR
Oversee and approve all aspects of book production, including layout, editing, index development, and interior design, for literature aimed toward an extremely high-tech audience. Maintain hands-on direction for computer books on the following subjects: Internet, AutoCAD, graphics, multimedia, and networking. Serve as a key contributor

in conceptualizing book presentations/formats including identifying potential target audiences, ensuring quality of writing, and developing overall marketing strategies. Work closely with Development Editors, Technical Editors, and Copy Editors during the entire process.

• Coordinate stringent and critical deadlines, frequently involving software releases.
• Conduct final editing, emphasizing consistency and ensuring style guidelines.
• Maintain close contact with authors regarding all editing and publishing deadlines.
• Manage the production of up to 3-5 books simultaneously; length range of 250-1,600 pages.
• Initially hired as Copy Editor, demonstrating acumen in overall editorial procedure.

THE COMMUNITY CENTER - Civic, USA   (1990-1991)
STAFF WRITER
One of 4 staff members to assist in the production of organization's newsletters and newspapers for a 2,000 readership distribution. Extensively interacted with the graphic designer in collaboration of layout and artist design. Personally authored several articles involving diverse subject matter, including local news, biographical sketches, and community issues. Solely responsible for conceiving ideas, investigating topics, and composing articles.

COMMUNICATOR CHANNEL - Hearme, USA   1988-1990
Executive USA & Reader World Magazines
ASSISTANT EDITOR
Promoted from an Editorial Assistant position. Comprehensively responsible for the writing, layout, copy-editing, and proofing of 4 departments for two monthly trade publications. Assisted with editing, proofreading, and layout of all other copy. Frequently composed news features and columns. Routinely screened hundreds of press releases, selecting news bits for publication.

THE READER - Readville, USA   1987-1988
EDITOR-IN-CHIEF
Selected by the Board of Publications to develop and edit the oldest college literary magazine in the country. Solicited and composed fiction, poetry, and essay submissions. Solely handled design and layout. Worked closely with the publisher. Significantly increased campus-wide exposure.

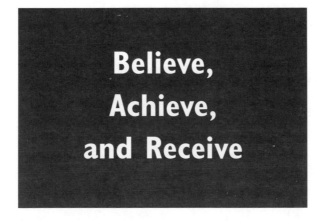

Believe,
Achieve,
and Receive

NOTES

Write down the results you want from your resume.

STEP 8

CHOOSING WHAT TO INCLUDE IN YOUR EMPLOYMENT HISTORY

Deciding what information to include in your employment history is another key area of concern, and there are many ways to approach this challenge. Remember, you want to show—as much as possible—that you have a proven record of success throughout your job history.

Since a resume is not a biography, it's not necessary to include every job you've ever held. So how do you decide? The first question to ask yourself is this: Does including information about this position provide evidence of my *overall* skills set? The jobs you held early in your career, for example, may give an employer very little information about your current qualifications, or the information may be irrelevant to the jobs you're currently seeking. In this case, it is perfectly acceptable to include brief summaries of your less relevant job experience, as in the two examples below. This will allow you more space to elaborate on the experience that is most relevant to your career goals.

▪ Additional experience includes substitute teaching for Chester County in 1989-91.

▪ Previously held a Receptionist/Bookkeeper position with a physician's office in Virginia and an English/Public Speaking Teacher position in Michigan.

Notice in the second example that no dates are included. This was done intentionally to avoid the possibility of age discrimination.

You may also want to eliminate positions you held for extremely brief periods unless they were relevant internships or summer/holiday employment characteristic of a recent graduate's background. Providing such information can work against you by suggesting that you have a tendency to "hop" from one job to another. Such information also takes up valuable space that could be used for more important information. Finally, these brief positions often don't serve as good employment references.

The logical question to ask yourself before eliminating any information is whether doing so will create gaps in your employment history. Many times this issue can be resolved simply by listing only the years, rather than the months and years, in which you were employed. Our recommendation is to eliminate full-time jobs that were held for less than a year, if at all possible.

For example, notice in the sample resume for John J. Seeker on page 85 that it shows he has held four jobs in four years. Now turn to page 86, which shows another resume for this same job seeker. Here, years, rather than months and years, are used for periods of employment. This allowed John J. Seeker to eliminate a position that was held for only six months without pointing out any gaps in employment. Also notice that the first position John held after college has been incorporated into a consolidated work statement in order to draw less attention to it. In this second version of the resume, a significantly different message is conveyed, and there is no longer the suggestion that John has held an unreasonable number of jobs in the years since he finished college. Having this new resume is certain to work to John's advantage during the screening process.

Unlike a job application, which requires that you document your employment history completely and chronologically, a resume is more of a summation of your background and highlights what you perceive to be your skills and abilities. On a job application, not disclosing every job you've held could be looked upon as misrepresentation or, at the very least, as failure to disclose information. Conversely, the goal of your resume is to present your background in the most persuasive light possible by emphasizing your skills, abilities, and credentials. However, if someone asks you for more details about your employment history (in an interview or on an application, for instance), you must provide the information he or she has requested, which may require providing specific dates of employment. After all, we are not suggesting that you misrepresent yourself in any way or that you alter your dates of employment.

Note: If you eliminate dates of employment for any positions, you may also want to omit your graduation date. This way, there won't appear to have been an employment gap between when you graduated from college and were employed in the earlier jobs.

Regardless of whether you include both months and years or years only in your employment history, it is wise to place your dates in the right-hand margin. Putting them in the left-hand margin highlights the dates of employment, rather than your employment experiences.

WORD OF CAUTION: Leaving out information from a resume is very different from including information that is inaccurate or incorrect.

> **The past reflects what you have been; the future reflects what you will become.**

JOHN J. SEEKER
123 Looking Hard Avenue
Top Dog, USA 20202
(555) 678-9101

PROFESSIONAL OBJECTIVE

Sales/Marketing position requiring a results-oriented individual with excellent leadership and interpersonal skills.

QUALIFICATION SUMMARY

- **Background includes experience involving outside sales, increasing sales and customer base, prospecting, cold calling, needs analysis, key account management, closing, negotiating, overcoming objections, exceeding budgeted sales revenues, and maintaining high levels of services.**
- **Excellent organizational, time management, interpersonal, and problem solving abilities, with proficiency in building and maintaining long-term client relationships.**
- **Computer literate (WordPerfect, Lotus 1-2-3, Excel)**

EDUCATION

SUCCESS STATE UNIVERSITY - Anytown, USA
Bachelor of Business Administration degree in Marketing

Professional Development Training
Completed ongoing training in Sales, Marketing, Product Knowledge Presentations, and Closing Techniques.

PROFESSIONAL EXPERIENCE

MEDICAL CONSULTANT
1/96-Present

AMERICAN PHYSICIANS, INC., Anytown, USA
- Increased sales throughout 3 states, calling on different medical organizations, selling permanent and temporary staffing services strictly for physicians.
- Opened new accounts by using effective cold-calling and presentation abilities.
- Perform extensive business management and development functions.
- Conduct sales presentations regarding company's services and pricing structure.
- Plan and develop advertising and promotional materials and coordinate telemarketing and mailing campaigns.

MEDICAL CONSULTANT
6/95-12/95

MEDICAL SERVICES, INC., Anytown, USA
- Assist in recruiting and placing physicians in positions with hospitals, clinics, medical groups, HMO's and other facilities throughout the United States.
- Successful in acquiring the Top Radiation Oncologist in the country as a Medical Director.
- Interact with Hospital CEO's and medical staff during scheduled visits and cold calls to assess organizational needs and personnel requirements.
- Attend national medical conventions to generate new clients.

MEDICAL CONSULTANT
5/93-6/95

PHYSICIAN SPECIALISTS, INC., Anytown, USA
- Major duties were similar to above position with Medical Services and involved extensive sales, telemarketing, and public relations while recruiting and placing physicians.
- Highly successful in achieving market penetration, including highest placement fee with the company in 5 years; attended national medical conventions.
- Generated two placements in two months, resulting in $45,000 gross revenue for company.
- Served as Regional Sales Manager for Northeast territory consisting of 9 states, achieving 50% increase in gross revenue.

ACCOUNT EXECUTIVE
8/92-5/93

SMITH-REYNOLDS, Anytown, USA
- Serviced existing accounts and generated new clients in commercial flooring.
- Prepared bid proposals in responding to building plans of general contractors.
- Negotiated and finalized contractual agreements.
- Ensured highest quality of flooring installations, bringing projects in on time.
- Performed extensive cold calls to schedule sales calls and obtain referrals.

OTHER EXPERIENCE

Golf Pro Assistant with USA Athletic Club, Fun City, USA (1985-92). Assisted Golf Officials in overseeing 1990 Major Women's Golf Tournament. Also, marketed and promoted annual Charity Golf Tournament.

PERSONAL

Born 5/29; single; excellent health.

REFERENCES

Excellent personal and business references will be provided upon request.

JOHN J. SEEKER
123 Looking Hard Avenue
Top Dog, USA 20202
(555) 678-9101

OBJECTIVE

To obtain an outside sales position where I may utilize my proven skills in all aspects of sales, marketing, business development, and account management to impact corporate growth and profits.

SIGNIFICANT SKILLS

- Proven skills in cold calling, facility assessment, needs identification, and contract negotiations.
- Demonstrated motivation and dedication pioneering a sales effort in an underperforming region.
- Developed all accounts from ground zero, strategically targeting and penetrating specific markets.
- Experienced in effectively managing the sales process from lead generation to closing.
- Demonstrate excellent skills in the areas of key relationship-building and account retention.
- Vastly experienced in interfacing closely with Presidents, CEOs, and Medical Staff Coordinators.
- Successfully target hospitals, clinics, private practices, multispecialty groups, managed care organizations, health networks, and urgent care centers in order to impact revenues.

EXPERIENCE

AMERICAN PHYSICIANS, INC. - Anytown, USA   (1996-Present)
SALES REPRESENTATIVE
Manage sales functions within a 3-state territory for a medical staffing company which includes locum tenens and permanent placement as well as credentialing verification services. Display strong proposal development, presentation, and negotiations skills necessary to solidify long- and short-term agreements ranging from one-week to 5-year staff assignments. Serve as a key liaison with in-house staffing specialists during contract fulfillment phase.

- Increased gross sales 150% within 3 months while maintaining one of the highest profit margins.
- Generated 25 new accounts and revived 10 previously deteriorated accounts within 6 months.
- Developed a key client base of national accounts and major MSOs, i.e., HMO Northwest, Major Health Services Corporation, and Major Medical Center.

PHYSICIAN SPECIALISTS, INC. - Anytown, USA   (1993-1995)
REGIONAL SALES REPRESENTATIVE
Managed a 9-state Northeast territory, promoting locum tenens with the Radiology Specialty. Quickly re-established and strengthened existing accounts, while developing 40 new accounts. Promoted to regional position based on success in the initial outside sales role.

- Consistently ranked as the #2 producer out of a national sales team.
- Earned two awards as Sales Rep of the Month; increased territory revenues by 110%.

SALES REPRESENTATIVE
Marketed permanent placement physician staffing services with an emphasis in aggressive business acquisition throughout U.S., Canada, and Puerto Rico. Fully accountable for marketing and contract development, while simultaneously managing recruitment and placement of physicians.

- Started in telemarketing role and earned two subsequent promotions in 8 months.
- Quickly achieved the highest fee in company history as a top-producing sales representative.

* Formerly an Account Executive in the commercial flooring industry with Smith-Reynolds, 1992-93.

EDUCATION

SUCCESS STATE UNIVERSITY - Anytown, USA
B.B.A. DEGREE IN MARKETING - 1992   *(Self-financed 100% of Degree)*

** During college worked as a Golf Pro Assistant with USA Athletic Club, 1986-1992.
Also assisted in managing and executing a Major Women's Golf Tournament.*

TRAINING

Completed extensive training in Sales, Marketing, and Account Management.

COMPUTER

• Windows	• Word	• WordPerfect
• PowerPoint	• Lotus 1-2-3	• Excel

QUICK RESUME-WRITING TIPS

There are three critical ways in which resumes differ from other kinds of writing.

1. Resumes never use the personal pronoun "I." It is still important to make sure the verb tense is correct, however. For example, it is appropriate to say "Manage a staff of 100" (first-person verb), but *not* "Manages a staff of 100" (third-person verb). The implied message is "I manage a staff of 100."

Below are three more examples. Each uses the present tense and first-person verbs to describe ongoing responsibilities.

■ Oversee a budget of $30K.
■ Develop a schedule for production.
■ Possess a wide variety of valuable qualifications.

In the examples below, the events being described have already taken place. Therefore, past tense verbs are used. Make sure to use the past tense even if the events you are describing occurred while you were in your current job.

■ Launched a strategic initiative that reduced costs by $30K.
■ Initiated a successful sales campaign.

2. Resumes do not use words such as "etc." and phrases such as "same as above." Although you have limited space in a resume, you don't want to seem lazy. You still need to create vivid impressions about your capabilities in the minds of potential employers. They need to know that previous employers appreciated your contributions and thought they were unique. "Etc." and "same as above" are shortcut phrases that sound vague and unoriginal.

3. Resumes don't include information that wastes valuable space. Including the following kinds of information is considered an outdated practice:

■ Your reasons for leaving a job
■ Street addresses of employers
■ Photographs
■ Your hobbies or other nonwork-related interests

Remember, every inch of space counts and, therefore, so does every word. Use every word wisely.

> Now it's time to complete several important resume-writing tasks. To begin, turn to your *Resume Worksheet* and fill out the qualifications and job history sections. You may want to refer to several worksheets you completed, such as *My Job History and Skills I've Acquired* (**WORKSHEET ONE**), *New Careers I'm Considering and the Skills They Require* (**WORKSHEET TWO**), *Developing the Key Phrases for Your Job Description* (**WORKSHEET FIVE**), *Your Work History Questionnaire* (**WORKSHEET SIX**), and *Power Words Worksheet* (**WORKSHEET SEVEN**).

If you will be writing a
chronological resume: Complete the job description section using the information you wrote down in earlier exercises, including your key phrases and the job descriptions you selected. You may also want to look at more samples of chronological resumes. Several are shown in the **Resume Library** section of this book, beginning on page 145.

If you will be writing a
combination resume: Complete the qualifications section of your **Resume Worksheet** using the skills/traits and key skills phrases you identified during the earlier exercises. Then complete the job description section of your **Resume Worksheet**. The combination resumes in the **Resume Library**, beginning on page 145, as well as the key phrases and job descriptions you selected in earlier exercises, should greatly assist you.

If you will be writing a
functional resume: Complete the qualifications and job history section of your **Resume Worksheet** using the skills/traits, key skills phrases, key job phrases, and job description information that you created during the earlier exercises. Remember, your bulleted items should include many examples of your work-related accomplishments and contributions to the companies where you have worked. Alternatively, you could include transferable skills you've gained through your work or other skill-building experiences. The sample functional resumes in the **Resume Library**, beginning on page 145, should assist you in formulating your bullet points. We suggest you group your skills and accomplishments into categories before writing these items.

NOTE: Recent graduates should refer to the section of the Resume Library, beginning on page 145, containing resumes for entry-level positions that include formatting and content ideas.

STEP 10

PRESENTING YOUR EDUCATIONAL BACKGROUND IN THE BEST LIGHT

How carefully an employer will evaluate your educational background will vary depending on whether the job you're seeking requires specific academic training. Many people assume that they must list their educational credentials, such as degrees earned or schools attended, at the top of their resume, right after their objective, mission, or career summary. This is not always necessary. Bear in mind that employers often scan the first half of a resume quickly before deciding whether to continue reading. Consequently, you want the material at the top to pique the employers' interest so they will not only continue reading but invite you in for an interview.

Before deciding whether to place your educational background at the top of your resume, answer the following questions:

1. Is academic training a fundamental qualification for the jobs you're seeking?
2. Are you a recent college graduate?
3. Do you have an advanced degree or very specific educational training as opposed to a lot of related work experience in the profession you're pursuing?

If your answer to any of the questions above is "yes," then you probably need to emphasize your academic background. Highlighting your education at the top of your resume, after your objective, mission, or career summary, is a good way to do this.

If you are a recent graduate, for instance, your academic background has given you the training that will enable you to excel in your chosen career. In this case, the example below is an effective way to present this information. To highlight it, you will want to include this information at the beginning of your resume.

UNIVERSITY OF CHICAGO - Chicago, IL
B.A. in Journalism, Minor in Marketing - 1998

The next example illustrates an ideal way to present your educational background if you have recently completed education or training relevant to the jobs you're seeking. In this case, the paralegal training is listed above the graduate and undergraduate degrees because it is most relevant to the job seeker's current career pursuits.

PARALEGAL TRAINING SCHOOL OF AMERICA -
Los Angeles, CA
Lawyer's Assistant Certificate, Litigation,
12/94 (A.B.A. approved)

VIRGINIA COLLEGE - Morgantown, WV
M.A. in English Literature, 8/85
(oral and written thesis required)
B.A. in English Language and Literature, 8/83

If you are enrolled in or recently completed a graduate program that relates more closely to your career goal than does your previous work experience, we recommend that you list your graduate and undergraduate degrees at the top of your resume. Your graduate degree should be listed first and your undergraduate degree second, as shown in the example below.

STATE UNIVERSITY OF NEW YORK - Buffalo, NY
M.B.A. in Management - 1997-Present
B.A. in Economics - 1995

If, on the other hand, you have completed some graduate coursework but don't intend to complete a degree, we recommend you present your education in a way similar to the example below. If you've been employed for any significant amount of time, however, you will probably want to put your education section at the end of your resume. This lets employers know you took some graduate courses, but it also shows that the skills you gained through your work experience far outweigh your educational background.

UNIVERSITY OF ALABAMA — Tuscaloosa, AL
B.A. in Political Science - 1992
* Completed graduate coursework in Economics.

If you started but did not complete a degree or certificate program, there are ways to deal with this. First, as shown in the following example, you can list your major or area of study, followed by the last year when you were a student. In many cases, an employer will mistakenly interpret this as your date of graduation, which can only work in your favor.

DUKE UNIVERSITY — Durham, NC
Majored in Business, 1989

Second, as shown in the following example, you can list the years you attended school. This option is considerably less effective, however, since an employer will know immediately that you didn't complete the requirements for a degree if you attended for fewer years than are typically required.

DUKE UNIVERSITY — Durham, NC
Business Studies, 1987-1989

It is also important to give some thought to whether or not to include graduation dates. These serve as an easy way for an employer to calculate your age, which could be used to discriminate against you. Certainly, if you are older than 45, it may be more effective simply to eliminate all dates from the education section.

If you did not attend college or have a general education degree (GED), it would probably be a good idea to eliminate the education section entirely. Not having an advanced degree may be viewed as a weakness, and your resume is the place to highlight only your strong points. However, don't let your level of education be an excuse for not pursuing the job of your dreams. Many employers will consider you for employment without a degree if you possess skills that outweigh their educational requirements. Remember, your goal in sending an employer your resume is only to get an interview. Once you are face-to-face with a potential employer, many factors will contribute to whether or not you are hired. These include your personality, your employment record, and your ability to fit into the organization. Use your resume to highlight your other assets and deemphasize your educational weaknesses. Once you get the interview, focus on your strengths and on projecting confidence in your ability to learn. After all, that is what education is all about!

Complete Worksheet Eight, entitled *My Educational Background*, on page 141, which will help you write the education section of your resume. Then complete the education section of your *Resume Worksheet*.

STEP II

PLANNING YOUR CATEGORIES

Each person's work history and background is unique, and you may want to include information in your resume that someone else may not choose to include in his or her resume. The challenge is to figure out how to group this information into logical categories so that employers can quickly locate the information they believe is most pertinent. For instance, in addition to obvious **Employment** and **Education** sections, you might want to include categories such as **Internships**, **Special Projects**, **Coursework**, **Civic/Community Activities**, **Honors/ Awards**, **Languages**, **Licenses**, **Certifications**, **Professional Development Training**, **Computer Skills**, **Campus Activities**, **Affiliations**, and **Travels**. Including these categories enables you to highlight critical skills and credentials or simply to provide a more comprehensive professional profile.

Before you can prioritize your categories, you must consider the "audience" for your resume. For example, in most cases, a Professional Development Training category would deserve much greater attention and higher priority than a Travel category. However, if you were applying for a position that involved extensive international travel, giving the Travel category higher priority might very well be warranted. Similarly, if you are just finishing college, you might want to include a Special Projects category. This would be an excellent way to provide information on related experience gained through academic studies. Again, the challenge is to learn as much as possible about the requirements potential employers are seeking and to tailor the resume categories accordingly.

Some employers value the information included in supplementary categories more than others. In any case, you probably won't want to include every category listed above. As a rule of thumb, we advise against adding pages to your resume for the sole purpose of including supplementary categories. Remember, the challenge is to use your space wisely and to include information potential employers will want to read.

A word of caution: We strongly discourage you from including personal information, such as your height, weight, age, hobbies/interests, or marital status. Why, you ask? Imagine, for instance, that one employer might prefer to hire a married person because, in her mind, being married is a sign of stability. Another employer, however, might prefer to hire a single person in the hope that she might be willing to work 70 hours a week. Since equal opportunity laws have made it illegal to ask questions about your marital status in an interview, volunteering such information on a resume is never a good idea. In fact, any highly subjective information could be used to screen you out of, rather than into, the interview process.

That's why we also advise against including information about your political or religious affiliations. The risk of discrimination is simply too great. Laws were developed to provide equal opportunity for all; don't allow employers to use their subjective biases against you.

Before you input your resume into a computer, be sure to allow space to include the categories future employers might think are relevant.

The *Category Planning Questionnaire*, Worksheet Nine, on page 142, will assist you in deciding what supplementary information to include in your resume. Complete the exercise, then prioritize the information on the questionnaire from most important to least important based on what you think makes you most marketable. Keep in mind that information you think is the least important should be placed at the very end of your resume or omitted altogether. Next, turn to your *Resume Worksheet*. Transfer the information you think is relevant from the *Category Planning Questionnaire*.

> # You are like a work of art, each brush stroke is an important part of what created the masterpiece.

DETERMINING THE RIGHT LENGTH FOR YOUR RESUME

"How long should my resume be?" It's a popular question. On the one hand, we live in a "microwave society" where "less is better." On the other hand, given the importance of your resume to your job search, it may be necessary to describe your qualifications and experience in some detail. In this case, you may need more than a one-page resume. Nevertheless, it's still important to describe your background concisely and to omit irrelevant information.

Before making a final decision about the ideal length for your resume, answer the following questions:

- **Does your job experience exceed 10 years?**
- **Does your earlier job history provide evidence of your total skills set?**

If the answer to both these questions is yes, then a two-page resume is probably appropriate.

Before making your final decision, ask yourself this question:

- **Can I highlight the most impressive points about my qualifications and experience in one page?**

If the answer to this question is also yes, then a one-page format may be suitable.

As in other decisions you have made about your resume, it is important to consider your audience when deciding how long your resume should be. For example, if you have 20 years of work experience but only 8 years in positions that are relevant to your current career, you don't necessarily need to include anything about the 12 years of unrelated experience. At the same time, you don't want to minimize the value of providing evidence of a steady job progression and including enough detail so that the reader understands the value of your earlier career endeavors. Readers will spend very little if any, time reading between the lines of your resume for information that is merely implied. You must tell them what you want them to know about you. If two pages are required to sell yourself fully, then take the time to draft a two-page resume. Just remember, "short is sweet," but sometimes "longer can be stronger."

Write down the top 10 reasons why someone should hire you.

STEP 3

MAKING YOUR RESUME VISUALLY APPEALING

As you should realize by now, having a resume that is well organized and well written is extremely important. But, equally important, your resume needs to be error-free and visually appealing. Would you want to read a resume that looked busy or confusing? Would you read a resume that was filled with typographical errors, or one that used headings and a typeface that was hard to read? Busy employers certainly don't. Visual appearance will never compensate for a poorly written resume, but a combination of dynamic wording and aesthetic appeal can optimize its impact.

Before the computer revolution, most people typed their resumes and then photocopied them. A few people gave their resumes to printers who typeset and print (or offset) them at considerable cost. Today, there are other options, and they'll save you both time and money.

The most widely accepted way to produce a resume today is on a computer. Computers allow you to produce a sharp, clean, quality resume that can be stored and easily customized, revised, or printed at any time.

There are many other advantages to preparing a resume on a computer. One is that you'll have many choices in the typefaces or fonts you use. This doesn't mean that every font is acceptable, however. Most important, the font should be easy to read and professional looking. Your resume is not the place to experiment with artsy or cute fonts. Aim, instead, for one with a polished-looking appearance.

Some people use a font called Courier simply because it's the default font on their computers. Courier has the appearance of typewriter print and for this reason gives a resume a somewhat old-fashioned appearance.

This is an example of Courier.

We strongly recommend that you use Times Roman or Helvetica. Both fonts are easy to read and professional looking.

This is an example of Times Roman.

This is an example of Helvetica.

Another advantage to preparing your resume on a computer is that you'll have a wide range of choices in font sizes—from very small to very large. You want to choose a font size that is easy to read and looks sharp.

We suggest that the text of your resume be in a 10- to 12-point typeface.

This is an example of 10-point Times Roman.

This is an example of 12-point Times Roman.

Your name and address should stand out at the top of your resume. For this reason, we recommend you use 13- to 15-point type for the header, or copy at the top.

This is an example of 13-point type.

This is an example of 14-point type.

This is an example of 15-point type.

In addition to a wide range of possible typefaces, there are a variety of papers on the market. We recommend that you use 25% cotton-based paper in a neutral or pale tone. These include natural, ivory, white, gray, beige, or light blue. The words, not the paper color, should get an employer's attention. When in doubt, err on the side of being conservative.

At this point you should have completed all of the workbook exercises and your **Resume Worksheet**. Now would be a good time to design your resume on a computer, if you have not already done so, using the CD-ROM version of the workbook. Use the word-processing soft-ware of your choice. Bear in mind that you may need to revise the information on your **Resume Worksheet** to fit a one- or two-page format. It may be necessary to condense thoughts or to reword sentences to maximize the amount of information you can include.

If you don't have access to a computer, you may want to contact a resume service or copy center for assistance in putting your resume into its final form. There are many such centers across the country, and many are open 24 hours a day.

We strongly recommend that you read Step 14 on proofing your resume before printing it out. We also urge you to complete the next sections of the workbook, on cover letters, salary information, references, and thank you notes, after you have prepared your resume.

REMEMBER:
Resumes Are About
First Impressions

STEP 14

PROOFING YOUR RESUME

The age-old adage "To err is human" is best ignored when it comes to writing your resume. In most cases, "forgiveness" is not forthcoming. The best rule of thumb is to consider errors absolutely unacceptable.

You may be wondering why having an error-free resume is so important. Remember, your resume is your calling card or tool for getting an interview. If your resume has typographical or other errors, the message you'll convey to employers is that you're not very conscientious. As a result, many employers will automatically disqualify you. In a competitive job market, there is no shortage of qualified applicants, and some will have strong qualifications and error-free resumes. Naturally, these are the applicants who will be selected for interviews.

We recommend the following tips for making sure your resume is error-free:

Run a computer spell check on your resume.

Remember, though, a computer spell check cannot distinguish between *there, they're,* and *their,* so be careful about using the proper words and correct grammar.

Check the names of people, companies, and other proper names, as well as phone numbers and dates, very carefully for accuracy.

Remember, a computer spell check can't tell you the correct spelling of proper names, such as the companies you worked for, and an employer will never be able to call you if your phone number is wrong. If you include a list of references, be especially careful that the names and phone numbers are correct.

Ask at least three people to proof your resume.

Ask them to review it for the content as well as for mistakes in spelling, grammar, syntax, and punctuation.

PROOF, REPROOF, AND PROOF AGAIN BEFORE PRINTING YOUR RESUME.

NOTES

Write down the names of at least 5 companies you would like to work for. Then ask yourself how

you can get your resume in the hands of key decision-makers.

STEP 15

COMPOSING YOUR COVER LETTER

An effective cover letter can have considerable impact on your job search. For instance, when one job applicant we know, named Susan, walked into an interview, the employer began by pointing to her cover letter and said, "This is the reason you're here." The interviewer went on to say, "I had not intended to interview any more candidates—until I read your cover letter. It convinced me to meet with you." Shortly after the interview, Susan was offered the job.

Having an excellent cover letter obviously paid off for Susan. It can pay off for you, too.

You may be wondering why it's even necessary to write a cover letter. "After all," you're thinking, "my resume says everything there is to know about me." In fact, there are five good reasons why a cover letter is essential:

1. A cover letter gives you a chance to introduce yourself to an employer and provides an excellent opportunity for you to market your skills and qualifications.

2. Since employers expect to see a cover letter with a resume, not including one is considered poor etiquette and shows a lack of professionalism.

3. Because a cover letter, unlike a resume, is a narrative, it can be highly descriptive and include persuasive sentences aimed at evoking emotion and a positive response in a reader.

4. A cover letter gives you a chance to describe how you could contribute to a company in the future. A resume simply highlights your contributions in the past.

5. A cover letter is extremely flexible because it can easily be adapted to fit different job opportunities.

Your overall goal in writing a cover letter is to clarify your reason for sending an employer your resume, provide additional information about yourself, and ask for an interview. At the same time, you want to make the employer eager to learn more about what you have to offer.

Your letter should have a confident tone and project a feeling of self-worth. This is definitely not the place to sound humble or unsure of yourself. You want to promote yourself in the most positive light possible.

Like a resume, a cover letter contains several critical components. Typically, these include: the **introduction**, the **body of the letter**, and the **closing**.

Introduction: The purpose of your introduction, the first section of your cover letter, is to clearly state your reason for sending the employer your resume. If you are applying for a specific position, be sure to include this information in the opening sentence. As in the example on page 100, this is also the place to highlight your key areas of expertise and to state that you are enclosing your resume.

Sample introduction:

In response to your advertisement for an engineering position, I have enclosed a copy of my resume. It briefly outlines my 10 years of experience in the mechanical engineering field.

Body of the Letter: The second component of a cover letter is the body. Typically, it contains one or two paragraphs of four to five sentences each. This is where you summarize your professional qualifications. The goal is to highlight your strongest assets and accomplishments so that the employer will want to interview you, even before reading your resume.

Although information in your resume and in your cover letter will sometimes overlap, ideally your resume and cover letter should complement one another. In general, your resume should contain far more detailed information than your cover letter, which primarily includes broad statements about your background. Notice the use of broad statements in the following example.

Sample body of a cover letter:

As evidenced by my consistently excellent performance in sales, I have significantly contributed to my employer's revenue growth and exceeded all corporate objectives. During my career with two highly successful companies, I have demonstrated an outstanding performance in all aspects of the sales process. Not only am I experienced in stimulating new revenue through prospecting and cold calling, but I have also excelled in positions requiring strong territory management and customer service skills. As a result, I have clearly established a track record and capacity for exceeding quotas, increasing sales volume, and raising profit margins. Given the opportunity, I am certain to become a valuable addition to your sales force.

It is sometimes tempting to omit information from a resume and include it in a cover letter instead. We do not recommend this since some interviewers will not read your cover letter in its entirety. Also, an employer is less likely to store a cover letter than a resume in a database.

Closing: The third component of a cover letter is the closing paragraph. This is where you request an interview, much as a salesperson asks for an order. As shown in the sample below, always assume that the employer will respond positively to your request and thank him or her in advance for granting you the interview.

Sample closing:

Realizing that I will become an immediate asset to your company, I am requesting a personal interview to discuss my qualifications in greater detail. Thank you in advance for your time, and I look forward to speaking with you soon.

TIP: Write your cover letter after you've written your resume. It's much easier to write broad sentences after composing a highly detailed resume.

One of the reasons many people don't like to write cover letters is that writing a great letter takes considerable energy. One solution is to write a standard cover letter and then personalize it as necessary. Your standard letter would include a general description of your skills and abilities. It would also highlight the most marketable aspects of your background.

The primary advantage to writing a strategically designed, well-thought-out standard cover letter is that you have to write only one great letter rather than many. This helps to:

■ Increase your response time to classified ads.

■ Reduce the chance of errors.

■ Eliminate procrastination, which results in a more aggressive job search.

A sample of a standard cover letter is shown on page 102.

Once you've created a standard cover letter, all you'll have to do is modify it slightly the next time you want to send your resume to a prospective employer. At the very least, you'll need to indicate the position you're interested in and insert the company's name. You don't want the employer to assume your letter was part of a mass mailing. Including the company's name personalizes your letter while making it appear as if it was written with the employer's company in mind. An example of how to a personalize a cover letter is shown on page 103.

Turn to the **Cover Letter Library**, beginning on page 255, which contains sample cover letters for a variety of positions. Take time to review these letters, even if you're not pursuing jobs in these areas. It will help you considerably when you write your own cover letter.

Using what you have learned about cover letters, you should now be ready to complete Worksheet Ten, the *Cover Letter Worksheet,* on page 143. Strive to describe your qualifications in the most positive, enthusiastic, and results-oriented way possible.

Remember, when it comes to getting a job, there are no prizes for second place. Your cover letter is a critical part of the job search process. It can have a powerful impact on your success in securing interviews. Without an effective cover letter, you may have difficulty getting an interview, and without that, it's tough to get a job.

REMEMBER:
Strangers only know about you what you bother to tell them.

SARAH J. SEARCH, CPA
123 Job Hunting Lane
Big Time, USA 10101
(444) 567-8910

Due to my keen interest in your organization, I have enclosed a resume that highlights my numerous qualifications and my thirteen years of proven accounting experience.

Please note that as a successful accounting professional, I offer a diverse range of practical experience that I am certain would be of significant value to your company. As the Owner of a financial consulting business, I have secured a broad base of clients, ranging from a real estate construction company to an international distribution firm. Throughout several long-term consulting relationships, I have performed a wide array of services, including financial reporting, payroll management, operations budgeting, projections/forecasting, procedures development, cash flow analysis, and full-charge bookkeeping. Not only have I demonstrated an undisputed ability to assess an existing operation's financial efficiency, but I have consistently impacted my clients' and employers' overall accounting procedures in a number of crucial and profit-enhancing ways.

Frequently, I have offered computer automation expertise that has clearly improved overall corporate accounting capabilities and financial effectiveness. Similarly, on many occasions, I have conceived and instituted policies and procedures that enhanced staff productivity while reducing fixed operating costs. Not only am I a highly committed professional who excels in multifaceted work environments, but I also possess outstanding organizational and prioritization skills that have ensured maximum levels of efficiency.

During my professional career, I have acquired in-depth accounting, financial management, and investment management experience in a number of highly visible roles within diverse industries and for multimillion-dollar companies with both national and international scope. My flexibility in quickly assimilating into an organization and rapidly contributing to the company's bottom-line profits is evidenced throughout each of my professional affiliations. I certainly believe that my unique set of qualifications may be fully utilized in an organization that values professionalism, integrity, quality performance, and dynamic leadership skills.

Confident that resumes provide only a brief overview of an individual's entire skills set, I am interested in arranging a meeting where we could discuss our mutual goals in some depth. Thank you in advance for your time in reviewing my credentials. I look forward to speaking with you soon.

Sincerely,

Sarah J. Search, CPA

SARAH J. SEARCH, CPA
123 Job Hunting Lane
Big Time, USA 10101
(444) 567-8910

Date

Name of Hiring Official
Title of Hiring Official
Company Name
Company Address
City, State Zip

Dear Name of Hiring Official,

Due to my keen interest in the (Job Title You Are Pursuing) position, I have enclosed a resume that highlights my numerous qualifications and my thirteen years of proven accounting experience.

Please note that as a successful accounting professional, I offer a diverse range of practical experience that I am certain would be of significant value to your company. As the Owner of a financial consulting business, I have secured a broad base of clients, ranging from a real estate construction company to an international distribution firm. Throughout several long-term consulting relationships, I have performed a wide array of services, including financial reporting, payroll management, operations budgeting, projections/forecasting, procedures development, cash flow analysis, and full-charge bookkeeping. Not only have I demonstrated an undisputed ability to assess an existing operation's financial efficiency, but I have consistently impacted my clients' and employers' overall accounting procedures in a number of crucial and profit-enhancing ways.

Frequently, I have offered computer automation expertise that has clearly improved overall corporate accounting capabilities and financial effectiveness. Similarly, on many occasions, I have conceived and instituted policies and procedures that enhanced staff productivity while reducing fixed operating costs. Not only am I a highly committed professional who excels in multifaceted work environments, but I also possess outstanding organizational and prioritization skills that have ensured maximum levels of efficiency.

During my professional career, I have acquired in-depth accounting, financial management, and investment management experience in a number of highly visible roles within diverse industries and for multimillion-dollar companies with both national and international scope. My flexibility in quickly assimilating into an organization and rapidly contributing to the company's bottom-line profits is evidenced throughout each of my professional affiliations. I certainly believe that my unique set of qualifications may be fully utilized in an organization that values professionalism, integrity, quality performance, and dynamic leadership skills.

Confident that resumes provide only a brief overview of an individual's entire skill set, I am interested in arranging a meeting where we could discuss our mutual goals in some depth. Thank you in advance for your time in reviewing my credentials. I look forward to speaking with you soon.

Sincerely,

Sarah J. Search, CPA

NOTES

Take a moment to celebrate your success in writing your own resume and cover letter.

Now you are ready to launch a more powerful job search.

Describe below how you feel about yourself after completing the process.

STEP 16

DECIDING WHAT SALARY INFORMATION TO DISCLOSE

Another question that may concern you is whether to disclose your salary history or salary requirements in your resume or cover letters. Before even discussing the pros and cons of doing this, it's important to understand the difference between these two terms. Your **salary history** is a chronological listing of how much you were paid in your previous jobs and, if you're currently employed, how much you are paid now. Your **salary requirement** is what you would need to be paid to accept another position.

We strongly advise against including any salary information in your initial correspondence with an employer. It may very well work against you. In some cases, you'll want to learn more about a position before deciding how much you think you should be paid. In other cases, you'll want to use the job interview as an opportunity to convince the employer of your worth. If you've already indicated your salary requirements, you significantly limit your ability to negotiate during the interview process and can eliminate yourself as a potential candidate.

Some classified ads state that you must include your salary requirements when you apply for the positions being advertised. Employers do this to help them prescreen candidates. If your demands are too high, they won't interview you. There is no need to include your salary history *unless* the ad states that "no one will be considered" without it. We suggest that, when-

ever possible, you politely request in your cover letter, as in the samples below, that you would like to discuss your salary requirements in a personal interview:

SAMPLE 1: I would prefer to discuss my salary requirements and related qualifications in our personal meeting.

SAMPLE 2: Realizing the confidential nature of salary information, I would like to meet with you personally before providing this information.

Although there is a risk in not disclosing salary information, discussing the topic face-to-face in an interview generally gives you more chance to negotiate and ultimately get a better salary and benefits package overall.

For those who feel they must include a brief salary history in their cover letters, here are two examples of ways to do so:

SAMPLE 1: My current compensation package includes a $30K base and a 10% annual bonus.

SAMPLE 2: My salary requirements would range from $36,000 to $40,000 annually depending on the other benefits included in my compensation package. *[Bear in mind that the lower figure is the one the employer is likely to focus on, so choose this figure carefully.]*

Turn to page 106 to review a sample of a more in-depth salary history.

JOHN J. SEEKER
123 Looking Hard Avenue
Top Dog, USA 20202
(555) 678-9101

Salary History

ABC Restaurant

Starting Salary: $26,000
Ending Salary: $55,000
Bonus Potential: $5,000
Total Package: $60,000

American Management Group

Starting Salary: $60,000
Ending Salary: $60,000
Bonus Potential: $10,000
Expenses: $5,000
Total Package: $75,000

Nation's Best Restaurants

Starting Salary: $73,000
Ending Salary: $100,000
Car Allowance: $6,000
Annual Expense Account: $12,000
Food Allowance: $15,000
Bonus Potential: $40,000
Total Package: $173,000

∎ **Negotiated new salary**
  (after company buyout)
  Base - $150,000
  Bonus - $75,000
  Car Allowance - $10,500
  Food Allowance and Expenses - $36,000
  Total Package: $271,500

∎ **Additional Benefits**
  Medical, Life, and Dental Insurance
  Stock Options - 2,500 Shares
  6 Weeks Vacation

STEP 17

PREPARING A REFERENCE LIST

Many of you have probably written or seen resumes that included a line that said "References available upon request." What does this really mean? According to some employers, very little. Some people believe it's unnecessary to include this phrase since it is standard practice to provide references when requested by a prospective employer.

Conversely, some resume experts say that by including the brief statement "References available upon request," you are simply alerting an employer that references are not enclosed. Others think that including the phrase is like saying "the end," since the statement is usually at the end of a resume.

Everyone agrees, however, that including a statement about references is certainly not essential. After all, space on a resume is limited. In the final analysis, it really doesn't matter; it's up to you whether to include a statement about references or not.

We advise against including a list of references in your initial correspondence—unless specifically asked to do so. Typically, references are presented to a potential employer during the interview process. It is usually requested by employers and is usually a sign of their extreme level of interest. Should you choose to include one, we suggest that you list your references on a separate sheet.

Ideally, your reference list will include three to five employers or other professionals who have knowledge of your background and expertise. Personal references are also acceptable but less preferable.

Turn to page 108 to review a sample reference list.

NOTE: Be sure to notify your references that you are including their names on your reference list. This will ensure they are prepared to answer questions about you and to reiterate all the reasons you are a valuable employee.

SARAH J. SEARCH
123 Job Hunting Lane
Big Time, USA 10101
(444) 567-8910

References

∎ Mr. John Doe (Current Supervisor/Mentor)
Senior Vice President
ABC University
123 Academic Road, NE
Schoolville, USA 11221
Office: 222-333-9090

∎ Ms. Jane Doe (Current Colleague)
Program Chair
The College for Success
345 Smart Road, NE
Richtown, USA 34568
Office: 231-444-0002

∎ Mr. James Doe, Ed.D. (Mentor/Consultant)
Associate Professor
Bright University
Department of Counseling Services
University Center
Sunshine, USA 33383
Office: 555-669-0000

∎ Ms. Jenny Doe (Former Colleague)
Associate Professor
Hard Knocks Community College
555 Challenging Drive
Hardworking, USA 33212
Home: 111-909-8888

STEP 18

WRITING
THANK YOU NOTES

Sending a thank you note after an interview is extremely important for several reasons. In addition to being a courteous gesture, it provides an excellent opportunity to reiterate why you are the ideal candidate for your desired position. It also gives you another chance to address any objections the employer might have raised during your meeting.

Always send your thank you notes one to two days after your interview. Although it is acceptable to hand-write them, it is more professional to word-process a letter.

A well-written thank you note allows you to leave a positive impression long after your interview is over. Don't overlook this golden opportunity.

Page 110 shows a sample thank you note.

SHORT STORY: A job candidate without industry experience was offered a job with a Fortune 500 company over a candidate with industry experience because of the quality of her follow-up correspondence. The company said that if the candidate approached the job with as much persistence and professionalism as indicated by her thank you notes, she would be a huge success in the company.

SARAH J. SEARCH
123 Job Hunting Lane
Big Time, USA 10101
(444) 567-8910

May 26, 1999

Mr. John Doe
President, National Sales Manager
ABC Mutual Fund Inc.
Mutual Fund Trade Center
Big Apple, USA 10011

Dear Mr. Doe,

I wanted to take a moment to express my sincere appreciation for your valuable time in meeting with me to discuss career opportunities with ABC Mutual Fund Inc. It was a pleasure meeting you, and I certainly value your insightful forecast regarding the changes we can expect in the industry.

After discussing the sales position in great depth, I am convinced that I would become a highly productive member of your sales force. As you know, not only do I possess nine years of industry experience, but I possess valuable industry contacts. I would be extremely proud to represent your organization in Northern Sunnystate or in any number of territories throughout the U.S.A. In short, I am confident that my wholesaling background and dynamic sales skills will provide the necessary framework for my future success with your excellent company.

Once again, thank you for your time and consideration. I look forward to possibly becoming a part of your team.

Sincerely,

Sarah J. Search

MY JOB HISTORY AND SKILLS I'VE ACQUIRED

Tear out and fill in the worksheet by writing down, in reverse chronological order, each position you have ever held and the skills you gained in each job. Then write down several phrases that describe the skills you possess. Refer to the *Skills Inventory* on pages 2-11 to assist you in completing the exercise.

JOB TITLE: _____

SKILLS/TRAITS: _____

_____

_____

PHRASES: _____

_____

_____

_____

_____

JOB TITLE: _____

SKILLS/TRAITS: _____

_____

_____

PHRASES: _____

_____

_____

_____

_____

JOB TITLE: _____

SKILLS/TRAITS: _____

_____

_____

PHRASES: _____

_____

_____

_____

JOB TITLE: _____

SKILLS/TRAITS: _____

_____

_____

PHRASES: _____

_____

_____

_____

JOB TITLE: _____

SKILLS/TRAITS: _____

_____

_____

PHRASES: _____

_____

_____

_____

JOB TITLE: _____

SKILLS/TRAITS: _____

_____

_____

PHRASES: _____

_____

_____

_____

JOB TITLE: _____

SKILLS/TRAITS: _____

_____

_____

PHRASES: _____

_____

_____

_____

JOB TITLE: _____

SKILLS/TRAITS: _____

_____

_____

PHRASES: _____

_____

_____

_____

NEW CAREERS I'M CONSIDERING AND THE SKILLS THEY REQUIRE

First, tear out the worksheet and write down new careers that interest you. Next, write down the skills/traits required in these positions. Then write down several phrases that describe the skills you feel you possess. Compare the skills required in the new career with the ones you feel you already possess. Refer to the *Skills Inventory* and the worksheet entitled *My Job History and Skills I've Acquired* to assist you in completing the exercise.

JOB TITLE: _____

SKILLS/TRAITS: _____

_____

_____

PHRASES: _____

_____

_____

_____

_____

JOB TITLE: _____

SKILLS/TRAITS: _____

_____

_____

PHRASES: _____

_____

_____

_____

_____

JOB TITLE: _____

SKILLS/TRAITS: _____

_____

_____

PHRASES: _____

_____

_____

_____

JOB TITLE: _____

SKILLS/TRAITS: _____

_____

_____

PHRASES: _____

_____

_____

_____

JOB TITLE: _____

SKILLS/TRAITS: _____

_____

_____

PHRASES: _____

_____

_____

_____

JOB TITLE: _____

SKILLS/TRAITS: _____

_____

_____

PHRASES: _____

_____

_____

_____

JOB TITLE: _____

SKILLS/TRAITS: _____

_____

_____

PHRASES: _____

_____

_____

_____

JOB TITLE: _____

SKILLS/TRAITS: _____

_____

_____

PHRASES: _____

_____

_____

_____

CHRONOLOGICAL RESUME WORKSHEET

First Name _____ Last Name _____

Address _____

City _____ State_____ Zip _____

Phone (   ) _____ - _____

Write either an objective, mission, or a career summary.

OBJECTIVE _____

MISSION _____

CAREER SUMMARY _____

_____

Fill out the Experience section in reverse chronological order. Include as many jobs as you feel are necessary to portray your skills and reflect your primary job history.

EXPERIENCE Company Name _____ City _____ State _____

Job Title _____ (Dates of Employment _____)

Write 4-5 brief sentences describing the scope of your job responsibilities.

_____

_____

_____

_____

List 3-5 bullet statements that describe your contributions or accomplishments in this job.

- _____
- _____
- _____
- _____
- _____

Company Name_____ City_____ State _____

Job Title _____ (Dates of Employment _____)

Write 4-5 brief sentences describing the scope of your job responsibilities.

_____

_____

_____

_____

EXPERIENCE
(Continued)

▪ _____
▪ _____
▪ _____
▪ _____
▪ _____

Company Name_____ City_____ State _____
Job Title _____ (Dates of Employment _____)

Write 4-5 brief sentences describing the scope of your job responsibilities.

_____
_____
_____
_____

List 3-5 bullet statements that describe your contributions or accomplishments in this job.

▪ _____
▪ _____
▪ _____
▪ _____
▪ _____

Company Name_____ City_____ State _____
Job Title _____ (Dates of Employment _____)

Write 4-5 brief sentences describing the scope of your job responsibilities.

_____
_____
_____
_____

List 3-5 bullet statements that describe your contributions or accomplishments in this job.

▪ _____
▪ _____
▪ _____
▪ _____
▪ _____

EDUCATION   College _____ City _____ State _____

Degree _____ Date of Graduation _____

GPA: (Only include if 3.0 or higher) _____

Related   ▪ _____   ▪ _____   ▪ _____
Coursework   ▪ _____   ▪ _____   ▪ _____
                        ▪ _____   ▪ _____   ▪ _____

Other possible headings: Fill out those that apply.

PROFESSIONAL   ▪ _____   ▪ _____   ▪ _____
TRAINING   ▪ _____   ▪ _____   ▪ _____
                             ▪ _____   ▪ _____   ▪ _____

COMPUTER/   ▪ _____   ▪ _____   ▪ _____
TECHNICAL   ▪ _____   ▪ _____   ▪ _____
SKILLS   ▪ _____   ▪ _____   ▪ _____

LICENSES   ▪ _____   ▪ _____   ▪ _____

CERTIFICATES/   ▪ _____   ▪ _____   ▪ _____
DESIGNATIONS   ▪ _____   ▪ _____   ▪ _____

LANGUAGES   ▪ _____   ▪ _____   ▪ _____

HONORS/   ▪ _____   ▪ _____   ▪ _____
AWARDS   ▪ _____   ▪ _____   ▪ _____

AFFILIATIONS   ▪ _____   ▪ _____   ▪ _____
                             ▪ _____   ▪ _____   ▪ _____
                             ▪ _____   ▪ _____   ▪ _____

CIVIC/   ▪ _____   ▪ _____   ▪ _____
VOLUNTEER   ▪ _____   ▪ _____   ▪ _____
ACTIVITIES   ▪ _____   ▪ _____   ▪ _____

*Remember, this worksheet is only a guideline to assist you in formatting your resume and does not reflect the actual space you will need to complete each category. Your information will be considerably condensed once it is word-processed. The goal is to create a one- or two-page resume.

FUNCTIONAL RESUME WORKSHEET

First Name _____ Last Name _____

Address _____

City _____ State_____ Zip _____

Phone ( ) _____ - _____

> Write either an objective, mission, or a career summary.

OBJECTIVE _____

MISSION _____

CAREER SUMMARY _____

> The purpose of the next section is to highlight your skills or experiences that enable you to excel in the next position you are pursuing. To help you organize your skills and accomplishments, choose categories, such as Administration, Sales, and Management, that reflect your qualifications. Then list these categories in the left-hand margin and write the corresponding bullet items.

QUALIFICATIONS

(Subheading)
- _____
- _____
- _____
- _____
- _____

(Subheading)
- _____
- _____
- _____
- _____
- _____

(Subheading)
- _____
- _____
- _____
- _____
- _____

Fill out the Experience section in reverse chronological order. Include as many jobs as you feel are necessary to reflect your primary job history.

EXPERIENCE

Company Name _____

City _____ State _____

Job Title _____ Dates of Employment _____

Company Name _____

City _____ State _____

Job Title _____ Dates of Employment _____

Company Name _____

City _____ State _____

Job Title _____ Dates of Employment _____

Company Name _____

City _____ State _____

Job Title _____ Dates of Employment _____

Company Name _____

City _____ State _____

Job Title _____ Dates of Employment _____

Company Name _____

City _____ State _____

Job Title _____ Dates of Employment _____

Company Name _____

City _____ State _____

Job Title _____ Dates of Employment _____

EDUCATION   College _____ City _____ State _____

Degree _____ Date of Graduation _____

GPA: (Only include if 3.0 or higher) _____

Related
Coursework

▪ _____   ▪ _____   ▪ _____

▪ _____   ▪ _____   ▪ _____

▪ _____   ▪ _____   ▪ _____

Other possible headings: Fill out those that apply.

PROFESSIONAL
TRAINING

▪ _____   ▪ _____   ▪ _____

▪ _____   ▪ _____   ▪ _____

▪ _____   ▪ _____   ▪ _____

COMPUTER/
TECHNICAL
SKILLS

▪ _____   ▪ _____   ▪ _____

▪ _____   ▪ _____   ▪ _____

▪ _____   ▪ _____   ▪ _____

LICENSES

▪ _____   ▪ _____   ▪ _____

CERTIFICATES/
DESIGNATIONS

▪ _____   ▪ _____   ▪ _____

▪ _____   ▪ _____   ▪ _____

LANGUAGES

▪ _____   ▪ _____   ▪ _____

HONORS/
AWARDS

▪ _____   ▪ _____   ▪ _____

▪ _____   ▪ _____   ▪ _____

AFFILIATIONS

▪ _____   ▪ _____   ▪ _____

▪ _____   ▪ _____   ▪ _____

▪ _____   ▪ _____   ▪ _____

CIVIC/
VOLUNTEER
ACTIVITIES

▪ _____   ▪ _____   ▪ _____

▪ _____   ▪ _____   ▪ _____

▪ _____   ▪ _____   ▪ _____

* Remember, this worksheet is only a guideline to assist you in formatting your resume and does not reflect the actual space you will be need to complete each category. Your information will be considerably condensed once it is a word-processed. The goal is to create a one- or two-page resume.

Worksheet Three (C)

COMBINATION RESUME WORKSHEET

First Name _____ Last Name _____

Address _____

City _____ State_____ Zip _____

Phone (   ) _____ - _____

Write either an objective, mission, or a career summary.

OBJECTIVE   _____

MISSION   _____

**CAREER
SUMMARY**   _____

The purpose of the next section is to highlight your skills or experiences that enable you to excel in the next position you are pursuing.

QUALIFICATIONS

- _____
- _____
- _____
- _____
- _____
- _____
- _____
- _____

If the above statements would be better organized into categories of skills, then group several statements together under subheadings, such as Administration, Sales, and Management. Then list these categories in the left-hand margin and write the corresponding bullet items.

Fill out the experience section in reverse chronological order. Include as many jobs as you feel are necessary to reflect your primary job history.

EXPERIENCE Company Name _____ City _____ State _____

Job Title _____ (Dates of Employment _____)

Write 4-5 brief sentences describing the scope of your job responsibilities.

_____

_____

_____

_____

List 3-5 bullet statements that describe your contributions or accomplishments in this job.

▪ _____

▪ _____

▪ _____

▪ _____

▪ _____

Company Name _____ City _____ State _____

Job Title _____ (Dates of Employment _____)

Write 4-5 brief sentences describing the scope of your job responsibilities.

_____

_____

_____

_____

List 3-5 bullet statements that describe your contributions or accomplishments in this job.

▪ _____

▪ _____

▪ _____

▪ _____

▪ _____

Company Name _____ City _____ State _____

Job Title _____ (Dates of Employment _____)

Write 4-5 brief sentences describing the scope of your job responsibilities.

_____

_____

_____

_____

EXPERIENCE
(Continued)

List 3-5 bullet statements that describe your contributions or accomplishments in this job.

- _____
- _____
- _____
- _____
- _____

Company Name _____ City _____ State _____
Job Title _____ (Dates of Employment _____)

Write 4-5 brief sentences describing the scope of your job responsibilities.

_____
_____
_____
_____

List 3-5 bullet statements that describe your contributions or accomplishments in this job.

- _____
- _____
- _____
- _____
- _____

Company Name _____ City _____ State _____
Job Title _____ (Dates of Employment _____)

Write 4-5 brief sentences describing the scope of your job responsibilities.

_____
_____
_____
_____

List 3-5 bullet statements that describe your contributions or accomplishments in this job.

- _____
- _____
- _____
- _____
- _____

EDUCATION   College _____ City _____ State _____

Degree _____ Date of Graduation _____

GPA: (Only include if 3.0 or higher) _____

Related
Coursework

▪ _____ ▪ _____ ▪ _____
▪ _____ ▪ _____ ▪ _____
▪ _____ ▪ _____ ▪ _____

Other possible headings: Fill out those that apply.

PROFESSIONAL
TRAINING

▪ _____ ▪ _____ ▪ _____
▪ _____ ▪ _____ ▪ _____
▪ _____ ▪ _____ ▪ _____

COMPUTER/
TECHNICAL
SKILLS

▪ _____ ▪ _____ ▪ _____
▪ _____ ▪ _____ ▪ _____
▪ _____ ▪ _____ ▪ _____

LICENSES

▪ _____ ▪ _____ ▪ _____

CERTIFICATES/
DESIGNATIONS

▪ _____ ▪ _____ ▪ _____
▪ _____ ▪ _____ ▪ _____

LANGUAGES

▪ _____ ▪ _____ ▪ _____

HONORS/
AWARDS

▪ _____ ▪ _____ ▪ _____
▪ _____ ▪ _____ ▪ _____

AFFILIATIONS

▪ _____ ▪ _____ ▪ _____
▪ _____ ▪ _____ ▪ _____
▪ _____ ▪ _____ ▪ _____

CIVIC/
VOLUNTEER
ACTIVITIES

▪ _____ ▪ _____ ▪ _____
▪ _____ ▪ _____ ▪ _____
▪ _____ ▪ _____ ▪ _____

---

* Remember, this worksheet is only a guideline to assist you in formatting your resume and does not reflect the actual space you will be need to complete each category. Your information will be considerably condensed once it is a word-processed. The goal is create a one- or two-page resume.

Worksheet Three (D)

First Name _____ Last Name _____

Address _____

City _____ State_____ Zip _____

Phone (___) _____ - _____

Write either an objective or a mission statement.

OBJECTIVE _____
_____

MISSION _____
_____

The purpose of the next section is to highlight skills or experiences that enable you to excel in the position you are pursuing. This section could appear in other locations if you prefer.

SKILLS ■ _____

HIGHLIGHTS ■ _____

■ _____

■ _____

EDUCATION College _____ City _____ State _____
Degree _____ Date of Graduation _____
GPA: (Only include if 3.0 or higher) _____ Major GPA: (Only if 3.3 or higher) _____

Related ■ _____ ■ _____ ■ _____
Coursework ■ _____ ■ _____ ■ _____

Related ■ Project Title: _____
Coursework ■ Project Description: _____
_____

■ Project Title: _____
■ Project Description: _____
_____

■ Project Title: _____
■ Project Description: _____
_____

■ Project Title: _____
■ Project Description: _____
_____

Studies   Program Title: _____
Abroad: Subjects Studied & Location: _____

Other possible headings: Fill out those that apply.

ADDITIONAL TRAINING	▪ _____ ▪ _____	▪ _____ ▪ _____	▪ _____ ▪ _____
COMPUTER/ TECHNICAL SKILLS	▪ _____ ▪ _____ ▪ _____	▪ _____ ▪ _____ ▪ _____	_____ _____ _____
LICENSES	▪ _____	▪ _____	_____
CERTIFICATES/ DESIGNATIONS	▪ _____ ▪ _____	▪ _____ _____	_____ _____
HONORS/ AWARDS	▪ _____ ▪ _____	▪ _____ ▪ _____	_____ _____
AFFILIATIONS	▪ _____ ▪ _____	▪ _____ ▪ _____	_____ _____
LANGUAGES/ TRAVEL	▪ _____ ▪ _____	▪ _____ ▪ _____	_____ _____
CIVIC/ VOLUNTEER ACTIVITIES	▪ _____ ▪ _____ ▪ _____	▪ _____ ▪ _____ ▪ _____	_____ _____ _____

Fill out the experience section in reverse chronological order. Include as many jobs or internships as you feel are necessary to reflect your primary job history.

EXPERIENCE   Company Name _____ City _____ State _____
                Job Title _____ (Dates of Employment _____)

Write 4-5 brief sentences describing the scope of your job responsibilities.

_____
_____
_____
_____

List 3-5 bullet statements that describe your contributions or accomplishments in that job.

▪ _____
▪ _____
▪ _____
▪ _____
▪ _____

EXPERIENCE
(Continued)

Company Name _____ City _____ State _____

Job Title _____ (Dates of Employment _____)

Write 4-5 brief sentences describing the scope of your job responsibilities.

_____

_____

_____

_____

List 3-5 bullet statements that describe your contributions or accomplishments in that job.

▪ _____

▪ _____

▪ _____

▪ _____

▪ _____

Company Name _____ City _____ State _____

Job Title _____ (Dates of Employment _____)

Write 4-5 brief sentences describing the scope of your job responsibilities.

_____

_____

_____

_____

List 3-5 bullet statements that describe your contributions or accomplishments in that job.

▪ _____

▪ _____

▪ _____

▪ _____

▪ _____

Company Name _____ City _____ State _____

Job Title _____ (Dates of Employment _____)

Write 4-5 brief sentences describing the scope of your job responsibilities.

_____

_____

_____

_____

* Remember, this worksheet is only a guideline to assist you in formatting your resume and does not reflect the actual space you will be need to complete each category. Your information will be considerably condensed once it is a word-processed. The goal is create a one-page resume if you are a recent graduate.

AN OBJECTIVE, MISSION, OR A CAREER SUMMARY:
Which Should You Use?

1. What field or industry are you currently in? _____

What fields have you been in during your career? _____

_____

2. Would you like to continue to work in your current field? _____

If not, in what field are you pursuing your job search? _____

3. Write a brief description of your ideal job. _____

_____

_____

4. Who will be reviewing and considering your resume for employment (e.g., director of sales, office manager, engineering manager, software development supervisor)? _____

Evaluating Your Answers

If you answered "yes" to question 2: You probably want to write a targeted objective or mission statement using the information from question 1. In this case, your current experience or related skills can help you advance in your field of interest.

If you answered "no" to question 2: Use the information from questions 3 and 4 to pinpoint the types of positions you might want to pursue. Once you determine a specific or general position, write a generalized objective or mission statement that highlights the skills you have gained that would be valued in that particular career.

If you answered "no" to question 2 and you don't know what direction your career will take: Write a one-sentence career summary that describes your overall background or the skills you have acquired that you believe would be important in a broad range of positions.

After you have completed the worksheet and evaluated your answers, turn to pages 21-26 to review a variety of sample objective, mission, and career summaries. Write your own objective, mission, or career summary at the top of your resume worksheet in the appropriate blanks. When you're finished, turn to page 27 and begin Step 4.

Worksheet Five

Complete this exercise by writing 5 key phrases that describe each position you have held. Begin with your current or most recent position and go as far back in your job history as you would like. Refer to the key phrases as necessary.

POSITION: _____

PHRASES: _____

_____

_____

_____

_____

_____

POSITION: _____

PHRASES: _____

_____

_____

_____

_____

_____

POSITION: _____

PHRASES: _____

_____

_____

_____

_____

POSITION: _____

PHRASES: _____

_____

_____

_____

_____

POSITION: _____

PHRASES: _____

_____

_____

_____

_____

POSITION: _____

PHRASES: _____

_____

_____

_____

_____

POSITION: _____

PHRASES: _____

_____

_____

_____

_____

POSITION: _____

PHRASES: _____

_____

_____

_____

_____

Worksheet Six

WORK HISTORY QUESTIONNAIRE

Fill out this form based on your current or most recent employment experience. Then, using additional sheets of paper, write the answers to these same questions for each employment period that you want to include in your resume.

NOTE: This is simply a guide to help you in developing your resume. Do not be concerned if you do not wish to answer all the questions.

■ Information Needed for Each Position Held

1. Where do you currently work or have you most recently worked? Include company name, city, and state. _____

2. How long have you been or were you employed there? From when to when? _____

3. Does your job title quickly give the reader a clear idea of the scope of your position? _____

If not, consider using a more functional job title that at first glance will give the reader an indication of your responsibilities. For example, instead of listing an official job title, such as Clerk Typist II, you might want to use a title such as data entry staff, which better indicates the scope of your job responsibilities. *Word of Caution*: Do not misrepresent your position. List your job title. _____

4. Did you start in this position? If not, what was your first title? _____

5. Have you been promoted? How fast and how often? _____
_____

6. What are your responsibilities and duties? _____
_____
_____
_____
_____

7. How is your performance measured? _____
_____
_____

8. In what ways have you had a positive effect on your company? _____
_____
_____

9. What acknowledgments, incentives, or performance awards have you received? _____

_____

_____

_____

10. What committees—internal or external—are you on? _____

_____

_____

11. What is the job title of the person you report to? _____

Please complete the questions that apply to your specific career.

Have you created any programs (i.e., marketing, sales, advertising, operational)? List them.

_____

_____

How have you reduced the company's operating costs, and by how much?

_____

_____

What special projects have you completed?

_____

_____

What specific industry expertise or knowledge of governing regulations do you have?

_____

_____

▌ Questions Related to Management Positions

What are your management responsibilities?

_____

_____

Have you streamlined or automated operations? How?

_____

_____

_____

How have you reduced employee turnover, and by how much?

_____

_____

Do you manage staff? How many?

_____

_____

Do you have hiring or training authority? What level of personnel?

_____

_____

Do you have budget responsibility? What is the amount?

_____

_____

Have you achieved budget and revenue goals? Explain and include dates.

_____

_____

_____

What problems have you solved? How?

_____

_____

_____

Have you revised policies, authored procedure manuals, improved training programs? If so, discuss.

_____

_____

_____

Do you have financial reporting responsibilities? What kind?

_____

_____

_____

Are you on any boards? Name them.

_____

_____

▌Questions Related to Sales Positions

Explain how you get new business (i.e., cold calling, networking, telemarketing).

_____

_____

How large is your territory (i.e., how many states or what region)?

_____

_____

Do you have to nurture a long sales cycle or is it an immediate close? Explain.

_____

_____

_____

_____

What size and types of companies are part of your customer base?

_____

_____

_____

Name some of your key accounts.

_____

_____

_____

Do you give presentations or create bids/proposals? If so, explain.

_____

_____

_____

_____

_____

Have you increased sales or revenue? If so, explain.

_____

_____

_____

_____

_____

_____

Have you achieved/exceeded quota? If so, include by how much and dates.

_____
_____
_____
_____
_____

How many new accounts have you opened? How much revenue have you produced?

_____
_____
_____

What types of incentives/bonuses have you earned?

_____
_____
_____
_____

What is your ranking among your peers? How large is this group?

_____
_____

Have you strengthened customer relations, improved customer retention, or received any documented feedback on your success?

_____
_____
_____

Do you attend or plan trade shows/conventions? You may want to include the show names.

_____
_____
_____
_____

Have you initiated any new sales or marketing strategies?

_____
_____
_____
_____

▮ Questions Related to Engineering/Technical Fields

List projects you have participated in and how you contributed to each. Where were they, and what were their dollar values?

_____
_____
_____
_____
_____
_____
_____
_____
_____
_____
_____
_____
_____
_____
_____
_____

Do you regularly achieve budgets? Explain how.

_____
_____
_____
_____
_____
_____

Do you regularly complete projects on deadline? Explain.

_____
_____
_____
_____
_____
_____

Do you manage any teams? What types, and how many people are in them?

_____
_____
_____
_____
_____

POWER WORDS WORKSHEET

List words you would like to be sure to include in your resume to give it impact. Select words that you feel most comfortable using or ones that are often used in your industry.

VERBS

▌_____	▌_____	▌_____
▌_____	▌_____	▌_____
▌_____	▌_____	▌_____
▌_____	▌_____	▌_____
▌_____	▌_____	▌_____
▌_____	▌_____	▌_____
▌_____	▌_____	▌_____
▌_____	▌_____	▌_____

ADJECTIVES

▌_____	▌_____	▌_____
▌_____	▌_____	▌_____
▌_____	▌_____	▌_____
▌_____	▌_____	▌_____
▌_____	▌_____	▌_____
▌_____	▌_____	▌_____
▌_____	▌_____	▌_____
▌_____	▌_____	▌_____

ADVERBS

▌_____	▌_____	▌_____
▌_____	▌_____	▌_____
▌_____	▌_____	▌_____
▌_____	▌_____	▌_____
▌_____	▌_____	▌_____
▌_____	▌_____	▌_____
▌_____	▌_____	▌_____
▌_____	▌_____	▌_____

Worksheet Eight

Do you have any degrees? If so, what are they?

_____

_____

What college/technical schools have you attended? When?

_____

_____

What courses have you taken that employers in your desired field might consider relevant?

_____

_____

Was your overall GPA or the GPA in your major 3.0 or better? If so, list your GPA.

_____

Was your minor or area of concentration or emphasis relevant to your desired field? If so, what was it?

_____

Did you study abroad? If so, where? _____

Independently or through an exchange program? _____

Did you do any special projects while you were in school? What were they?

_____

_____

Did you participate in any internships? If so, where, and what did you do?

_____

_____

Did you complete a thesis? If so, what was the title?

_____

_____

Alternatively, information about special projects and internships could be included in the work experience section.

CATEGORY PLANNING QUESTIONNAIRE

Have you ever participated in seminars, workshops, or professional development programs? If so, what were they and who sponsored them?

_____

_____

What computer/technical skills do you possess?

_____

_____

Do you have any designations/licenses/certifications? If so, which ones?

_____

_____

Which, if any, foreign languages do you speak fluently? _____

Which do you speak conversationally? _____

What industry/job-related accolades, honors, or awards have you earned?

_____

_____

Which professional or career-related organizations are you involved in?

_____

_____

In which organizations have you held leadership roles? What skills did you gain and what did you accomplish in these roles?

_____

_____

_____

What civic organizations or volunteer activities are you involved in?

_____

_____

_____

Are you willing to relocate? _____

Worksheet Ten

COVER LETTER WORKSHEET

First Name _____ Last Name _____

Address _____

City _____ State_____ Zip _____

Phone ( ) _____ - _____

Introduction: Write 1-2 sentences that state your purpose in sending your resume to the reader's attention.

_____

_____

_____

Body: Write 4-5 sentences (more if necessary) that summarize your career or general skills. The goal is to convince the reader that you are qualified for the specific position or the field you are pursuing.

_____

_____

_____

_____

_____

_____

_____

(* If you need two paragraphs for the body of your letter, fine.
Ideally, there should be a logical break in the content.)

Closing: Write 2-3 sentences that summarize why your skills are extremely well suited for the position and 1 sentence that clearly requests a personal meeting to discuss your credentials in more detail.

_____

_____

_____

_____

_____

Sincerely,

Name (First and Last) _____

Resume
Library

Resumes are categorized in alphabetical order
according to a variety of professions

SARA J. SEARCH
123 Job Hunting Lane
Big Time, USA 10101
(444) 567-8910

MISSION   A challenging position where I can fully utilize my proven claims processing and office automation experience coupled with strong project management and customer service skills.

EXPERIENCE   INSURANCE OPERATION - Insured City, USA   (9/93-Present)
DATA PROCESSING SPECIALIST
Created and implemented all aspects of a paperless filing system from ground zero and trained customer service representatives on system usage. Manage high volume of accuracy-critical record-keeping without back-up paper documentation. Perform extensive alpha-numeric data entry and information processing of claims, new business submissions, and policy changes/reinstatements, which includes uploading and downloading data daily from the headquarter's mainframe system.

- Developed a forerunning transactional and chronological-based filing system which included establishing all system-related processes and procedures.
- Successfully converted all client records to a new automated database, which involved data processing critical information associated with 13,000 accounts.
- Earned maximum performance bonuses based on dependability and a devoted work ethic.
- Consistently awarded excellent employee evaluations from the management team.
- Entrusted to operate a virtual office due to efficiency, accuracy, and integrity.

LOCAL INSURANCE - Agencyville, USA   (9/85-9/93)
ACCOUNT REPRESENTATIVE
Managed a base of 3,000 accounts for an independent agency representing multiple lines of P&C, commercial, life, and health insurance. Maintained heavy customer contact, quickly responding to diverse customer inquiries and requests. Handled policy instatements/modifications, claims processing, and quoting new business rates. Also acted as primary liaison between insurers and insureds, performing account research and facilitating problem resolution.

- Designated Head Account Representative charged with jointly overseeing department operations.
- Analyzed claim-specific coverage criteria to accurately process and report claims to providers.
- Maintained knowledge of underwriting regulations for up to 20 major insurance carriers.
- Consistently processed highly detailed account information with accuracy and efficiency.
- Fielded up to 50 customer service calls per day, providing exceptional account follow-up.
- Promoted in succession from Receptionist, to Assistant Customer Service Rep, to Account Rep.

OFFICE, INC. - Quicktown, USA   (11/83-9/85)
RECEPTIONIST
Handled multifaceted office administration functions, i.e., clerical support, typing, mail processing, and multiline communications system management, for a small equipment manufacturer.

TRAINING   • Sub Agent License   • Mainframe Uploading

COMPUTER   • Windows 95   • AMS for Windows   • MS Word
                 • Insurnet   • Applied Systems   • Redshaw

REFERENCES AVAILABLE UPON REQUEST

SARAH J. SEARCH
123 Job Hunting Lane
Big Time, USA 10101
(444) 567-8910

EXPERIENCE

<u>BIG NAME CONSULTING COMPANY.</u> - Sunshine City, USA　　　　　　(7/97-Present)
Consulting Division
Consultant with 2 years' progressive responsibilities serving client companies in the areas
of banking, consumer goods, software sales, transportation, and healthcare.
Key accountabilities and accomplishments include:

• Designed and streamlined reporting procedures for incident tracking system for conversion of
banking systems. Facilitated communications between users and systems management to verify
accurate and acceptable conversion of C&S Sovran systems to BigBank systems. Documented
all reporting procedures and trained client personnel in the tracking system.

• Acted as administrative contact for project management of 120 Big Name Consulting personnel on
BigBank transition team. Designed and organized executive presentations, solely responsible for
billing, monitoring evaluation of personnel, and conducting orientation for new project members.

• Expanded Southeastern Regional Sales database by 50% for Big Name Consulting Co. national
software sales. Involved researching key statistical information for target markets.
Supervise 2 inexperienced staff in gathering vital statistics via research and personal contact.

• Conducted benefits analysis for multimillion-dollar food retail chain post-conversion to
determine post-software implementation savings.

• Programmed online Cobol II programs to implement terminal usage to improve the efficiency
and accuracy of the aircraft maintenance division at Flyaway Airlines. Conceived and constructed
test packages to determine program's overall utility. Documented functionality report for the
program user, detailing procedures and purpose of modules.

• Selected to act as liaison between the consulting staff, partners, and administration as a
member of the Staff Advisory Committee in representation of diverse issues and topics. Organized
quarterly informal training sessions for 50 to 100 consultants. Proposed in-house training,
which was accepted and implemented, for more cost-efficient education of seniors and managers.

**COLLEGE
EXPERIENCE**

<u>International USA Trade Center</u> - Job Town, USA　　　　　　　　(Spring 1990)
Intern
Researched international companies within assigned categories of products and services to
identify possible exporting opportunities.

<u>G & S Food Brokerage Company</u> - Job Town, USA　　　　　　　(Summer 1986)
Marketing Representative
Serviced retail accounts for U-Can Products. Increased market share by 60%.

EDUCATION

<u>USA UNIVERSITY</u> - Job Town, USA
Bachelor of Science in Corporate Finance 1990　**Summa Cum Laude**

COMPUTERS

Completed over 600 hours of training in the areas of systems integration,
installation, and design. Computer capabilities in the following:

• Paradox	• Power Point	• Mac Draw	• Persuasion
• Microsoft Word	• Excel	• Install I	• DB2

**HONORS/
ACTIVITIES**

• Wall Street Journal Award for outstanding student in the school of business
• *Who's Who in Outstanding American College Students*
• USA University Finance Association, President　• OK Sorority, Fund Chairman

REFERENCES AVAILABLE UPON REQUEST

SARAH J. SEARCH, M.S., CRC
123 Job Hunting Lane, #1
Big Time, USA 10101
(444) 567-8910

EDUCATION	<u>STATE UNIVERSITY</u> - Sunshine City, USA **Master of Science Degree in Rehabilitation Counseling**, 1994 **GPA: 4.0** <u>USA UNIVERSITY</u> - Sunshine City, USA **Bachelor of Arts Degree**, 1966
CREDENTIALS	• Certified Rehabilitation Counselor (CRC) • Nationally Certified Counselor (NCC)
AFFILIATIONS	• American Counseling Association • National Rehabilitation Association • Sunshine State Rehabilitation Association • National Rehabilitation Counseling Association

**PROFESSIONAL
EXPERIENCE**

<u>Any State, Division of Rehabilitation Services</u> 1995-Present
Rehabilitation Counselor, Business Enterprise Program Anytown, USA

Rehabilitative counseling and case management of blind vendors who operate snack
bars under the Randolph-Sheppard Act. Supervision of approximately 14 vendors and
11 helpers. Facilitated the initial installation and ongoing operation of snack bars
as small business enterprises which have total annual gross sales of approximately
$1 million. As advocate for blind vendors, provide referrals to community resources
as needed, select vendors for locations, hire helpers, and develop sites and resources.
Utilize the guidelines of the Americans With Disabilities Act. Represent the Business
Enterprise Program on the DRS Research Committee.

<u>Unknown County Department of Family and Children Services</u> 1993-1995
Social Services Specialist, Anytown, USA
Ongoing Treatment, Child Protective Services

Managed a caseload of 25 families with the goal of rehabilitating family members
and improving family systems functioning. Priority was assessment and reduction of
risk factors for children. Provided extensive crisis intervention and ongoing individual
and family counseling. Case management required community support, teamwork, and
oversight of service delivery. Developed, with parents' participation and with
a prevention focus, the case treatment plan, which included clients' strengths, needs,
goals, and corrective steps.

<u>Any State USA, Division of Rehabilitation Services</u> 1990-1993
Disability Adjudicator Anytown, USA

Determined eligibility for Social Security disability benefits. Reviewed medical and
psychological records, communicated with healthcare and social agencies, and counseled
with claimants during the decision-making process.

PROFESSIONAL EXPERIENCE (Cont.)

<u>Any State USA, Division of Rehabilitation Services</u> (Cont.)
Documented each case and arranged evaluations with medical and psychological providers. Utilized the DSM III-R for psychological claims. Completed residual functional capacity and transferable skills analyses, utilizing the *DOT* (*Dictionary of Occupational Titles*).

<u>Unknown County Department of Family & Children Services</u>   1979-1990
Caseworker Principal, Homemaker Services   Anytown, USA

Assessed individual needs of elderly and disabled clients in their home settings. Evaluated eligibility for home health and household maintenance services. Developed and implemented individual service plans. Counseled individuals and families. Worked with medical and social community agencies to arrange appropriate in-home services and provided case management.

Caseworker Principal, Adult Protective Services

Investigated allegations of neglect, abuse, and exploitation of aged and disabled persons. Assessed disabilities and determined eligibility for various services. Extensive fieldwork was required. Developed case plans and coordinated rehabilitation services. Caseload consisted of 30 clients and included legal guardianship and representative payee case management duties. Filed, organized, and presented guardianship petitions in Probate Court; represented the state agency in a variety of matters as acting guardian. Provided individual counseling and client follow-up.

Caseworker Principal, Special Job Program

Evaluated training and employment potential for AFDC recipients. Worked closely with a Department of Labor Counselor in developing joint individual service plans. Coordinated all aspects of job training and job placement in order to remove obstacles to employment. Case management included individual counseling. Arranged day-care services, monitored children's participation, and authorized payment for day care, training, and other job-related services.

PREVIOUS EXPERIENCE

<u>Statewide Retardation Center</u>
Program Specialist   Sunshine City, USA

Designed and implemented educational, recreational, and social programs for mentally retarded and developmentally disabled inpatient residents. Assisted in developing individual service plans. Provided client counseling and monitored individual progress.

REFERENCES AVAILABLE UPON REQUEST

149

SARAH J. SEARCH

123 Job Hunting Lane   Big Time, USA 10101   (444) 567-8910

OBJECTIVE

To obtain a position with an interior design firm where I may utilize the full scope of my creativity, training, and industry-related experience toward future contributions.

EDUCATION

THE COLLEGE FOR THE GOOD ARTS - Sunshine City, USA
Bachelor of Fine Arts Degree in Interior Design - June 1996 *(FIDER Approved)*
* Thesis required an in-depth Design Project from inception

UNIVERSITY OF SOUTHERN USA - Beachville, USA
Bachelor of Fine Arts Degree in Painting - December 1993

SPECIAL PROJECTS

- **Hospital Design Project** - Conducted in-depth research of specific medical conditions and conceptualized facility interior from ground zero utilizing a horseshoe floor plan.
- **Residential & Commercial Projects** - Utilized knowledge of ADA design specifications.
- **Feng Shui Project** - Created a residential design using the Chinese art of furniture placement.
- **Historic Restoration Project** - Developed floor plan characterized by Greek Revival Era design for Briarpatch House from ground zero; ultimately developed structure into a conference center.
- **Day Care & Office Building Design Projects** - Utilized architectural graphics skills.

RELATED EXPERIENCE

FUN INTERIORS - Rocking Chair Town, USA   (1997)
Designer
Performed highly creative interior design consulting primarily for new construction, residential projects. Demonstrated strong needs identification, design evaluation, client relationship-building, and project management functions. Utilized excellent interior selection, space planning, and tile design skills in fulfilling diverse client objectives.

BIDDLE AND DAUGHTERS - Sunshine City, USA   (1996-1997)
Showroom Coordinator
As one of 2 showroom consultants, performed multifaceted design support and office management functions for an upscale design showroom. Primary corporate liaison and design coordinator for trade professionals. Utilized creativity and trusted design expertise to provide high level of service, including recommending fabric, wallpaper, and furniture to designers. Interacted closely with head office in facilitating ordering, which included securing pricing information, ensuring stock availability, and resolving customer credit issues. Demonstrated an impressive knowledge of available design elements, particularly of designer fabrics.

YOUR ASSOCIATES - Sunshine City, USA   (1994-1995)
Design Assistant
Progressed rapidly to higher levels of accountability in this architectural and design firm. Researched fabrics through the design showroom, prepared pricing information, and scheduled vendor appointments/presentations. Assisted in the development of marketing portfolios which contributed to new client procurement. Controlled various office support functions.

FIDO BROTHERS - Beachville, USA   (Summer 1992)
Drafting Intern
Handled drafting projects for this nationally recognized advertising agency, servicing key clients such as Money Bank, Car Co., and Fitzhugh. Project involvement included conducting on-site surveys, extracting measurements, developing sketches, and preparing final signage drafts.

* As a former Assistant Draftsman with Alaska Fish Co., became adept at reading blueprints and interpreting floor plans involving power/communications, lighting, and electrical.

COMPUTERS/ AFFILIATIONS

- Proficient in CAD and MS Word
- USID, Student Member; American Cancer Society, Volunteer, 1994-1995

PORTFOLIO & REFERENCES AVAILABLE UPON REQUEST

JOHN J. SEEKER
123 Looking Hard Avenue
Top Dog, USA 20202
(555) 678-9101

OBJECTIVE

A challenging Chef/Sous Chef position where my culinary training and related experience will offer the opportunity for growth and advancement.

EDUCATION

COOKING INSTITUTE OF AMERICA - Tasty, USA
Associate of Arts Degree in Culinary Arts, June 1994
• Future Chefs of the Nation, President (5th Quarter)
• Future Chefs of the Nation, Co-Chairman (6th Quarter)

Completed two-year vocational course in Culinary Arts, 1981-1983

CERTIFICATIONS

• Certification in Safety & Sanitation (NRA)

**PROFESSIONAL
EXPERIENCE**

ROWDY SPORTS BAR & GRILL   Good Food, USA
Kitchen Manager   5/94-8/94
Responsible for all aspects of creating, implementing, and maintaining efficient kitchen environment for a new operation. Created menu, recipes, and plate sets for steak, hamburger, and seafood menu. Ordered and maintained inventory and cost control. Handled scheduling, training, and supervision of staff of 6.

THE EXPENSIVE TAVERN   Upscale, USA
Line Cook   2/94-6/94
Responsible for preparing, serving, and operating pantry, fryer, saute, and inside expeditor for an open kitchen at a high-volume restaurant.

YUMMIES BISTRO   Yum Yum, USA
Assistant to Pastry Chef   11/93-2/94
Assisted the Pastry Chef in preparation of Mediterranean and French desserts and breads for a fine dining restaurant.

CAFE GOOD FUN   Pick up, USA
Buffet Cook, Part-time   11/93-2/94
Prepared and plated for large parties in a fine dining restaurant.

LUXURY GOLF & COUNTRY CLUB   Pamperville, USA
Line Cook/Buffet Cook   4/93-10/93
Served on 2-person high-volume line and prepared buffets for private parties of 60-600 at a members-only country club.

**AFFILIATIONS/
ACTIVITIES**

• Culinary Fest Convention, Chef's Assistant to Chef Boy, C.E.C., 2/93
• Assisted Chef Hungry, C.E.C., in preparation for culinary competition, 3/93
• Bartown 500, Cook for Chef Good Food, C.W.C., 10/93
• Culinary Fest National Food Show, Salon Cook for Chef Boy, C.E.C., 10/93
• Culinary Fest USA, Junior Member, 1/94
• Sports Challenge, Station Cook for Chef Speedy, C.E.C., 3/94

MILITARY

AMERICAN MILITARY, E-4,
Honorable Discharge, 11/86

REFERENCES AVAILABLE UPON REQUEST

JOHN J. SEEKER
123 Looking Hard Avenue
Top Dog, USA 20202
(555) 678-9101

OBJECTIVE   To continue a highly successful Engineering career where I may fully utilize my proven experience and knowledge of control systems toward future contributions.

EDUCATION   SUCCESS STORY UNIVERSITY - Tall Tales, USA
B.S. in Mechanical Engineering, 5/92
Emphasis: Control Engineering   * *Scholarship Recipient*

RELATED
COURSEWORK
- Microprocessor-Based Control Systems
- Design of Modern Control Systems
- Automatic Control Systems
- Model & Analysis of Dynamic Systems

COMPUTER   • AutoCAD   • "C"   • Fortran   • DOS   • Lotus 1-2-3   • WordPerfect   • Basic   • Assembly

EXPERIENCE   ENVIRONMENTAL CORPORATION - Fresh Air, USA   (6/92-Present)
Formerly Environmental Associates

PROJECT ENGINEER
Comprehensively manage a wide range of electrical engineering projects in the areas of power distribution and refrigeration. Perform and coordinate all aspects of testing, evaluating, designing, reporting, and installing. Develop price quotes and bid presentations. Interface closely with clients throughout the design process from inception. Direct the technical staff during on-site installations.

- Successfully completed 50+ assignments during tenure.
- Managed projects ranging from $30K to $400K.
- Consistently complete projects within budget and in accordance with deadlines.
- Conceived and instituted custom-designed software programs to assist in the design process.
- Gained valuable experience with refrigeration and energy management controllers.
- Effectively purchase and integrate controllers into power distribution systems; handle all aspects of troubleshooting and quality management of controllers.
- Work with major corporations including CheapMart, Best Grocery, and Food City.
- Received excellent performance reviews from management.

TECHNOLOGY OF THE UNIVERSE - Cosmos, USA   (5/91-8/91)

INTERN
Conducted extensive testing of various electrical systems, including heat pumps, air conditioners, and furnaces. Personally contributed to the redesign of several air conditioning systems.

REFERENCES AVAILABLE UPON REQUEST

JOHN J. SEEKER
123 Looking Hard Avenue
Top Dog, USA 20202
(555) 678-9101

**CAREER
MISSION**

A challenging position where I may fully utilize my business development, credit analysis, financial modeling, and solutions-selling skills to strategically position clients for growth.

EXPERIENCE

OFF-SHORE CREDIT BANK - Sweetwater, USA   (8/96-Present)
ASSOCIATE - *Americas Division*
Partner with Vice President to originate, structure, review, and execute underwriting agreements for major Fortune 500 companies in a 5-state Western Region for a $350B global banking operation. Key contributor during entire underwriting process in securing capital and financing at all levels including refinances and acquisitions. Prepare detailed internal negotiation memo documents, meeting critical deadlines and achieving maximum allocations.

- Underwrite over $100M in capital for 40 active accounts including Soda, Inc., Cellular +, Good Merchandise, Deliline, Good Health Systems, and Aero Space, Inc.
- Utilize computer modeling skills to determine best growth investment strategies for specific clients.
- Establish solid relationships with targeted Fortune 500 corporations to drive new business development and strategically network, while simultaneously maintaining large existing portfolio.
- Develop numerous SVP, CEO, and CFO relationships; effectively interface with legal counsel.

BANK OF BIG CITY - Waterville, USA   (10/94-8/96)
ASSISTANT VICE PRESIDENT - *Corporate Banking Group*
Provided comprehensive financial services to major accounts in the Eastern marketplace for a $60B super-regional banking operation headquartered in Waterville. Performed financial analysis/modeling, formulated/confirmed credit structures, established pricing, and negotiated term sheets/loan documentation. Profitably managed diversified portfolio of existing middle-market accounts. Closely interacted with legal teams, CFOs, and CEOs in negotiations and in planning and executing strategies to resolve problematic loans.

PAUL BUNYAN BANK - Bridge City, USA   (6/93-8/94)
CREDIT TRAINEE
Selected and sponsored by a Senior Vice President of a banking operation to participate in this prestigious industry training. Acquired strong credit management background in Credit Analysis, Underwriting, Industry Analysis, and Corporate Finance. Performed case analysis and underwriting for corporate/real estate financings.

NATIONAL BANK OF SOUP CITY - Soup City, USA   (5/90-8/91)
TEAM MANAGER
Developed, trained, and supervised a Direct Deposit Sales Team providing a wide array of marketing strategies, in-depth product knowledge, and sales/customer service techniques targeting retail accounts. Received Outstanding Sales Award in the department.

INTERNSHIP

PAUL BUNYAN BANK - Bridge City, USA   (5/92-9/92)
Provided key support to the Banking Group, including analyses of financial statements and evaluations of up to $500K loans, ensuring compliance with company policies.

EDUCATION

GOOD STUDIES UNIVERSITY - Sweetwater, USA
Master in Business Administration, 1993 *Concentration: Finance*   **GPA: 3.5/4.0**

ANOTHER GOOD COLLEGE - Sweetwater, USA
B.A. in Banking and Finance, 1990

TRAINING

- Bank of Big City Seminars: Corporate Finance; International Trade Finance; Risk Management

COMPUTER

• Windows 95	• Internet	• WordPerfect	• Excel	• KMV Monitor
• Lotus 1-2-3	• MS Word	• Power Point	• RAROC	

SARAH J. SEARCH
123 Job Hunting Lane
Big Time, USA 10101
(444) 567-8910

SUMMARY

Highly effective, multitalented professional with a strong human resources background emphasizing recruitment, management, benefits, and policy development.

QUALIFICATIONS

**Recruitment/
HR Management**

- Experienced in all aspects of staffing including screening, testing, interviewing, and selection.
- Organized job fairs, marketing, and promotional events to further expand an existing labor pool.
- Created human resources departments from ground zero requiring development of recruitment, training, employee policies, regulatory compliance, and payroll functions; set up logistics under strict time constraints, including computer operations and work-related procedures.
- Experienced in employee benefits and defined contribution plans with extensive knowledge of laws governing diverse benefits programs acquired through tenure as an ERISA Paralegal.

**Policy/
Administration**

- Drafted complex internal and administrative documents addressing employee/employer issues.
- Created corporate policies and employee manual; developed pay structure aligning with cash flow.
- Oversaw payroll process including calculating compensation, handling payroll taxes, preparing government-regulated employee forms, administering payments, and developing incentives.
- Experienced in resolving employee disputes with Department of Labor to minimize liabilities.
- Demonstrate knowledge of regulations related to EEO, ADA, OSHA, and Workers' Compensation.

EXPERIENCE

GREAT STAFFING, INC. - Talent, USA   (8/94-Present)
Personnel Recruiter
Solely direct recruitment efforts for Big City District consisting of 4 offices and manage off-site group staffing assignments on a national scale for key accounts. Provide critical support to District in increasing labor pool, strengthening client relationships, and handling staff placements. Create and implement widespread marketing, advertising, and promotional efforts to attract high-quality talent and impact revenues through increased billable hours. Direct the start-up of remote human resources departments at client locations, requiring rapid logistical planning, operations development, and procedural implementation.

**Major
Projects**

- *Major Warehouse* - Currently recruiting employees for a start-up assignment in Big City.
- *Major Retailer* - Developed an account into 2,000 billable hours per week within 2 months.
- *Major Consumer Manufacturer* - Produced 4,000 billable hours per week within 3 months.

MAIDE SERVICES, INC. - Cleanup, USA   (6/91-8/94)
Business Manager
Developed a start-up personal service operation which targeted residential and commercial markets. Prepared all bids and sales proposals, successfully generating 100 accounts within one year. Recruited, trained, and managed staff of up to 20 and all business administration functions.

ATTORNEY & PARTNERS - Legalville, USA   (3/90-6/91)
Employee Benefits Department/ERISA Paralegal
Provided tax and employee benefits support to internal Human Resources Department, fielding questions regarding coverage. Served as a client liaison drafting summary plan descriptions, amendments, and resolutions related to employee benefits programs. Prepared administrative packages and Internal Revenue Service forms.

* Also served as an ERISA Paralegal for Attorneys & More from 2/89 to 2/90.

EDUCATION

ACADEMIC UNIVERSITY - Studytown, USA
Bachelor of Arts in English - 5/87

**ADDITIONAL
TRAINING**

- A.B.A. Approved Lawyers Assistant Certificate, USA Center for Paralegal Training
- Experienced in Lotus 1-2-3, WordPerfect, Microsoft Word, dBase III

JOHN J. SEEKER
123 Job Hunting Lane
Top Dog, USA 20202
(555) 678-9101

MISSION   An attorney position that capitalizes on my strong legal track record.

LEGAL   **PHARR & COOLIDGE**   Sweetwater, USA
EXPERIENCE April 1994 - Present
                Associate - Manage a diverse case load, including large products liability, personal
                injury, and general liability cases in insurance defense practice. Conduct depositions
                in wrongful death, personal injury, and other tort cases. Experience includes
                extensive motions practice and substantial client contact.

                JONES & JONES, P.C.   Sweetwater, USA
                June 1991 - March 1994
                Associate - Managed all aspects of substantial civil litigation case load and worked
                extensively in all areas of commercial and construction litigation, corporate, real estate,
                domestic relations, and personal injury. Drafted and orally argued motions, conducted
                depositions, and presided over condominium association and board meetings.

                SMITH & SMITH   Sweetwater, USA
                June 1990 - October 1990
                Summer Associate - Conducted comprehensive research and wrote legal memoranda
                in the areas of insurance defense, corporate law, and family law. Also worked
                on all aspects of plaintiffs' personal injury suits and pre-trial litigation.

                JOHN DOE, P.C.   Mountain City, USA
                June 1989 - August 1989
                Law Clerk - Researched and wrote briefs, motion papers, complaints, and memoranda
                in the areas of real estate, tort, family, and corporate law. Attended trials,
                depositions, land partition, and domestic hearings.

EDUCATION   **EXCEL UNIVERSITY SCHOOL OF LAW**   Sweetwater, USA
                Juris Doctor Degree, May 1991
                Outstanding Grades:
                Civil Procedure-90, Criminal Law-90, Products Liability-87
                Activities and Honors:
                Dean's List, Fall 1990; Merit Scholarship Award, 1989-1990; Finalist, Fall Moot
                Court Competition; Moot Court Special Teams; Excel Rep., Intra-State Moot
                Court Competition; Moot Court Society; Fall Orientation Counselor.

                ELITE UNIVERSITY   Newtown, USA
                Bachelor of Arts in Economics with Finance Option, May 1989
                Activities & Honors:
                Dean's List five of eight semesters; Kau Epsilon (Economics Honor
                Society); Hall Government; Intramural Sports.

ADMISSIONS/ Admitted to State and Superior Courts, Court of Appeals, Sunshine State
MEMBERSHIPS Supreme Court, U.S. District Court for Northern and Middle Districts, United States
                Court of Appeals for the Eleventh Circuit, and District of Columbia Court of
                Appeals. Member, State Bar of Sunshine (Younger Lawyer and Entertainment and
                Sports Law Sections), Sweetwater Bar Association (Olympic Committee; Litigation
                Section; Sweetwater Council of Younger Lawyers - Elected Board Member-At-Large
                and Social Committee), American Bar Association (Entertainment Law, Sports Law
                and Insurance Law Divisions, Litigation Section),The Elite Alumni Association,
                Elite Club of Sweetwater, Sweetwater Jewish Federation.

REFERENCES References and writing samples available upon request.

SARAH J. SEARCH
123 Job Hunting Lane
Big Time, USA 10101
(444) 567-8910

OBJECTIVE

A demanding Paralegal position which utilizes my in-depth related academic background in combination with proven research, writing, and information management acumen.

EDUCATION

<u>PARALEGAL TRAINING CENTER</u> - Sweetwater, USA
A.B.A. Approved Civil Litigation Certificate - 5/96   **GPA: 3.5/4.0**
Healthcare Elective * *Simultaneously employed full-time.*

<u>SELBY COLLEGE</u> - Selby, USA
A.S. Degree in Paralegal Studies (ACICS Accredited) - 2/95   **GPA: 4.0/4.0**
* *Nationally recognized 2-year program.* * *Worked full-time while pursuing education.*

<u>UNIVERSITY OF SOUTH NEW ENGLAND</u> - Ficus, USA
A.A. Degree in Liberal Arts - 5/93 * *Specialized in Mass Communications*

**LEGAL
EXPERIENCE**

<u>FITZ & FLOYD</u> - Sweetwater, USA   (3/95-Present)
Formerly Bloch Floyd & Swift
Assistant to Attorneys
Provide support for a 6-attorney litigation firm specializing in insurance defense and products liability. Contribute to paralegal functions, such as conducting document searches and reviews. Analyze and interpret case information to determine relevance. Provide direct administrative and discovery support, including processing billing. Key contributor in preparation of the first issue of a company newsletter; compiled articles, ensured accurate citings, and assisted in layout. Selected to write an article on a complex legal issue requiring in-depth research on collateral estoppel and *res judicata*.

<u>LEGAL TEMP STAFFS</u> - Ficus, USA   (11/94-2/95)
Administrative Assistant/Contract Administrator
Assisted a variety of law firms on a project basis. Provided the staffing company with applicant test administration, contractor orientation, and communication of policies.

*Contract
Assignments:*

Muss, & Garty; *Land & King:* Monitored a 44-line phone system and handled extensive client reception for a major Ficus law firm; supported the Accounting Department in the creation of vendor and personal expense files.

<u>STATE OFFICE OF HEARINGS & APPEALS</u> - Ficus, USA   (7/94-10/94)
Social Security Administration Hearing Clerk
Attended hearings involving Social Security appeals process. Prepared detailed records of testimony to supplement audio record-keeping. Worked with claimants to interpret files in the absence of an attorney. Prepared files for submission to Administrative Law Judge.

**OTHER
EXPERIENCE**

<u>ENVIRO EQUIPMENT, INC.</u> - Ficus, USA   (5/93-7/94)

Office Manager
Provided comprehensive administrative support for distributor of specialized equipment and services. Developed strong customer service, troubleshooting, and administrative skills.

COMPUTER

- Lotus
- Windows
- dBase
- DOS
- Westlaw
- Lexis
- WordPerfect
- Inmagic

AFFILIATIONS

National Federation for Paralegals; State Association of Legal Assistants

---

REFERENCES AVAILABLE UPON REQUEST

SARAH J. SEARCH
123 Job Hunting Lane
Big Time, USA 10101
(444) 567-8910

CAREER SUMMARY

Multifaceted professional with demonstrated success in management and operational reporting
as well as key executive support roles.

EXPERIENCE

CONSULTANTS USA - Advisors, USA   (1992-Present)
Client Service Measurement Process Manager
Direct a wide array of functions related to performance and satisfaction measuring
and tracking, particularly client and partner surveys, for the consulting group.
Ensure timely production and distribution of monthly reports company-wide. Interface
with up to 175 partners to determine and accommodate their specific reporting needs.

- Spearheaded all internal methodologies and procedures for a start-up department.
- Comprehensively analyzed, cleansed, and redeveloped the existing client database,
  which required extracting critical client data from the field.
- Established controls for the survey process and identified new reporting requirements.
- Highly adept with computers, evidenced through self-education of 4 programs; solely
  customized database, database management, reporting, and client information software.
- Recognized for exceeding performance of counterparts during first year of the start-up.
- Created training materials and facilitate sophisticated formal field training.
- Analyze and interpret extensive statistical data, then author and distribute critical
  client-driven reporting to upper-level management teams.

Operational Reporting Specialist, National Center of Processing
Produced division financial statements as well as internal accounting and customer
service response reports which assessed efficiency of all business administration functions.
Conducted departmental audits to ensure quality and accuracy of internal procedures.

- Significantly expanded monthly operational reporting distributed to over 50 partners
- Created 30 different reports involving spreadsheets, charts, and graphs from ground zero.
- Promoted from a position as Executive Assistant providing management support to Controller.

INTERNATIONAL FINANCE, INC. - Moneytime, USA   (1990-1991)
Assistant to Controller/V.P.
Assisted the Controller with diverse financial and reporting functions including preparing
lines of credit, wire transfer, cash analysis, and salary reports. Other accountabilities included
reconciling A/R, filing state taxes, and handling bank deposits. Simultaneously provided a
wide range of executive support functions to the V.P., frequently demanding confidentiality.

USA WHOLESALE FOODSERVICE, INC. - Bargain, USA   (1987-1990)
Supervisor
Promoted from Assistant to the President to a multifaceted management role. Directed a
24-hour computer operation, ensuring critical accuracy and efficiency, related to order
processing, invoicing, inventory, purchasing, and reporting. Concurrently managed all A/P,
A/R, collections, payroll, and benefits administration functions. Hired and supervised
staff; also developed a training manual. Key contributor in all aspects of automating
the operation from a manual system. Interfaced closely with clients involving sales,
pricing updates, and customer troubleshooting.

COMPUTER

• Access	• WordPerfect	• PowerPoint	• Contact Management System
• MS Word	• Windows 95	• PC Tools	• Client Score Card
• Oasys	• KMAN	• Allways	• Executive Information System
• Excel	• Lotus 1-2-3	• Quicken	• CC Mail

EDUCATION

Cajun University, Majored in Computer Science

JOHN J. SEEKER

123 Looking Hard Avenue
Top Dog, USA 20202
(555) 678-9101

CAREER SUMMARY

Multitalented professional with a proven track record in all phases of operations, marketing,
and personnel management, including an expertise in transportation and distribution.

EXPERIENCE

FREIGHT CARRIERS CORPORATION   (1985-1995)
District Manager, Truck City, USA, 1993-1995
Comprehensively managed a multi-tiered transportation operation consisting of terminal,
sales, linehaul, maintenance, satellite terminals, and increased local territory.
Maintained full P&L accountability, which required strong leadership and executive
decision-making to ensure the achievement of bottom-line profit goals.

Terminal Manager, Truck City, USA, 1990-1992
Served as a key contributor in the planning and development of this highly visible Big City
facility which supported 45 satellite terminals. Directed the efforts of over 700 employees
for this 230-door Distribution Center. Coordinated the daily operations to maximize
efficiency and productivity. Maintained responsibility for sales, customer support,
and office administration activities. Acquired extensive knowledge of human resources
and government-regulated labor policies.

Terminal Manager, Truck City, USA, 1988-1990
Managed the operations, sales, and staffing for a 90-door terminal. Utilized
strong team-building and motivational skills to achieve corporate objectives.

Operations Manager, Transport Town, USA, 1986-1988
Oversaw a 2-terminal facility, one with 224 doors and the other with 150 doors. Managed
8 Supervisors and 100 dock personnel. Earned promotion from a Dock Supervisor role.

Dock Supervisor, Transport, USA, 1985-1986

TRUCKERS COMPANY - Delivery, USA   (1982-1985)
Operations Manager/Dock Supervisor
Completed an in-depth sales and management training program which resulted in
extensive knowledge of operations, dispatch, maintenance, labor, and sales.
Promoted rapidly to a Dock Supervisor position and subsequently to a position
of increased responsibility as Operations Manager. Directed a 200-door facility
which included 5 Supervisors and 60 dock personnel per shift. Efficiently
handled all operations and financial record-keeping.

EDUCATION

UNIVERSITY OF SUCCESS - Success, USA
B.A. Degree in Economics, 1982

**ADDITIONAL
TRAINING**

Attended numerous company-sponsored seminars in the following areas:

• Operations	• Leadership	• Human Resources
• Sales Management	• Quality	• Hazardous Materials
• Labor Relations	• Employee Relations	• Communications
• Affirmative Action	• Sales	

REFERENCES AVAILABLE UPON REQUEST

SARAH J. SEARCH

123 Job Hunting Lane
Big Time, USA 10101
(444) 567-8910

Confidentiality Requested

SUMMARY

Vastly talented professional with over 20 years of experience in an international business setting who demonstrates proven operational and personnel management expertise.

EXPERIENCE

<u>BANK INTERNATIONAL SERVICES, INC.</u> - Bankers, USA   (11/81-Present)
Group Vice President
Commercial Letter of Credit Department
Comprehensively manage all activities related to the issuance and negotiation of Letters of Credit (L/C). Primarily work with major corporations in a tri-state area including Countrytown, Peachstate, and Surfersville. Consult customers on opening L/Cs, including methods of payment on export/import operations. Supervise a staff of 31 in all aspects of L/C documentation. Identify client needs and ensure an efficient/accurate issuance. Manage the L/C functions for 8 affiliated institutions.

• Fully accountable for a departmental issuance of $80M per month in L/Cs.
• Ensure documentation and procedural compliance with strict regulations.
• Consistently achieve high standards of performance related to productivity.
• Maintain an outstanding record of undisputed payments with customer base.
• Possess in-depth knowledge of diverse banking regulations and guidelines.
• Key contributor to the development of various new/improved operational policies.
• Participated in a staff expansion; hired 8 people and wrote job descriptions.
• Realigned the structure of a newly developed operation after a consolidation.
• Utilize strong training skills/evaluation expertise to ensure proper staff
  placement; maintain a high staff retention rate.
• Employed effective strategic planning and crisis management skills in coordinating
  the merging of 8 different banking operations during a major restructuring project.
• Successfully maintained strong customer relations during consolidation; required
  extensive documentation of customer-related procedures to ensure smooth transition.

First Vice President, *International Banking*
Maintained accountability for numerous functional areas of operation including Standby L/Cs, international wire transfers, foreign exchange operations, and international check collections. Managed a staff of 26, including employee hiring and evaluation.

• Provided strong training, mentoring, and staff development guidance.
• Contributed to marketing efforts aimed toward corporate and civic groups.
• Conducted import/export seminars both internally and externally.
• Issued $5-9M per month in import L/Cs and $2-5M per month in export L/Cs.
• Maintained a high level of efficiency and synergy among staff members.
• Achieved multiple standards of performance within a complex operation.
• Initiated and remained instrumental in the automation of back-office L/C functions
  involving 4 banks; contributed to standardizing procedures, testing, and
  implementation of new system.

* *Previously employed in international banking operations as Vice President, USA
National Bank, 1978-81, and Assistant Vice President, Overseas Bank, 1968-78.*

EDUCATION

<u>SUCCESSVILLE COLLEGE</u> - Successville, USA
Bachelor of Arts Degree * *Majored in Business* * *Minored in Spanish*

AFFILIATIONS

• Executive Board of the Council on Bankers USA, Member
• Grievance Committee, Surfer State Bar Association (One of 3 Lay Persons Appointed)
• Orange City Air Cargo Association, Treasurer

PERSONAL

• Extensive international travel including Europe, Asia, Costa Rica, Canada

SARAH J. SEARCH
123 Job Hunting Lane
Big Time, USA 10101
(444) 567-8910

Confidentiality Requested

CAREER SUMMARY

Results-oriented marketing and advertising expert with a broadcasting background.

EXPERIENCE

<u>International Broadcasting Leaders, Inc.</u> - Satellite, USA   (1/92-Present)
International Broadcasters, 6/93-Present
Advertising and Marketing Manager
Provide a diverse range of advertising and marketing support to 12 global field offices.
Report to the V.P. and Senior V.P. of Marketing and Advertising. Strategically plan,
develop, and implement global network and broadcasting/syndication sales campaigns
from point of inception to completion for 3 international regions; Latin America,
Asia/Pacific, Europe. Design and produce numerous print, promotional, video, and
direct mail materials. Promote and advertise 3 networks, ABB International, URS,
and Fun City Network, as well as the syndication of MFM and Warner Sisters
libraries. Manage creative development, direction, and placement of trade and
publication advertising.

- Maintain full accountability for multiple project budgets up to $200K+.
- Work closely with agencies and in-house public relations/legal personnel.
- Disseminate crucial marketing/advertising information, affiliate updates,
  and collateral materials to 12 global field offices.
- Key contributor in organizing and participating in 3 annual marketing
  conferences for the international marketing personnel.
- Personally created and developed a Marketing Handbook outlining corporate
  guidelines for global marketing.
- Coordinate and execute aspects of International Network's participation in
  trade shows, conventions, exhibitions, and special events.
- Interface with high-level corporate and international personnel as well as maintain
  extensive ongoing communication/relationship with regional Marketing Directors.

International Cable Network Sales, Inc., 1/92-6/93
Event Marketing Coordinator
Comprehensively managed a wide array of conventions, trade shows, and special events for
ICNS, a highly visible division which sells all 7 International networks to cable companies
nationwide. Capable of organizing events from inception to completion. Handled
diverse responsibilities, including exhibits planning, booths/facilities selections, vendor
negotiations, booth configurations/floor plan development, production of C-prints and
duratrans, detailed logistics planning, registration of company delegates, and on-site
event supervision.

- Experienced in successfully managing budgets of up to $280K per event.
- Managed International Broadcasting's participation in regional conventions:
  Cowboytown, Great Rivers, Westville, Midwestern America, Centralized; also manage
  Cowboy Cable Show and International Cable Association Show.

SARAH J. SEARCH
123 Job Hunting Lane
Big Time, USA 10101
(444) 567-8910

EXPERIENCE, Continued...

- Personally coordinated all phases of visible events, i.e., Hall of Fame Game, Headliners - Local Copies - Weekend Anchors, Duckbills Opening Night Party.
- Assisted Marketing Director in planning additional events, i.e., Bowl Game of USA, Armball Allstar Game, Money Makers Foundation, and Annual Sales Meeting.
- Organized 12 ABL pre/post-game parties for cable operators/clients.
- Planned and implemented 30 local ad sales workshops throughout the nation.
- Successfully managed numerous projects simultaneously.
- Consistently achieved all budget management goals and project deadlines.
- Received excellent performance reviews and continued acknowledgment from management.

<u>Cold Valley Foundation</u> - Rocky Hill, USA   (8/88-7/89)
Intern, 1989 Ski Mountain Championships
One of 30 staff members handling various aspects of event management for Overseas premier biennial event with 300 million viewers globally. Personally wrote press releases and athlete biographies. Credentialed in excess of 2,000 press and broadcast personnel. Acted as a liaison with Host Broadcasting agencies, including BBC, INS, and Overseas Broadcast Union. Organized and conducted broadcaster briefings, coordinated pre-event and event broadcast coverage production schedule, and planned guest lists. Assisted in orchestrating and implementing major event sponsor and donor functions. Received 12 college credits.

<u>Cycling America Championships</u> - Bicycle, USA   (2/86-9/86)
Assistant to Team Services Director
Liaison between Team Services Director, major sponsors, and in excess of 57 International Cycling Teams. Organized training schedules, housing interviews, and outside functions. Assisted in production during 2-week Championships.

**OTHER
EXPERIENCE**
- Started and currently manage own wedding planning company, Best Weddings.
- Previously assisted in numerous sporting events, primarily sponsored by IPN.
- Gained experience as a Production Assistant with National Armball League games, several cycling venues, and the 1983 World Athlete Festival.
- Worked with XYZ Sports during National Skiing Championships, 1988, 1989, 1990.

EDUCATION
<u>University of Chillville</u> - Chilly, USA
Pursued a Bachelor of Science degree in International Affairs

- Former Member of Omega Pega Sorority, President of Junior Panhellenic Council

REFERENCES AVAILABLE UPON REQUEST

SARAH J. SEARCH

123 Job Hunting Lane
Big Time, USA 10101
(444) 567-8910

SUMMARY

Proven public relations and marketing background in agency and in-house settings.

EXPERIENCE

<u>CORN COUNTY CONVENTION & VISITORS BUREAU</u> - Shucksville, USA   (1996-Present)
PUBLIC RELATIONS & COMMUNICATIONS MANAGER

Comprehensively manage the creation and production of all print communications
for a convention and visitors organization. Strategically formulate an
annual marketing and advertising plan with respective department budgets.
Work in close collaboration with sales management and the President.

• Conceptualize, develop, write, and coordinate distribution of press releases,
   industry-specific and visitor guidebooks, monthly newsletters, event calendars,
   direct mail campaigns, and other special project publications.
• Secure increased publicity through local, national, and international press;
   serve as the key media liaison and department spokesperson.
• Coordinate Bureau-sponsored events and press familiarization programs.
• Represent the Corn Bureau as a speaker in the hospitality industry.

<u>THE CONCEPT AGENCY, INC.</u> - Creative, USA   (1995-1996)
CONTRACT ACCOUNT EXECUTIVE

Managed and supported account activities for 3 major clients in a reputable public relations
firm. Conducted market research and created proposals in alignment with accounts' goals.
Experienced in investigating case histories to formulate campaign ideas and track
performance. Wrote and edited news/press releases and compiled comprehensive press kit
materials. Developed extensive contact and distribution lists. Planned and scheduled
client meetings as well as organized clients' participation in press conferences.

• Produced both display and audio-visual materials for client presentations.
• Contributed to client development and devised effective account strategies.
• Cultivated strong press relations crucial for client sponsored PR events.

<u>THE FINE RESTAURANTS, INC.</u> - Dinnertown, USA   (1993-1995)
PUBLIC RELATIONS/MARKETING COORDINATOR

Solely managed all aspects of public relations and marketing aimed at promoting
this well-respected hospitality leader. Worked closely with outside agencies in
strategically developing various customer-focused events, including new store openings.
Conducted extensive market research involving focus groups. Conceptualized and
implemented advertising campaigns for both print and radio in conjunction with an
outside agency. Planned and executed numerous promotional events, supervised photo
shoots, coordinated corporate trades, and approved all charitable donations.

SARAH J. SEARCH
123 Job Hunting Lane
Big Time, USA 10101
(444) 567-8910

EXPERIENCE

THE FINE RESTAURANTS, INC. (Cont.)

- Gained valuable experience in media placement functions while supervising creative staff.
- Skillfully managed press relations by updating distribution lists, writing press releases, and pitching new story ideas aimed at restaurant promotion.
- Positively contributed to the successful opening of 10 restaurants in a multistate area.
- Effectively managed a public relations budget, ensuring most cost-efficient spending.
- Developed corporate newsletter to strengthen inter-department communications.

SUITE HOTELS INTERNATIONAL - Peach Pie, USA   (Summer 1992)
MANAGEMENT IN TRAINING

Trained extensively in all departments within the organization, including sales, customer service, personnel supervision, and profit/loss reporting. Illustrated strong financial aptitude and crucial management capabilities during this internship program.

MAYOR GOOD LEADER - Peaceville, USA   (Summer 1990)
PERSONAL ASSISTANT

Gained strong speech-writing skills and schedule management experience during an assignment with the Mayor Por Tempora. Also served as an office representative at public relations events. Contributed to a successful political campaign for Mayor.

LAWYERS, ETC. - Analytical, USA   (Summers 1985/89)
LIBRARIAN ASSISTANT/ACCOUNTANT

Provided legal research assistance and administrative and billing support to attorneys.

BANKING WORLDWIDE - Moneytown, USA   (January 1988)
PERSONNEL INTERN

Contributed to various interviewing, job applicant screening, and computer-related functions.

EDUCATION

ALL GIRLS UNIVERSITY - Boyville, USA
BACHELOR OF ARTS IN COMMUNICATIONS, 1993
Concentration: Public Relations and Advertising

AFFILIATIONS

- Convention & Visitors Bureau of America
- Public Relations Society International
- Peachie Press Club
- Peach State Press Club
- Intown Partnership, Former Executive Board Member
- Intown Restaurant Association, Former Member

COMPUTER

• MS Word	• Pagemaker	• WordPerfect	• Excel
• Quicken	• Professional File	• Lotus 1-2-3	

REFERENCES AVAILABLE UPON REQUEST

SARAH J. SEARCH, R.N.
123 Job Hunting Lane
Big Time, USA 10101
(444) 567-8910

OBJECTIVE

To secure a nursing position in a hospital setting where I may fully utilize my practical nursing skills to provide quality patient care and excellent treatment management.

EDUCATION

COAST COMMUNITY COLLEGE - Seabound, USA
A.D. in Nursing, 12/95

UNIVERSITY OF SOUTHERN STATE - Nicetown, USA
Pre-Nursing Studies (One Year)

**LICENSE/
CERTIFICATION**

• Registered Nurse, #R117326, 2/96
• CPR, 11/94

**RELATED
EXPERIENCE**

HEALTH CARE, INC. - Sweetwater, USA   (2/96-Present)
Registered Nurse
Manage a diverse range of daily living activities including administering medications as well as educating and counseling patients on behalf of this living assistance home health provider. Efficiently manage an assigned patient load with accountability for implementing care plans and accurately documenting patients' progress.

• Astute at identifying and reporting health abnormalities to prevent health-related tragedies.
• Successfully cultivate an atmosphere of trust and credibility with patients and families.

CROSBY HOSPITAL - Singing River, USA   (10/95-12/95; 8/94-12/94)
Extern
Worked in a variety of units, including Medical-Surgical, which emphasized caring for post-surgical and medical patients, and Intensive Care, which involved primarily treatment and medications to trauma and critically ill patients. Also, gained valuable experience observing Operating and Recovery Room activities.

**PRACTICAL
TRAINING**

SERVICEMEN'S HOSPITAL - Veterans, USA   (8/95-10/95)
Psychiatric Unit
Conducted patient assessments and therapeutic communication in order to identify patients' coping mechanisms. Provided critical documentation while dealing with severe mental illness. Served as a valuable resource in recommending external community-based referral programs.

NABISCO MILITARY BASE - Brereton, USA   (1/95-5/95)
Pediatric and Women's Health Unit
Handled a variety of functions, including patient evaluations, medications, charting, ambulating, and patient education/consultation. Worked closely with families and patients. Gained valuable experience in Neonatal ICU and Nursery, which involved newborn assessments and general care. Also, provided nursing assistance during labor and delivery, ultimately documenting the stages of labor, reporting abnormalities, and providing patient support. In the Post-Partum Unit, monitored patient recovery and post-labor health issues.

MILITARY SERVICES - Brereton, USA   (1/94-5/94)
Medical-Surgical
Performed a variety of ADL duties including skin and oral care. Diverse accountabilities included post-surgical and medical treatment implementation, medications, and ambulating. Experienced in turn, cough, and deep-breathing treatments.

**OTHER
EXPERIENCE**

ABC CORPORATION - Sometown, USA   (1/89-12/95)
Administrative Assistant
Efficiently performed bookkeeping, client relations, and administrative support duties.

SARAH J. SEARCH, MCR

123 Job Hunting Lane
Big Time, USA 10101
(444) 567-8910

CAREER SUMMARY

Dynamic, highly skilled professional possessing a proven track record in the real estate industry.

**REAL ESTATE
EXPERIENCE**

HEALTHCARE CORPORATION - Medicalville, USA   1994-Present
REAL ESTATE MANAGER

Direct a wide array of asset management and property management functions for
this services provider specializing in the healthcare industry. Asset Manager for
350 commercial properties encompassing 1.3 million sq. ft. in office space
throughout a 39-state region with total rental liability of $42M. Handle all
lease renewals, relocations, new branch development, and surplus property disposals.
Coordinate the acquisition and integration of new properties into the corporation.

- Report to the Vice President of Real Estate for this $467M company.
- Effectively manage 47 ongoing renewal and relocation lease negotiations simultaneously.
- Successfully executed 121 lease agreements in 1995.
- Managed the disposal of 44 properties, resulting in corporate savings of $853,100 in 1995.
- Research and identify 20 ongoing surplus property-disposal opportunities requiring
  expertise in sales, subleasing, and buyout transactions.
- Interface frequently with Branch, Regional, and Divisional Management as well as
  numerous other landlords, brokers, and outsourcing professionals.

SECURITY CORPORATION - Protection, USA   1989-1994
PROPERTY MANAGER

Comprehensively managed 550+ commercial properties consisting of 1,500,000 sq.
ft. throughout 48 states, with full accountability for $69 million in long-term lease
commitments. Authorized $15 million in annual lease payments. Simultaneously
responsible for all surplus property asset management and surplus property lease
negotiations for 25 corporately owned properties. Diverse range of responsibilities
included challenging real estate taxes, reconciling common area maintenance charges,
supervising all maintenance/repair and construction projects, leasing office space,
rent collection, restructuring outstanding debts, and surplus property disposal.

- Facilitated $85,000 in company savings through aggressive lease audits.
- Maintained superior surplus property disposal rates; 1992-89%; 1991-73%; 1990-63%.
- Facilitated exceptional surplus property savings; 1992-$628,813; 1991-$340,865; 1990-$280,855.
- Designed and implemented a property summary database system that maximized
  operational efficiency and resulted in improved work flow.
- Personally instituted automated reporting methods to expedite distribution of information.
- Out of 8,000 corporate employees, received an Employee of the Month award.
- Achieved 3 Team Cooperation Awards based on outstanding performance.
- Interfaced frequently with 550 Branch Managers, 500 Landlords, and senior management.
- Generated 20-year lease commitment projections for each property on an annual basis.
- Performed Phase I environmental inspections for properties entering/exiting lease commitments.

RELATED EXPERIENCE

<u>USA REALTY COMPANY</u> - Property Town, USA — 1980-1984

Held a highly visible position as Assistant to the President of this personal holding company with multibillion-dollar real estate holdings. Interfaced regularly with senior management. Acted as a liaison between Property Manager and President. Other duties included controlling company stock records, preparing quarterly reports, supervising fundraising projects, and managing office functions.

<u>OK MORTGAGE CORPORATION</u> - Loan City, USA — 1978-1979

Recruited to this company to manage up to $4M in loan packages. Fully responsible for the amortization and secondary marketing of million-dollar loan pools. Ensured accuracy of all documentation according to federal guidelines.

<u>BEST MORTGAGE CORPORATION</u> - Loanville, USA — 1976-1978

Gained extensive knowledge of the mortgage business by qualifying loan packages to meet FNMA or GHLMC standards. Managed amortization and secondary marketing process. Assisted in new employee training.

EDUCATION

<u>Society of Real Estate Executives</u>
MASTER OF CORPORATE REAL ESTATE, 1992
* *Only 300 individuals hold this designation nationally.*
* *Completed a thesis on the Americans With Disabilities Act (ADA).*

<u>Study More University</u> - Learningville, USA
B.B.A. IN REAL ESTATE 1989 Double Minor Concentration: Finance and Law
* *Self-financed 100% of Education.*

CERTIFICATIONS

- **CCIM Candidate**
- **Commercial MAI Certification A-1, A-2**
- **Residential RM Certification 8-1, 8-2, 8-3**

ADDITIONAL TRAINING

- Real Estate Market Analysis
- Corporate Real Estate Finance
- Commercial Real Estate Leases
- Real Estate Brokerage
- Principles of Real Estate
- Commercial Management & Leasing
- Negotiating Real Estate Transactions
- Real Estate Law
- Financial Investment Analysis
- Business of Corporate Real Estate
- Contracts in Corporate Real Estate
- Real Estate Investment Management
- Real Estate Appraisal
- Real Estate Mortgage Banking
- Real Estate Property Management
- Commercial Tenant Leasing
- Managing the Construction Process
- Legal Environment of Business
- Deming Total Quality Management
- Financial Analysis of Commercial Real Estate

COMPUTER

- Microsoft Office • Lotus 1-2-3 • Paradox • Dbase • EZ Analyzer

AFFILIATIONS/ ACTIVITIES

- SCRE, Society of Corporate Real Estate Executives:
  - Chair of Surplus Property Disposal Round Table Discussion for a National Convention
- WIRE, Women in Real Estate
- Study More University Real Estate Alumni Association, Former Treasurer
- Study More University, Guest Lecturer for Graduate Real Estate Class
- Published Author, *The Professional*, October 1992, Article on ADA.

REFERENCES AVAILABLE UPON REQUEST

SARAH J. SEARCH
123 Job Hunting Lane
Big Time, USA 10101
(444) 567-8910

OBJECTIVE

To secure a sales position within the computer industry where I may utilize my proven account management skills, lead-generation strategies, and superior customer service techniques.

EXPERIENCE

TECHNOLOGY TREND SETTERS - Creative, USA   (3/95-Present)
ACCOUNT MANAGER
Maintain full responsibility for all aspects of account management and development as a manufacturers' representative for 10 computer software companies. Supervise client activities throughout the Peachstate/Birdstate territory, primarily focusing on Fortune 1000 companies. Participate in new business development through cold calling, target market identification, sales presentations, and product demonstrations. Negotiate terms of contracts and cultivate strong customer relations throughout a lengthy sales cycle.

- Represent highly visible software vendors, i.e., ABC Interactive, Innovative Software, Software USA, WordSoft, TechnoSoftware, Computer Brains, and ClientWare.
- Possess in-depth knowledge of technologically advanced products, i.e., quality assurance automated testing tools, Internet security, data warehousing, legacy extension, Unix systems management, software configuration, and application development tools.
- Skillfully secured accounts with Softdrink USA, Reporting USA, America's Fabrics, Men's Power Tools, and Busted Reserve Bank of America.
- Initiated up to $750K in potential revenue within just 6 months of employment.

COMPUTERWORKS - Chipville, USA   (3/93-3/95)
ACCOUNT EXECUTIVE
Managed a diverse range of account responsibilities within an 11-state Northeastern region. Conducted extensive phone sales and lead-generation activities for outside sales associates. Sold computer product, maintenance, and training services to senior and mid-level management as well as various technical experts. Participated in prospect planning and marketing efforts, including trade show coordination and research.

- Generated and managed over 50 key accounts, i.e., Computer Busters, Geeksville Software.
- Developed a VAR channel of distribution which involved securing 11 VAR accounts.
- Consistently ranked in the top 10 sales representatives based on superior performance.
- Personally generated over $500K in sales revenues through annual telemarketing campaigns.
- Selected by management to provide comprehensive sales training to other representatives.

ABC INDUSTRIAL SUPPLY - Toolmaker, USA   (11/91-3/93)
ACCOUNT EXECUTIVE
Gained extensive inside sales experience by managing aspects of account development and expansion for an industrial tools wholesaler. Illustrated in-depth product knowledge in an organization which offered 250K different products. Handled service-related issues such as credit/billing discrepancies and researched client complaints to ensure rapid resolutions.

- Managed 5 of the top 10 company accounts; developed them into the key revenue producers.
- Displayed outstanding upselling techniques, relationship-selling strategies, and persuasive closing skills; generated $350K per month in product revenues.

* Previously managed/owned a start-up company with $400K annual revenues. Supervised 5 employees and handled all marketing and sales for Lots of Fun Yacht Service, 6/89-9/91.

EDUCATION

STUDY STATE UNIVERSITY - Booktown, USA - **Business Major**, 1989

AFFILIATIONS

- Member of Spontaneous Speakers International

JOHN J. SEEKER
123 Looking Hard Avenue
Top Dog, USA 20202
(555) 678-9101

CAREER SUMMARY

Vastly talented sales professional with a proven track record in all phases of the sales process,
with an emphasis in highly technical and regulated product lines.

EXPERIENCE

<u>ENERGY AMERICA CORPORATION</u> - Lightning Rod, USA   (2/87-8/98)
Engineers International Enterprise
Formerly Engineers Elite - Energy Process Division

NATIONAL SALES REPRESENTATIVE
Hired initially as a Sales Trainee for this steel company specializing in nuclear
power plants. Rapidly promoted to increased accountability as a Manager for 4 years
during tenure. Subsequently promoted into a Sales position. Successfully pioneered a
new sales market throughout a national territory. Aggressively cold called and pursued
key relationships with engineers and quality control personnel. Utilized sales and
account management skills in establishing and servicing over 40 accounts. Additional
responsibilities included purchasing, bid development, corporate presentations, product
testing, specifications compliance, extensive follow-up, and troubleshooting.

ACHIEVEMENTS:

- Ranked as one of the top 3 Sales Representatives 6 out of 11 years.
- Generated annual sales volume of up to $2.5M and negotiated 40% profit margins.
- Achieved status on top supplier lists among 10 out of 12 major accounts.
- Ranked in the top 1% out of 10,000 vendors with Edison Energy account.
- Ranked as one of the top 5 suppliers out of 2,000 with Baywatch Nuclear
  Operating Enterprise account.
- Developed major utility and subsupplier accounts, i.e., Going Electric,
  Edison Energy, Electric Illumination.
- As a Sales Representative, negotiated product purchases of up to $500K annually.
- Developed a sales forecasting method to better identify corporate strategies.
- Personally oversaw the redesign of a major warehouse facility, including developing
  all initial transportation/distribution and warehousing systems and procedures.
- Experienced in managing over $3M in inventory with crucial product traceability.
- Consistently maintained comprehensive knowledge of in-depth regulating guidelines.
- Demonstrate excellent planning and management skills based on coast-to-coast travel.

* Previously employed by the Bulletville Club as an Assistant Athletic Director in
  Bullet, USA from 1983 to 1987.

EDUCATION

<u>UNIVERSITY OF LEARNING</u> - Hard Work, USA
Bachelor of Science Degree, 1983

**PROFESSIONAL
TRAINING**

Completed various seminars related to Total Quality Management,
Sales, Public Speaking, Computers, and Product Knowledge.

CIVIC

Little League Coach, West Sports County Youth Center

SARAH J. SEARCH
123 Job Hunting Lane
Big Time, USA 10101
(444) 567-8910

OBJECTIVE

To continue in a challenging career where I may utilize strong sales, marketing, account management, and creative skills toward impacting future profits.

**RELATED
EXPERIENCE**

Communications Experts - Surfers, USA   (1995-Present)
Account Executive
Aggressively drive corporate revenue growth through new business development strategies involving advertising radio sales for national campaigns. Strictly target advertising agencies within an assigned region. Identify stations which align with the agency's client-specific advertising goals. Compile extensive market-related research, prepare promotional collaterals, and negotiate advertising rates, as well as develop and present proposals.

• Ranked as the #2 highest producer in the nation out of a sales force of 45.
• Solely generated over $3M in revenues within first 8 months.
• Cultivated and continuously manage critical relationships with major advertising
  agencies, e.g., Advertising Innovators, Media Makers, and International Agency.
• Maintain knowledge of nationwide radio stations with respect to diverse market profiles.

Radio Store - Sunnyside, USA; Peachstate, USA   (1993-1995)
Account Executive
Employed highly effective account management skills for this third-party media resource service. Actively developed new business throughout an assigned Sunny State territory. Served as a key liaison between advertising agencies and radio stations. Demonstrated strong persuasive selling skills, negotiations strategies, and needs-identification techniques. Interfaced frequently with primary decision-makers, which included providing top-notch client service. Adept in all aspects of the sales process.

• Key contributor in 100% achievement of a $2.4M group sales budget.
• Personally produced $800K in revenues on an individual basis.
• Recognized for establishing profitable relationships with 2 advertising
  agencies previously uninterested in outsourcing media placement functions.
• Analyzed target audiences and conceptualized promotions in conjunction with radio stations.
• Hired initially as Advertising Sales Assistant, providing ongoing sales support for
  the nation's largest radio advertising sales and marketing company.

Cable Network Monsters, Inc. - Big Company, USA   (1992)
Marketing Intern
Assisted in the development of marketing materials for 5 major networks:
NTN, SBT, NNC, News in a Flash, Laughing Network. Demonstrated an ability to interface well with creative staff and upper-level personnel.

• Summarized press releases and created print promotions as part of the ABC Kit.
• Wrote copy and selected photographs for the programming highlighting calendars.
• Contributed to proofing of print and film advertising prior to production.
• Worked with ad agencies and participated in a cable advertising campaign.
• Compiled survey information and prepared a summary report for the V.P. of Marketing
  which provided the foundation of Cable Network Monsters' new marketing strategy.

EDUCATION

University of Peaches - Peachville, USA
B.B.A. Degree in Marketing, 1993 * Peaches, Peaches, Peaches Sorority, Alumni

COMPUTER

• WordPerfect • Lotus 1-2-3 • Strata • Donovan • Windows • PowerPoint

JOHN J. SEEKER
123 Looking Hard Avenue
Top Dog, USA 20202
(555) 678-9101

CAREER SUMMARY

Multitalented individual demonstrating a wide array of professional expertise in management, public and community relations, public speaking, and writing.

RELATED EXPERIENCE

NOW RADIO - Sunshine City, USA   (1994-1998)
Assistant Program Director
Key contributor in managing all aspects of taped and live programming, including conceptualization, writing, formatting, and production of on-air news specials, interviews, contests, and public service spots. Managed staff and conducted daily programming meetings.   Developed and directed widespread public relations and community action programs.

Special Projects:
• Conducted on-air interviews with experts, addressing numerous politically, economically, and socially charged issues.
• Organized community meetings to welcome newcomers into the Sunshine City area.

CAR TOWN - Sunshine City, USA   (1991-94)
Editor, *Cars of the Future*
Personally managed the production of an internal publication designed to communicate with an employee population of 7,000. Researched and conceived story lines, conducted interviews, and wrote articles. Handled all design, layout, and editing functions. Also, supervised print production and circulation. Utilized strong writing skills in targeting diverse readership. Magazine recognized as the "top" publication company-wide.

USA WIDE SCHOOL SYSTEM - Cottontown, USA   (1987-91)
Instructor
Successfully taught Journalism and English courses to high school students.

* Additionally held a position as an Adjunct Instructor at Uknow College from
   1980 to 1990 with accountability for teaching a Broadcast Journalism course.

EDUCATION

LEGAL STUDIES COLLEGE OF LAW - Sunshine City, USA
DOCTOR OF JURISPRUDENCE

REALLY GOOD UNIVERSITY - Cottontown, USA
MASTER OF ARTS IN ENGLISH LITERATURE (Pending Final Thesis)
BACHELOR OF ARTS IN ENGLISH

MILITARY

UNITED STATES SERVICE - **AVIATION MAINTENANCE ADMINISTRATOR**

LANGUAGES

Working knowledge of French

SPEAKING ENGAGEMENTS/ PUBLICATIONS

• *Sunshine City Business Scene*, National Association of Minority CPAs, Sunshine City
• *Green Capitalism*, Unique Institute of Entrepreneurship & Management, Sunshine City
• *Combating Drano*, XYZ-TV, Cottontown
• *Creative Writing for Media* (Lecture Series), The College, Sunshine City, USA
• "Characteristics of the Green Scene," Sunshine City Chamber of Commerce

AFFILIATIONS/ CIVIC

• 100 Striped Men of America, Sunshine City Chapter, North Metro
• Veteran's Administration, Vet Counselor

SARAH J. SEARCH
123 Job Hunting Lane
Big Time, USA 10101
(444) 567-8910

CAREER OBJECTIVE

To pursue a challenging career in surety underwriting with a growth-oriented organization that values
proven financial experience, analytical expertise, and strong computer skills.

EXPERIENCE

<u>INSURANCE UNITED COMPANY</u> - Snow City, USA   (8/94-7/95)
Underwriter Trainee
Comprehensive involvement in a year-long training program designed to introduce
newly hired underwriters to the major components of fidelity, surety, and
commercial lines underwriting.

Fidelity (Completed training, 1995)
Finalized training in underwriting primarily for financial institutions, insurance companies,
mortgage companies, and brokerage houses. Utilized extensive knowledge of financial
institutions' fidelity and insurance products. Carefully conducted complete and accurate
financial analysis of applicants' profiles, then rated and coded companies to determine
premium amounts. Employed a broad range of computer skills to analyze applicants'
financial stability using custom-designed software.

Surety (Completed training, passed exam in 1995)
Evaluated submissions and made decisions on whether to approve/decline bonds based
on financial analysis, risk evaluation, and other underwriting criteria. Also rated and
coded submissions to determine premium amounts. Performed extensive financial and
trend analyses. Utilized essential data-entry skills for work-in-process analysis.
Visited off-site agencies that offer contractor bonds. Met with contractors at annual
meetings to clarify account status and ensure account stability. Expertly compiled
meeting reports and contractor summaries.

Commercial (Completed training, passed exam in 1995)
Carefully analyzed financial statements to determine feasibility of bond offerings for
specific businesses and professions. Examined Dun & Bradstreet reports and determined
company net worth according to standards set by Insurance United. Presented final
recommendations based on findings.

**SPECIAL
PROJECTS**

• Assigned to carefully track commissions and calculate new commission schedules.
• Provided annual reviews of accounts for submission for recommendation to increase
  bond amounts for those accounts whose limits exceeded approval authority.

EDUCATION

<u>GREAT STATE UNIVERSITY</u> - Wonderful, USA
B.S. Degree in Finance and International Business, 1994
GPA: 3.43/4.0   Major GPA: 3.8/4.0   * *Studied Abroad in Europe, 1993*

ACTIVITIES

• Equestrian Team   • Go Girls Social Sorority   • Dean's List
• Orientation Leader   • Cool Guys Little Sister   • CPR Certified

COMPUTER

• Microsoft Word   • Windows   • Excel   • Lotus 1-2-3

**LANGUAGES/
PERSONAL**

• Fluent in French, Spanish, and Arabic
• Formerly resided in France, Yugoslavia, and Lebanon

REFERENCES AVAILABLE UPON REQUEST

SARAH J. SEARCH
123 Job Hunting Lane
Big Time, USA 10101
(444) 567-8910

OBJECTIVE

A challenging position where I utilize my proven background in the areas of customer service and administration management combined with expertise within the office furniture industry.

SKILLS & STRENGTHS

• Proficient in Word for Windows and in managing multi-line communications systems.
• Exceptionally organized and talented at prioritizing heavy workloads.
• Proven problem-solving and decision-making skills in high-pressure environments.
• Articulate and poised individual demonstrating excellent interpersonal skills.

EXPERIENCE

<u>ABC Graphics & Interiors</u> - Designer, USA   (1995-Present)
Customer Service Representative
Manage all customer service functions related to office furniture catalog telephone sales for an organization with 2 major wholesale suppliers. Research and gather industry comparison data to prepare revenue-generating customer proposals. Perform key support functions including purchasing, communications management, credit processing, and delivery coordination.

• Establish effective client relationships with over 200 vendors due to outstanding customer service.
• Maintain current knowledge of office furniture product information from 300+ manufacturers.

<u>Data Systems, USA</u> - Information, USA   (1990-1995)
Administrative Assistant
Performed a diverse range of support functions with an emphasis in invoicing vendors, posting payments, and processing payables. Other key duties included coordinating new accounts as well as shipping/receiving. Administrative functions included ordering office supplies, data entry, multi-line phone management, and office reception functions.

• Handled inventory control of over $200K in highly technical equipment.
• Managed detailed records of customer equipment/coordinated pre-installation product distribution.
• Demonstrated excellent troubleshooting/problem resolution skills related to back orders/returns.

<u>Learning Center of America</u> - Educators, USA   (1988-1990)
Assistant Manager
Assisted in personnel and operations management for this educational system retailer. Accountabilities included purchasing, inventory control, shipping/receiving, and merchandising. Handled bank deposits, opening/closing, and computer work. Consulted educators and customers in product selections.

• Acted as account liaison with school accounts in 5-county area ranging up to $30K in gross sales.
• Worked within strict time constraints regarding vendor research and price negotiations.

<u>XYZ Office Equipment</u> - Comfort, USA   (1983-1988)
Assistant Manager/Sales Representative
Comprehensively assisted in managing all daily operations for this office supply and equipment retailer. Performed outside and inside sales duties with an emphasis in customer service. Handled ordering, coordinated deliveries, and resolved billing issues.

• Personally serviced high-volume accounts with gross sales of up to $20K monthly.
• Utilized strong price negotiation and inventory control skills purchasing from 3 major suppliers.
• Received merchandise deliveries, processing all paperwork including returns.
• Interfaced with upper-level management personnel within diverse industries.

* Previous experience includes an additional Sales and Administrative staff position.

JOHN J. SEEKER

123 Looking Hard Avenue
Top Dog, USA 20202
(550) 678-9101
johnseeker@internet.com

CAREER SUMMARY

A multitalented system architect with an extensive technical background that emphasizes
business automation design projects.

SIGNIFICANT QUALIFICATIONS

- Multi-platform system development expertise in multi-threaded environments combined with a vast
  understanding of the latest object-oriented (OO) programming languages, tools, and design methodologies.
- Unique experience encompasses working with industry leaders, who have previously defined
  leading-edge OO technology, in formulating the basis of forerunning programming patterns/frameworks.
- Experienced technical trainer with excellent presentation, teaching, and public speaking skills.
- Technically astute with a high level of programming skill and team programming experience.
- Proven client management strengths required to collaborate with senior management in evaluating
  change requests, defining project requirements, prioritizing projects, and allocating resources.
- Highly skilled in conceiving, planning, executing, and instituting technology improvements.
- Adept at using development methods that ensure project control, user acceptance, and quality.

EXPERIENCE   TECHNICAL DEVELOPMENT, INC. - Tech Town, USA   (2/95-Present)
**CONSULTANT/LEAD SYSTEM ARCHITECT/
TECHNICAL TRAINER**
Pursue and secure a variety of highly technical, visible assignments with major corporations.
Impressive track record of on-site software development and joint development projects. Serve as a
Contract Trainer instructing on C++ and Visual Studio topics at various A-Tech Centers worldwide.
Set up a corporate Intranet NT network solution that required establishing a corporate Web Server
and designing a Web system that included an Informix Database along with JAVA and HTML.

*Project
Highlights:*

LOGIC - LEAD ARCHITECT
Led a team of 6 Developers in constructing an application framework developed in C++
and ATL environments for this software reseller to utilize in designing a new suite of
logistics applications written in Visual Basic and C++.

- Designed core framework using UML and Rational Rose in addition to developing company's
  first commercially distributed application utilizing the newly designed framework.
- Instrumental in transitioning company from procedural to OOA/D development environment.
- Delivered C++ and ATL development training and provided mentoring to enhance Developers'
  skills in utilizing the newly designed core framework in developing new applications.

TOO TECHNICAL, INC. - OO FRAMEWORK ARCHITECT
Recruited to a unique assignment spearheaded by a well-known author and some technology experts.

- Assisted in developing an innovative new scripting language designed to more effectively
  express business logic while enforcing EBTs with frameworks that expedite development.
- Key contributor in building a rules manager framework called RM3 using OOA/D written with C++
  language and using Visual Age/C++ compiler in a cross-platform NT, 95, and OS/2 environment;
  based on project success, the new framework has been sold commercially to XYZ's clients.

CREDIT SERVICES, INC. - LEAD DESIGN ARCHITECT
Recruited as the OS/2 programmer and expert to manage a struggling PC-based automation
project, which involved revising a time-critical, high-volume card-replacement application.
Coordinated and completed heavy programming, project management, and a phased roll-out,
which included system installation and end-user training, within a strict 3-month time frame.

Project Highlights:

<u>CREDIT SERVICES, INC</u>. (Cont.)
- Championed a major shift in programming strategies to include design patterns and OOA/D.
- Provided key staff mentoring and training responsibilities for the programming team.
- Wrote software which automated call center update processes and reduced staffing requirements.
- Designed updates using OOA/D, utilizing Booche and UML methodologies and Rational Rose.
- Developed enhancements that reduced call time 50% and helped salvage disgruntled accounts.
- Utilized Visual C++, Internet Explorer, VBScript, COM, and Active X technologies.

XXX - LEAD DESIGN ARCHITECT
Critical member of a large programming team which developed diverse business applications for senior management. Identified technical requirements and produced multi-language software.

- Built customized charting and graphing software in a real-time environment using LU 6.2.
- Developed complex software involving GUI for managing transportation workstations to ensure critical on-time deliveries, contract compliance, and internal efficiency.
- Initiated a voice-recognition component while writing an Executive Interface software system.
- Collaborated with author of C++ and FAQs in implementing an extended Railroad Management framework which utilized GUI and design patterns.

<u>DATA CONTROL SYSTEMS, INC.</u> - Peachtown, USA   (6/92-2/95)
SENIOR SOFTWARE DEVELOPER
One of a 4-member programming team to devise a factory control software product which regulated various environmental-specific process, production, and equipment maintenance controls. Performed in-depth application coding which included on-site programming and client troubleshooting in the field, using OS/2 PM and involving GUI development.

- Programmed customized clients' bid-specific software according to critical time frames.
- Wrote main system initialization software involving multi-threaded programming solutions.
- Built system security manager applications to govern user access rights.

<u>CREDIT SERVICES, INC.</u> - Splash, USA   (2/89-6/92)
SENIOR TPF ONLINE SPECIALIST
Hired initially as TPF Online Specialist monitoring a mainframe operating system prior to earning a promotion to a Senior technical role. Conceived and launched a mainframe automation using multi-threaded C++ programming in OS/2 to create an PC-based application that reduced mainframe downtime and streamlined reporting.

- Created software that facilitated significant savings during an inter-facility mainframe migration by eliminating errors and associated high-cost-per-minute time delays.
- Earned two employee recognition awards based on outstanding contribution and performance.

EDUCATION

<u>UNIVERSITY OF WESTERN CITY</u> - Lighthouse, USA
B.S. IN COMPUTER SCIENCE, 1988

CREDENTIALS

- **Microsoft Certified Solutions Developer (MCSD)**
  Specializing in Visual C++ and OLE Development using MFC

- **Microsoft Certified Trainer (MCT)** - Able to Facilitate MOC Classes:
  (1012) Mastering COM Development Using Visual C++
  (1011) Mastering MFC Fundamentals Using Visual C++
  (1015) Mastering MFC Development Using Visual C++
  (1298) Developing Distributed Applications with Visual Studio 6.0

PUBLICATIONS

- Published in *URTECHNICAL Online Magazine* (1991)
- Contracted by Wren book publisher to author "Designing Dynamo Stuff: Applications with Design Patterns in ATL Using Visual Studio 6.0" (In progress)

JOHN J. SEEKER
123 Looking Hard Avenue
Top Dog, USA 20202
(555) 678-9101

CAREER SUMMARY

Dynamic, multitalented professional possessing vast experience in counseling,
human resources, training and development, and event planning.

SIGNIFICANT QUALIFICATIONS

Human Resources
- Talented counselor with a proven track record of assisting individuals in surmounting debilitating problems which limit professional and personal success.
- Possess extensive recruiting, staff relations, and employee record-keeping experience.

Training & Development
- Demonstrated success in originating management and professional development training programs from ground zero using both formal and informal formats.
- Excellent instructor with a keen insight into learning curves and audience receptivity.

Management
- Effectively direct the activities of a large staff due to strong leadership skills.
- Outstanding operations and resource management abilities due to advanced organizational, time management, and financial skills.

Event Planning
- Experienced in all phases of event planning including budgeting, event marketing, sponsor solicitation, vendor negotiations, and logistics coordination.
- Successfully planned and implemented numerous employer training programs and association-sponsored workshops.

EXPERIENCE

HEALTH COUNSELING CLINIC - Sunshine City, USA   1995-Present
Director/Counselor
Successfully initiated and developed a private counseling/consulting practice employing up to 8 Counselors. Personally manage all personnel functions including staff recruiting, training, and supervision. Comprehensively manage all operational functions including marketing, advertising, promotions, business administration, and community/patient relations. Full P & L accountability.

- As a form of public relations and promotions, conduct extensive public speaking and develop articles for publication.
- Experienced presenter/lecturer for audiences of up to 500; topics include sales, motivation, management, health, employee training.
- Personally developed all marketing materials and collateral speaking materials, including audio-visual presentations.
- Actively consult corporations and entrepreneurs in a variety of industries on their business practices in order to improve bottom-line profitability.
- Solely secured all new business, cultivating strong business-community relations.

XYZ CENTER - Sunshine City, USA   1990-1995
Human Resource Director/Instructor
Performed multiple job responsibilities for this state-approved instructional institution/ counseling center. Hired initially as a Staff Therapist and promoted rapidly into a management role. Acted as an Instructor, School Counselor, and Director of Therapist Relations. Gained vast experience in human resources management including recruiting, training, evaluation, and staff supervision. In addition, developed personal client base by providing therapeutic recovery.

EXPERIENCE
Continued...

U. R. HEALTHY - Sunshine City, USA   1986-1990
Training Coordinator
Assumed this newly created position, gaining full accountability for originating corporate training procedures for an $80 million company with 2,500-plus employees. Conceived and implemented all formal training programs with an emphasis in management, sales, product knowledge, customer relations, policies and procedures, union avoidance, safety, and security topics. Actively participated in management recruitment and manpower planning. Managed all phases of training and development from logistics planning, to structuring curriculum, to administering follow-up. Selected as member of the Training Council.

MILITARY DEPARTMENT - Uncle Sam, USA   1983-1986
Combat Development Experimentation Command, Captain
Rapidly promoted to increasing levels of responsibility and rank. Directed a staff of up to 53 and managed up to $11.2 million in facilities and equipment. Acquired valuable experience in operations management, planning, personnel supervision, and international relations. Exercised strong decision-making skills and crucial diplomacy.

EDUCATION/
RELATED
TRAINING

BEST UNIVERSITY - Eastern, USA
B.S. Degree in Secondary Education 1975
* *Self-financed 100% through employment.*
* *College employment emphasized retail sales.*

• Completed extensive training through the military, associations, and private
  institutions regarding Human Resources, Training and Development, Management,
  and Counseling.

HONORS/
AFFILIATIONS

• Nominated by XYZ Center for an ASTD Torch Award for Contributions to Employer
• Nominated twice by Sunshine City Chamber of Commerce and *Sunshine City Business
  Chronicle* for Entrepreneur of the Year Award
• Nominated by Sunshine State Speakers Association as Member of the Year
• Received a U.S. Military Commendation Medal and other performance accolades
• National Society for Performance & Instruction
• American Society for Training & Development
• Sunshine State Society of Professional Graphologists, Executive Director
• National Speakers Association; Sunshine State Speakers Association, Board of Directors
• Behavioral Research Laboratories, Director
• American Hypnosis Association, President
• The Northern Medical Center, Director of Behavior Modification
• Elected to Who's Who of Men of Achievement
• Appointed to the Advisory Board of popular men's health magazine
• Co-hosted and Hosted two television broadcasts
• Published Author in numerous publications including *Sunshine City Business
  Chronicle* and *Sun City News*

OTHER
CREDENTIALS

• Certificate, Behavioral Graphology
• Diploma, Clinical Hypnotherapy

REFERENCES AVAILABLE UPON REQUEST

JOHN J. SEEKER
123 Looking Hard Avenue
Top Dog, USA 20202
(555) 678-9101

OBJECTIVE A challenging position where I may fully exercise my creative aptitude and technical expertise toward professional development.

QUALIFICATIONS

Education Mountain University - Stone Village, USA
Bachelor of Fine Arts in Studio Art
Emphasis in Photography   Expected Graduation: Summer 1999

Coursework Includes Photography...Computer Imaging...Applied Theater...
Acting...Costume Design...Dance (Modern)

Old Time College - Old Time, USA
Associate of Fine Arts in Studio Art 1994

Computer
- Super Paint 2.0
- Image Studio
- Digital Dark Room
- Aldus Freehand
- Mac Word 4.0

Activities/ Affiliations
- Photographer for Quantrek, an outdoor organization.
- Program Council, student organization, **Assistant Production Manager** with total management responsibility for Old Time Chapel Theater. Other positions include Stage Technician, Film Series Usher and Projectionist, Photo Editor for the Calendar, and Assistant to the Media Department.
- Technical Positions at Old Time Theater include Assistant Director, Stage Manager, Lighting Director, and Carpenter for *You Can't Take It with You, Buried Child, The Rivals, Rashmon,* and *Places in the Heart.*
- Actor at Old Time Theater, played the Grand Duke in *Cinderella* and the Prime Minister in *Emperor's New Clothes.*
- Member of the Drama Club (Vice President) and Olga Omega, a dramatic honor society.

EXPERIENCE

Photographer Mountain University - Stone Village, USA (1995 - Present)
Photographer Lab Monitor
Responsibilities include preparing chemicals and stocking supplies for the Fine Arts Photo Lab. Assist students with resolving both technical and creative problems.

Reflections - Stone Village, USA (Summer 1997)
Assistant to Still Photographer
Worked with the Still Photographer in developing black and white photographs for this motion picture which was filmed on campus.

The School - Old Time, USA (1992 - 1993)
Photographer, School Newspaper

Stage Technician Figgy Auditorium, Mountain University - Stone Village, USA (1994 - Present)
Mountain Green Amphitheater - Dine Out City, USA (Summers 1995, 1996)
Rock Theater - Stone Village, USA (1995)
The Ionia - Dine Out City, USA (1995)
Extensive technical knowledge regarding set up, strike, sound, lights, staging, band gear, and rigging. Proficient in operation of lighting and sound boards for diverse types of performances. Expertise in musical concerts.

Projectionist Figgy Auditorium, Mountain University - Stone Village, USA (1994 - Present)
New Cinemas - Sunshine City, USA (1992)
Experienced in 16 mm projectionist duties as well as 35 mm and 70 mm film.
Effective in areas of splicing and minor projector maintenance.

JOHN J. SEEKER
123 Looking Hard Avenue
Top Dog, USA 20202
(555) 678-9101

CAREER SUMMARY

A multitalented executive with a proven track record in the areas of operations management,
sales, and service coupled with exceptional abilities in personnel leadership and training.

SIGNIFICANT QUALIFICATIONS

**Operations
Management**

- Display strengths in articulating mission-critical goals, implementing the tactical activities
  required to achieve success, and managing corporate resources within approved budgets and plans.
- Quantify objectives, rank solutions, conduct vendor negotiations, recommend viable action plans
  with back-up alternatives, and facilitate the attainment of defined results.
- Utilized RFP to develop business cases for mission-critical projects using NPV or IRR criteria.
- Apply mature management practices leading a diversified work force toward goal achievement.
- Nurture a resourceful and innovative atmosphere to create a staff culture that manifests
  consensus and shared ownership of both objectives and accomplishments.
- Act on solid understanding of staff productivity and commitment levels required for goal achievement.

Training

- Demonstrate distinctive skills in course development and delivery, instructor skills development,
  and training program management at domestic and international locations.
- Identified and applied emerging training methodology developing 25 professional instructors.
- Possess certified expertise in the development and delivery of cutting-edge computer-based
  technical/sales training course materials and textbooks utilized worldwide.
- Authored mainframe CAI tools that achieved outstanding learning effectiveness.
- Originated CAI training needs analysis modules used system-wide by international airline carriers.

**Sales &
Service**

- Skilled at conceptualizing and implementing methodologies that deliver effective service.
- Leverage knowledge capital toward strengthening an organization's competitive positioning.
- Developed and implemented industry-specific service-level agreements supported by infrastructure.
- Strategically apply effective sales techniques including customer qualification, product offering,
  assumptive close, recap, and conscientious service after the sale.
- Cultivate partnerships through consultative selling skills to foster account growth and retention.
- Adept at client service needs identification, accurate problem diagnoses, and prompt resolution.

EXPERIENCE

TOOL TIME   Farmville, USA
DIRECTOR OF CUSTOMER RELATIONS   (1996-Present)
Launched an efficient and centralized customer relations center from ground zero,
serving 5,000+ lawn/garden dealers nationwide, with full accountability for a capital and expense
budget in excess of $1M. Merged finance, credit, sales, service, and technical support functions
into one "blended" call center operation. Hired, trained, and directed a management staff of 3
and 45 account specialists. Leveraged focus group-based research.

- Met or exceeded $25M variable monthly revenue goals by astute start-up operations management.
- Oversaw all aspects of 30,000 sq. ft. facility build-out, i.e., ergonomic layout, staffing, technology
  architecture, and application selection, in 3 months, at $600K budget, without service interruption.
- Installed an advanced telephone switch functionality to accomplish *one-call-does-it-all* philosophy.
- Achieved business-business and business-consumer service-level agreement goals relative to
  the quantity and quality of calls answered and efficiency of customer handling time.
- Successfully gained support of executive committee for all sales and service methodologies.

LIVEWORLD   Sunshine City, USA
MANAGER, BUSINESS/INFORMATION SYSTEMS   (1991-1996)
Developed innovative applications and managed systems support of internal multi-site
call center operation and field sales. Systems support resulted in efficient handling of
1.2 million calls annually by 250 agents in an airline mainframe/client server environment.

EXPERIENCE
Continued...

LIVEWORLD - (Cont.)

- Centralized 3 airlines' customer support operations through load balancing supported by technology.
- Optimized customer support tools to service 12,000 subscribers on 36,000 terminals.
- Key player in leading-edge LAN/WAN and CTI implementations using major vendors such as ABC, XYZ, and UP at Flyaway, Courteous, and OBC airline sites.

USA TRAVEL SYSTEMS
MANAGER, TECHNICAL/SALES TRAINING

Alltowns, USA
(1986-1991)

Managed all aspects related to training staff of 25 that delivered state-of-the-art technical and sales training to 3,000+ travel agents annually at 3 domestic hubs and international sites. Accountable for trainer competencies on continually evolving curriculums and training methods. Oversaw logistical coordination of trainee lodging, transportation, and entertainment needs.

- Pioneered cutting-edge Hunter EEI methodology to develop world-class, competent trainers.
- Elevated corporate training effectiveness to top performance from lowest within one year.
- Negotiated contracts directly with Huntley & Cook Hotel's domestic and international local site management staffs to secure optimum pricing/benefits on 15,000+ room nights annually.
- Met stringent worldwide Courteous/OBC training goals by utilizing zero-based budgeting.

OBC, INC.

Sardine, USA; Alltowns, USA
(1976-1986)

REGIONAL RESERVATIONS SALES/SERVICE MANAGER, 1984-1986
Directed the reengineering of business processes to create more efficient and sales-effective airline reservations operation. Streamlined frontline and back office prior to corporate spin-off.

- Served as Project Lead pioneering and instituting from ground zero a benchmark remote call center program that saved costs, gained national exposure, and triggered similar programs.
- Achieved #1 ranking in system productivity nationally within highly competitive environment.
- Led initiatives on entire set of operational goals related to sales, answering quality, performance, loss control, budget, and absenteeism that resulted in achievement of maximum effectiveness.

CENTRAL OFFICE/TRAINING SUPERVISOR, 1976-1984
Implemented capacity management strategies to handle 700 flights daily and achieve optimum revenue gain. One of 12 on corporate task force conducting on-site visits in 16 OBC offices worldwide. Monitored service operations and front-line impact. Mandated and ensured effective performance of process improvement changes based on observations reported to management teams. Developed and supervised implementation of training for 2,000 employees.

* Prior experience as OBC Reservations Sales Agent/Team Leader, Ville, USA, during college. Consistently exceeded performance goals.

EDUCATION

UNIVERSITY OF LEARNING - Alltowns, USA
Pre-MBA in Business

UNIVERSITY OF ACADEMIA - Ville, USA
B.A. in English Language/Literature   ** Speak Fluent Trainer Language*

TRAINING/
SEMINARS
- Knowles Adult Learning
- Flyaway CBI Authoring
- Transactional Analysis
- Reference Materials
- Programmed Instruction
- Hunter EEI Methods

AFFILIATIONS
- American Society for Training, 18-year member; Program Chairperson

COMPUTER
- Numerous Office Productivity Software Tools
- ABC UNIX
- XYZ O/S2
- Informix SQL
- HP-UX

179

SARAH J. SEARCH
123 Job Hunting Lane
Big Time, USA 10101
(444) 567-8910

OBJECTIVE

To continue a successful career where I may fully utilize my proven customer service, account management, sales, and negotiation skills toward impacting future profits.

KEY QUALIFIERS

- Outstanding account management skills useful to nurturing an existing customer base.
- Strong problem-solving and troubleshooting abilities, crucial to customer service.
- Demonstrated effectiveness in detail-oriented positions based on organizational skills.
- Excellent decision-maker with proven experience in fast-paced, diverse work environments.
- Talented sales professional with strong negotiation and persuasive selling techniques.

RELATED EXPERIENCE

NETWORK USA - Communications, USA   (2/95-Present)
Account Relations Representative
As a sales/support representative, call on upper-tier management within diverse industries. Present new communications products during product roll-outs which emphasize account development through marketing of value-added services. Manage customer base of 160 accounts, including 20 major accounts which bill up to $60,000 annually.

- Consistently achieve sales goals in the highly competitive telecommunications industry.
- Earned three significant performance-based raises within one year totalling 18%.
- Conduct account analysis and drive revenues through negotiation of long-term agreements which increase monthly commitments.
- Possess knowledge of voice, pager, and cutting-edge teleconferencing communications.

Customer Service Representative
Handled sales support functions for a staff of 10, including order processing, vendor management, service activation, and credit authorization. Successfully managed a work load previously handled by 3 staff. Provided key account management for major customers.

MEDICAL SUPPLIERS - Healthcare, USA; Medical Town, USA   (1/93-2/95)
Medical Equipment Company
Inside Sales/Customer Service Representative
Promoted to the Big City district to manage inside sales activity in state of Rest. Provided support to an outside sales force of 8. Directly impacted revenues through equipment fees and reimbursement coverage negotiations with hundreds of major insurance companies. Marketed equipment services to hospitals, physicians, and nursing homes.

- Facilitated and managed district revenues of $500K per month.
- Cultivated long-term, loyal relationships with physicians, PT/OTs, and hospital staff.
- As Quality Assurance Chairperson coordinated patient surveys to ensure service standards.
- Key contributor in preparing the Medical Town office for an industry-related accreditation.
- Successfully controlled high-priced equipment inventory, requiring detailed recordkeeping.
- Gained valuable knowledge of property and casualty, medical, and workers' comp insurance.

* Previous nursing background includes various LPN positions from 11/83 to 1/93.

EDUCATION

Practical Nurse Program, Nursing City Schools - Caretakers, USA
Nursing Degree, 1983   * Licensed Practical Nurse (LPN)

TRAINING/ COMPUTER

- Courses: Time Management, Effective Public Speaking, Case Management
- Software: Windows 95, Excel, Word, and customized telecommunication programs

REFERENCES AVAILABLE UPON REQUEST

JOHN J. SEEKER
123 Looking Hard Avenue
Top Dog, USA 20202
(555) 678-9101

Confidentiality Requested

CAREER MISSION

A position where I may utilize my full-cycle international-scale project management skills,
leveraging my expertise in mechanical and aerospace engineering as well as advanced technologies,
combined with proven strengths in the areas of custom solutions management and client/vendor relations.

SUMMARY OF QUALIFICATIONS

- Possess diverse international project management experience directing turn-key design processes from inception.
- Adept at building strong customer and vendor relationships to accurately identify needs and customize products.
- Effectively communicate complex technical information to multi-tiered levels from mechanics to top CEOs.
- Demonstrate proactive decision-making abilities and leadership throughout full cycle of project development.
- Proficient in industry-essential computer programs, software, applications, i.e., CAD and Finite Element Method.
- Adapt to rapidly changing customer demands, utilizing analytical problem-solving and engineering background.
- Key experience managing strategic business planning and R&D strengthened by in-depth understanding of high-tech aerospace engineering, lightweight design, composite materials, as well as technical and flight mechanics.
- Proven product analysis, design, troubleshooting, and staff training skills with cutting-edge international projects.

PROFESSIONAL EXPERIENCE

AERO CORPORATION - Sweetwater, USA   (12/94-Present)
Subsidiary of Aero, AG of Citytown, Europe
APPLICATION ENGINEER
Manage all aspects of turn-key product design and implementation projects of customer-specific
automotive and industrial engines for U.S. branch of leading global manufacturer of engines. Direct
multiple project teams simultaneously throughout all phases of product development from defining the
project to market implementation and testing. Interface with up to 20 OEM customers concurrently to
design and develop new components, engine packaging, and unique power unit configurations from
inception to market fruition. Negotiate vendor price quotes for complete packages including
manufacturing plus components. Perform on-site supervision of entire manufacturing process in plants
throughout the U.S. Report to Chief Engineer.

*Critical
Accountabilities:*
- Handle all phases of product management from trends and cost analysis, to initial design and manufacturing, follow-up, market acceptance, and strategic planning for future sales/marketing.
- Initiate and direct prototype production plan jointly with engineering, sales, and service teams in the U.S., Europe, as well as a South American joint venture group.
- Cultivate strong relationships with numerous industrial and automotive customers including O-Ring Corporation, Blast Off, Inc., and Shuttle Performa.
- Provide expert engine-testing troubleshooting and field support to customer project managers.
- Oversee entire engine implementation process, involving intense communications about functional modifications required to meet customer-specific product installation needs.
- Initiate and closely supervise customized testing process to ensure highest functional product performance in each of several diverse environmental conditions from polar to desert areas.

*Selected
Highlights:*
- Key contributor to revenues increasing significantly for several consecutive years and gaining industry-wide reputation for service and product excellence.
- Personally designed and developed 5+ comprehensive industrial engine field component packages.
- Built and maintain 50+ vendor relationships, ensuring optimum products for customer specs.
- Serve as executive decision-maker on initial design and final product acceptance as well as final authority on warranty status following full-cycle management.
- Structure custom engine package pricing and rebate selling, ensuring best product at lowest price.
- Utilize technical expertise to conceive and develop product solutions within customer budgets.

PROFESSIONAL EXPERIENCE (Cont.)

UP IN THE AIR AIRLINES - Little Village, Europe (4/93-12/93)
AEROSPACE ENGINEER
Chosen to execute diverse aspects of highly technical research project for DLR government group in cooperation with Super University of Eurotown. Studied the influence of high-flying, long-range aircraft exhaust emissions on the atmosphere and specifically on the ozone layer.

Project Highlights: Determined and calculated the volume and ultimate distribution trajectory of C Air 747-200 and DC 29's atmospheric gas emissions over the North Atlantic. Interpreted and converted technical test results to report format.

* Relocated to U.S., explored career opportunities, and acclimated to culture/language, 12/93-12/94.

COLLEGE EXPERIENCE

Special Project: FIGARO - Pickleville, South America (3/91-11/91)
ENGINEER
Invited by the Department of Technical Mechanics of Figaro to join forces with a team of doctoral candidates during an 8-month water research and implementation project. Analyzed and verified a diversity of highly technical factors to develop and implement a crucial condition monitoring and problem detection system for a local water resource department. Utilized vibration analysis defect prediction concept to enable accurate estimation of shortest total down times with optimized labor efforts.

Internships: ABC - Little Village, Europe (Summer 1990)
Performed specific gas analysis testing of satellites and satellite subsystems within a cutting-edge, extremely low pressure space simulation chamber for ABC Department of Government Organization. Handled short-term project during development timeframe of 5 commercial satellite transports. Initiated and monitored testing cycles daily for one shift of 24-hour process, checking for residual gas emission, high radiation impact, and other measurable gas-related effects utilizing scientific and technologically advanced tests.

(Summer 1989)
Key player in ABC Department simultaneously researching causes of military aircraft crashes while analyzing specific prototype test vehicle problems of leading-edge high-speed magnetic field trains. Performed aircraft failure analysis, aircraft components service life calculations, and tests related to technical mechanics and materials science.

EDUCATION

YOU STUDY UNIVERSITY - Sweetwater, USA
Master's Degree in Technology Management (Candidate, 1998)

HIGH TECH UNIVERSITY - Sweetwater, USA
Mars Bar Business College - Snickers School of Management
Mid-Management Certification, 1997

TECH TOWN UNIVERSITY - Little Village, Europe
M.S. in Aerospace Engineering, 4/93
B.S. in Mechanical Engineering, 4/89

COMPUTER SKILLS

Programming:	• Fortran	• Pascal	• Basic	• MS-DOS	• NOS/VE
Software:	• MS Office	• Lotus 123	• Freelance	• Ami Pro	• Corel Draw
CAD:	• AutoCad	• MegaCAD	• Prime Medusa	• Proren	• Euklid
Finite Element:	• SET	• NOS/VE			

LANGUAGES/PERSONAL

• Fluent in Spanish and English; Conversant in French and Russian.
• Permanent United States Resident

JOHN J. SEEKER
123 Looking Hard Avenue
Top Dog, USA 20202
(555) 678-9101

CAREER SUMMARY

A talented professional with proven strengths in the critical areas of sales, project management,
and computing technologies combined with a passion for winning.

SIGNIFICANT QUALIFICATIONS

- Possess significant sales experience within varied markets including government, education, and corporate.
- Superbly manage long sales cycles requiring detailed needs analysis and complex multivendor bid responses.
- Proven ability to self-educate on new "relevant" products/technologies necessary to remain at peak performance.
- Highly skilled in various aspects of both project and product management.
- Extensive knowledge of Novell, NT, UNIX, TCP/IP, WAN/LAN, Windows, Macintosh, and Internet technologies.
- Ability to translate complex technologies into sellable features and benefits that meet specific customer needs.

EXPERIENCE   XYZ COMPUTERS - Sunshine City, USA   (1990-Present)

REGIONAL CONSULTING ENGINEER - 1995-Present
Manage the growth of a $400M region and a partnering sales effort involving a team of 50
sales managers, account executives, systems engineers, development executives, and education
consultants. Maintain a primary focus on high-level strategic sales, providing critical assistance
in major account tactical selling and closing of sales opportunities. Serve as the conduit between
a 13-state regional sales team and corporate headquarters.

Accountability
Highlights:

- Provide regional technology leadership to sales force, communicating market-specific
  product positioning and competitive solution advantages.
- Facilitate regional customer roundtables to identify customer requirements and collect
  qualified customer input which directly influences product development.
- "Top Gun" presenter during high-level customer briefings that reveal on XYZ's future
  products and demonstrator of advanced technologies that emphasize XYZ's vision and leadership.
- Direct technical development of 12 Sales Engineers; identify needs and facilitate training.
- Remain abreast of industry trends and technologies through attendance at industry trade shows
  and extensive self-education which includes reading 4-5 trade publications per week.

Results:

- Recognized as System Engineer of the Year out of a 60-member national sales team and earned
  the 1995 President's Award for Excellence.
- Consistently exceeded quotas for 5 consecutive years and achieved the highest incentive levels.
- Key contributor in exceeding sales goals and ensuring growth that surpasses the industry
  average for each market.

SENIOR SYSTEMS ENGINEER - 1990-1995
Managed a variety of pre- and post-sales technical support functions to assist 3 sales
representatives in maximizing business development opportunities throughout an assigned
South Florida territory. Maintained team accountability for ensuring the achievement of
an annual quota of $25M.

EXPERIENCE (Cont.)

Accountability
Highlights:

- Assisted in identifying customers' needs and conducted initial client assessments and evaluations.
- Key participant in developing sales proposals and conducting executive-level sales presentations.
- Contributed to sales by overcoming technical obstacles and promoting products' capabilities.
- Provided post-sales technical solutions and consulting support to ensure customers' satisfaction.
- Established crucial relationships with key technology figures within territory-specific accounts.

Results:

- Driving force in winning a $14M RFP, recognized as the largest single bid in the company's history, then served in the project manager role overseeing the solution implementation.
- Critical leader in ensuring cutting-edge products were marketed in most effective light possible.
- Selected as System Engineer of the Year in 1994, earning a President's Award for Excellence.
- Achieved regional accolades, i.e., Excellence Award for Being a Team Player-1993, Excellence Award for Quality-1991, and a Regional Award Based on Customer Empathy-1992.

COMPUTER CORPORATION - Happy, USA   (1985-1990)

SALES SUPPORT/SYSTEMS ANALYST - 1987-1990

Provided post-sales support for a new UNIX-based operating system. Analyzed customer needs and recommended strategic sales methodologies. Traveled occasionally and worked closely with a nationwide sales teams in business development and account support functions.

- Earned company-wide recognition as the #1 Systems Analyst supporting HCX/UX system.
- Provided critical sales support to Account Executives and System Engineers in the field.

SENIOR TEST ENGINEER - 1985-1987

Developed complex solutions to automate the manufacturing process of complex PCBs. Demonstrated strong project management and scheduling skills. Managed the development of software and hardware required to test up to 50 different complex circuit boards.

- Served as Project Manager, accumulating engineering specifications, overseeing development of test fixtures, writing test programs, and conducting hardware testing.
- Successfully automated and streamlined the circuit board testing process.

EDUCATION

UNIVERSITY OF UPPER LEARNING - Cloudless, USA
Bachelor of Science in Electrical Engineering - 1985
Concentration: Computer Science/Programming

CERTIFICATES

- Certified Netware Engineer (Earned within 6 days) - 1994

TRAINING

- Anthony Robbins Successful Selling
- Xerox SPIN Selling Techniques
- Completed extensive internal training related to management, sales, and interpersonal relationships

---

REFERENCES AVAILABLE UPON REQUEST

SARAH J. SEARCH
123 Job Hunting Lane
Big Time, USA 10101
(444) 567-8910

CAREER SUMMARY

Experienced professional possessing exceptional skills in the areas of special events coordinating and management combined with extensive background in public relations, marketing, and publicity management.

SIGNIFICANT QUALIFICATIONS

- Vast event management background which incorporates an extremely visible and diverse array of events.
- Possess astute logistical planning, purveyor selection, negotiations, financial, and personnel management skills.
- Extremely meticulous and organized individual with essential prioritization and time management skills.
- Fluid sales abilities combined with a proven track record in publicity, promotions, and public relations.
- Adept troubleshooting abilities related to critical security, organization, and communications issues.
- Experienced in all aspects of facility operations management during production of live national broadcasts.

EXPERIENCE   <u>MASSIVE MARKET CENTER</u> - Spacious, USA   (1/98-Present)
A Big Deal Company

Sports Facility
EVENTS/MARKETING MANAGER
Solely accountable for the facility management as well as planning and implementation of a variety of events held in this 100,000 sq. ft. plaza. Direct an administrative staff and effectively manage approximately 25 events annually, including corporate dinners, award ceremonies, private/public functions, trade shows, incentive events, and fundraisers. Demonstrate strong interdepartmental coordination skills working with trade show and building management teams. Report to Senior V.P. of Operations for the Massive Market Center.

- Managed the entire facility during the 1998 Sporting Games, providing critical credentialing for temporarily leased space, identifying security needs, and handling tenant relations; interfaced with key clients, i.e., Snap Shot, Eye Products, USA Tomorrow, Roadsweeper, and Movie Town.
- Produced quarterly newsletters, providing assistance in coordinating complex facility events.

**Project
Highlights**

Sports Show Events - *Sports Event 1998/Sports Dinner and Award Ceremony*
Hosted 2 events for the largest sports manufacturing trade show in Sunnybrook. Managed combined budgets of $100K, coordinating events from inception to execution. Developed themes, marketed, promoted, and advertised events, supervised operations, and handled on-site event management. Planned and implemented the highly visible formal Sports Dinner for 500 international business executives, recognized as a first-time event in Sunnybrook and hosted by J. Smith.

1996 Sporting Games - *Talking Telephone Press Center*
Fully accountable for all operations involving a 100,000 sq. ft. center. Being a joint venture with Talking Telephone, participated in selling temporary space to media and corporations. Served as a liaison to 50 companies. Managed the booking and oversight of sought-after press briefing rooms. Worked closely with Sporting Committee related to press credentialing and badging functions. Coordinated technical installations/dismantling and supervised facility during live broadcasts.

- Facilitated an exclusive agreement with Sporting Committee to provide tenant access to Press Center becoming the only on-line system for non-accredited media.

EXPERIENCE
Continued...

• Interacted daily with CBA Hello America, SBS Radio, Hollywood Today, Extra Special, GAWA-TV, and variety of international media.
• Interfaced with Press Center's corporate sponsors, including Big Bank, Copy USA, and Credit USA.
• Managed a budget of $600K; recruited and trained Press Center staff and a security team of 15.

Other Event Planning Highlights:
• Heavily involved in preliminary planning and on-site event management in conjunction with external event planners for a Sporting-sponsored event, Gymnastics Team Exhibition.
• Intensely involved in supporting planners for the Big Guy Film premier with 1,600 attendees.

<u>B&B PUBLISHING & PRODUCTIONS</u> - Glamourtown, USA   (2/95-10/97)

MARKETING DIRECTOR
Assisted this publishing company in the coordination of all publicity, public relations, and special event planning to drive revenues of their printed publications. Coordinated book signings and media publicity to promote authors' books. Wrote press releases and coordinated press briefings. Served as an Account Executive for 3 authors. Supervised a marketing team of 4.

• Increased sales by 37% through the design and implementation of effective marketing strategies.
• Attained publicity which positioned an author as a subject matter expert in national publications such as *Beautiful, Sexy*, and *Stylin'*.
• Pursued and secured author appearances on national broadcasts, i.e., *Talk Show USA, Serious News Network, Funtime Tonight*, and *CBB News*.
• Designed and instituted a newsletter and press pack to promote author's practice.

<u>HITMAKER/CLASSEY RECORDS</u> - Songville, USA   (11/93-2/95)
Subsidiary of Golden Records

ASSISTANT PROJECT COORDINATOR
Performed extensive business and personal planning and coordination for professional songwriters and musicians, primarily Songbird, a music producer and Senior V.P. of Golden Records. Worked with publishers to secure publishing rights and submit artists/label releases in order to prevent legal liabilities. Served as a key liaison between artists, managers, and publishers. Also, planned and implemented special events such as charity fundraisers. Traveled extensively.

• Handled coordination of artists' demo and recording schedules for production projects which included booking studios as well as hiring programmers, composers, and creative staff.
• Assisted in the production of Easy to Hear and Got to Hit the Top soundtracks.
• Worked directly with artists, including Long Hair, Smooth Sounds, Shreiker, Soft Tones, and Country Boy, on various albums and single recordings.

* Previously employed by Jane Doe, M.D., as a Media Relations Specialist, 1/91-11/93.

EDUCATION   <u>UNIVERSITY OF SUNSHINE</u>
Bachelor of Arts in Communication - 6/93

COMPUTER
• MS Word   • MS Office   • WP 5.1   • Lotus 1-2-3   • MS Excel
• JD Edwards   • PowerPoint   • Elite   • Act (DOS/Windows)

AFFILIATIONS
• Special Event Society of Sunshine - *Member*
• Celebrity Assistants Society - *Associate Founder*
• Good Cheer Foundation - *Volunteer*
• Event Planners over Sunshine - *Member*

REFERENCES AVAILABLE UPON REQUEST

JOHN J. SEEKER, CPA

123 Looking Hard Avenue
Top Dog, USA 20202
(555) 678-9101

CAREER SUMMARY

Accomplished, highly effective executive manager experienced in all phases of
finance and accounting.

SIGNIFICANT QUALIFICATIONS

- Successful professional track record in both entrepreneurial and corporate environments.
- Possess diverse public accounting experience with private and publicly traded companies.
- Extremely talented in streamlining existing operations and developing start-up operations.
- Adept in all aspects of computer automation projects to maximize operational efficiency.
- Outstanding personnel management strategies which emphasize training and team-building.
- Consistently provide strategic and effective executive direction for multifaceted companies.
- Capable of identifying innovative methods and procedures to increase bottom-line profits.

**PROFESSIONAL
EXPERIENCE**

<u>CLEVER CONSULTANTS, INC.</u>   Projectville, USA
CORPORATE CONTROLLER   (7/96-Present)

Comprehensively manage all finance and accounting functions for this
international recruiting/consulting firm which contracts over 500 employees.
Managed financial personnel. Participated in and directed budgeting,
forecasting, month-end/year-end reporting, tax preparation, financial
statements, payroll, and benefits administration. Personally managed all
revenue and banking relations.

- Successfully negotiated a line of credit which increased financing by 250%.
- Initiated and directed a major computer conversion project to accommodate
  an expanding workload during a 60% organizational growth.
- Determined a strategy to reduce third-party accounting fees by over 50%.
- Instituted new policies and procedures and streamlined accounting functions
  to maximize staff productivity.
- Utilized strong cash flow management skills during crucial periods.

<u>ABC HOLDINGS, LTD.</u>   Secretsville, USA
**CORPORATE CONTROLLER/
SENIOR MANAGEMENT CONSULTANT**   (8/92-7/96)

Directed an accounting staff of 16 for this privately held security transportation
company which primarily serviced Fortune 500 companies. Evaluated all existing
systems and implemented numerous turn-around strategies for 11 subsidiaries.
Accountabilities included corporate tax returns, audits, financial statements,
closings, banking, and cash management for 50+ operating accounts.

- Reversed a floundering accounting operation into a highly efficient business.
- Immediately brought bookkeeping current from 8 months in arrears and
  reconciled one year of outstanding bank statements.
- Negotiated cost-effective benefit contracts and secured additional financing.
- Purchased and installed a cutting-edge hardware and software system.
- Revised procedures and standards to strengthen nationwide accounting controls.
- Key contributor in maximizing company operations during a 40% annual growth.
- Personally managed CEO's investment properties and handled strategic tax
  planning, both corporate and individual, for corporation's officers.

PROFESSIONAL EXPERIENCE Continued...	<u>NORTH POLE ARMS, INC.</u> **CONTROLLER**	Frigidtown, USA (2/89-7/92)

Managed all accounting operations for this importing and manufacturing company. Supervised a staff of 10 with full responsibility for A/P, A/R, payroll, purchasing, inventory control, customer service, and data processing functions.

- Planned and facilitated extensive reductions in operating expenditures.
- Impacted bottom-line profitability by 200% within 3 years.
- Developed accounting systems and integrated operations subsequent to a $12M corporate buy-out.
- Directed a major computer conversion from a mainframe to a PC environment, which required selecting and negotiating new hardware and software.

<u>AMERICAN MANUFACTURING INDUSTRIES, INC.</u>
ASSISTANT CONTROLLER

Stichesville, USA (8/86-2/89)

Promoted within 2 years to a management position with supervisory responsibility for a staff of 7 and reporting directly to the V.P. of Finance of this $65M manufacturing and distribution company. Handled all accounting functions for 3 subsidiaries and 14 manufacturing plants. Gained valuable experience in loan compliance, letters of credit, cost accounting, 10Q/10K SEC filing, and investment planning.

- Directed an automation project from manual to computer-operated systems.
- Successfully managed a multimillion investment portfolio for the company owner.

<u>ACCURATE, CPA's</u>
SENIOR ACCOUNTANT

Financialtown, USA (11/80-8/86)

Performed various auditing and tax preparation responsibilities for a diverse client base including banks, hospitals, and governmental institution. Managed three Accountants.

<u>METICULOUS & CAREFUL, CPA's</u>
STAFF ACCOUNTANT

Right City, USA (7/78-11/80)

EDUCATION	<u>NUMBERS COLLEGE</u> **B.B.A. DEGREE IN ACCOUNTING**	Numbersville, USA 1977

* Self-financed 75% of Educational Expenses.

CERTIFICATION   Certified Public Accountant, Financial State, 1982

COMPUTER
- Lotus 1-2-3
- RealWorld
- Basic Four
- Paradox

- Excel
- ProWrite
- Harvard Graphics
- ASC

- Quattro Pro
- Dataflex
- Mass 90
- Report Writer

AFFILIATIONS
- Peachstate Society of Certified Public Accountants
- USA Institute of Certified Public Accountants

REFERENCES AVAILABLE UPON REQUEST

SARAH J. SEARCH

123 Job Hunting Lane
Big Time, USA 10101
(444) 567-8910

OBJECTIVE

A challenging position where I may utilize my master's degree in accounting combined with extensive experience in positions requiring complex data analysis and interpretation.

QUALIFICATIONS

- Accustomed to the demands of critical accuracy; regularly prepare reports requiring strong deductive reasoning abilities which influence crucial management decisions.
- Strong computer skills and excellent aptitude for new software.
- Extremely familiar with an impressive array of intense numerical data analyses.
- Self-disciplined, detail-oriented individual with intense interest in corporate finance and accounting where strong financial skills are essential.

EXPERIENCE

ABC INTERNATIONAL - Anytown, USA   (4/95-Present)

Analyst, 3/97-Present
Collect and analyze complex data regarding nuclear fuel cycle for nuclear and engineering consulting company. Prepare supply and demand analyses based on critical interpretation of data. Compile and prepare the *Enrichment Status Report*, one of six crucial volumes distributed as a valued resource quarterly to nuclear power plants and uranium suppliers.

- Conduct research and extrapolate detailed data from 12 major U.S. utility companies and 4 additional utilities in Asian countries.
- Write published articles that interpret commodity data for trade magazines.
- Direct research efforts of consulting teams to ensure accumulation of specific data.
- Update and maintain OS/2 and FoxPro databases; experienced in running status reports.

Analytical Aide, 4/95-3/97
Part-time position while enrolled in graduate school. Reviewed reports for accuracy of information and provided efficient administrative support to Analysts.

XYZ, INC. - Nowhere, USA   (5/94-12/94)
                                                                     (Summers 1990-93)

Computer Operator/Tape Librarian
Encoded insurance policies to an electronic medium to permit company which initialized in-house printing. Operated mainframe and accompanying equipment. Managed entire tape inventory system, including taping, documentation, and transportation to an off-site storage location.

EDUCATION

SUCCESS UNIVERSITY - Sometown, USA
MASTER OF BUSINESS ADMINISTRATION, 1995
Concentration: Accounting   Major GPA: 4.0/4.0

RELATED COURSEWORK

- Auditing
- Individual Income Tax
- Corporate Finance
- Managerial Accounting
- Decision Theory

CONFIDENCE UNIVERSITY - Successville, USA
BACHELOR OF ARTS DEGREE IN PSYCHOLOGY, 1990

CERTIFICATION

- *Preparing to sit for CPA exam in November 1998.*

COMPUTERS

- Excel 5.0 • Lotus 1-2-3 • FoxPro • MS Word 6.0 • WordPerfect 5.0

REFERENCES AVAILABLE UPON REQUEST

SARAH J. SEARCH, CPA

123 Job Hunting Lane
Big Time, USA 10101
(444) 567-8910

CAREER SUMMARY

A top-notch professional with 13 years of diverse management and financial experience.

SIGNIFICANT QUALIFICATIONS

- Highly adept at performing numerous accounting functions including operations budgeting, financial analysis, tax compliancy, audit preparation, payroll generation, production planning, and sales projection.
- Proven expertise in the implementation of computerized accounting systems resulting in maximized efficiency.
- Utilize keen analytical abilities in reviewing complex financial data and providing effective recommendations.
- Experienced in handling accounting concerns for various business types working on a national/international level.
- Provide excellent leadership and staff guidance; conduct ongoing training to ensure lasting client satisfaction.

EXPERIENCE

FINANCIAL ENTERPRISES - Consulting, USA   (1994-Present)
FINANCIAL CONSULTANT
Provide full-charge accounting services including financial reporting, reconciliations, budgeting, and tax compliancy to various privately held businesses. On and off-site projects.

Current Projects:
ABC Distributer

Comprehensively manage all accounting procedures for this $75M international distributor, including G/L, A/P, A/R, payroll, tax reporting, inventory control, monthly/yearly financial statements, operations budgets, sales projections, and production volume planning. Invest 30 hours per week in this long-term consulting assignment. Monitor aspects of international trade distribution, track cash flow, handle wire transfers, and perform bank reconciliations. Present financial reports during annual/semi-annual board meetings as well as prepare company for year-end financial and insurance audits. Remain a bank account signatory.

- Created entirely new financial database to eliminate corrupt information.
- Successfully brought a 6-month delinquent general ledger to current status.
- Conceived and implemented new sales and forecasting reporting systems.
- Established procedures/controls to maximize internal efficiency.

XYZ Contractors

Perform wide array of financial procedures for this $2M construction contractor consisting of 4 separate operations. Conduct job costing and performance analyses, generate month-end and year-end reports, and complete G/Ls for 4 companies. Contribute 20 hours per week during this long-term consulting assignment. Improved cash flow management by creating customized spreadsheets.

Previous Projects:
Accountants USA

Completed multiple accounting functions, including job costing, for a real estate construction company. Updated financial ledgers which were 6 months behind.

Architects Group

Contributed to G/L, financial reporting, and payroll management for an architectural/ construction company consisting of three separate entities.

MUTUAL FUNDS, INC. - Investors, USA   (1991-1994)
CONTROLLER/MUTUAL FUND ADMINISTRATOR
Managed a diverse range of financial accounting and mutual fund administration functions. Coordinated automated check-writing procedures, prepared weekly financial reports, analyzed cash flow, managed A/P and A/R, and handled bank reconciliations. Provided in-depth client investment tracking, including loss/gains analysis, daily net value generation, and balance sheet preparation. Initially hired as a Portfolio Manager with supervisory capacity over 75 accounts with assets of $250K+ each. Prepared investment analysis/summary statements and handled client investment trading.

EXPERIENCE
Continued...

- Installed improved accounting software and automated bookkeeping procedures.
- Implemented numerous financial controls to increase accuracy of record-keeping.
- Instituted accounting policies/procedures which maximized operational efficiency.
- Eliminated need for outside accounting team, resulting in a savings of $30K/year.
- Reinstated 2 companies and acted as an officer for all 3 operations.
- Reduced company auditing costs through comprehensive preplanning strategies.
- Expedited A/R functions; developed spreadsheets to automate mutual fund management.
- Simultaneously served as System Administrator; researched and made recommendations for software/hardware installations and upgrades.
- Provided continuous computer training/system support for all staff members.

REVENUE COLLECTORS OF AMERICA - Scary City, USA   (1989-1991)
SENIOR TAX EXAMINER
Coordinated all tax return screening/coding and ensured accurate completion of information prior to data entry; qualified returns for auditing. Conducted performance reviews of 25 examiners and contributed key troubleshooting strategies within a high-stress atmosphere. Assisted with employee hiring and served as vital information resource for staff examiners. (*Simultaneously employed with ABC, Inc.*)

- Promoted from Tax Examiner position based upon superior production and efficient completion of project goals.
- Conducted training for seasonal employees within the Document Perfection Branch.

ABC ADVISORY CORPORATION - Advisors, USA   (1986-1989)
ACCOUNTING ASSISTANT
Implemented a client billing system which efficiently serviced 250 accounts and prepared complex quarterly billing reports and handled A/R. Reviewed files to ensure correct settling of trades. Performed daily mutual fund trade operations, working with brokers to confirm figures and record information into the system. Tracked dividends per individual client account and coordinated monthly portfolio reconciliations.

INVESTMENT INTERNATIONAL COMPANY - Spenders, USA   (1984-1986)
ACCOUNTANT
Maintained full accounting authority for operations consisting of an investment corporation, partnership, 2 subsidiaries, and a non-profit organization. Completed all corporate, state, local, county, and personal tax returns; prepared a total of 100 returns. Started company's G/L and implemented computerized accounting systems. Conducted investment analysis and distribution of investment income. Brought G/L from 12 months behind to current.

EDUCATION

COLLEGE OF BRIGHTSVILLE - Brightsville, USA
B.S. in Accounting, Business Administration, and Economics, 1986

BRIGHT COMMUNITY COLLEGE - Brightsville, USA
A.A.S. in Accounting, 1984
A.A.S. in Business Administration, 1980

CERTIFICATIONS
- Certified Public Accountant, 1995
- Series 6-Investment Company Products License, 1989
- South State Real Estate Broker License, 1984

COMPUTER

• Solomon III	• Great Plains	• Small Systems Design
• Excel	• Word	• Quickbooks
• Lotus 1-2-3	• WordPerfect	• Shaw Data

PERSONAL
- Marathon Runner
- Interior Design Background

REFERENCES AVAILABLE UPON REQUEST

SARAH J. SEARCH

123 Job Hunting Lane
Big TIme, USA 10101
(444) 567--8910

CAREER SUMMARY

A uniquely qualified professional possessing 13 years of proven experience in human resources
with expertise in the areas of benefits and PeopleSoft HRIS software, coupled with
astute project management and process re-engineering skills.

SIGNIFICANT QUALIFICATIONS

**Human
Resources**

- Possess in-depth knowledge of benefit plans, including experience in benefits administration.
- PeopleSoft expert related to HR, Benefits, Ad Hoc Reporting, Crystal Reports, and Query.
- Maintain a vast knowledge base of continuously changing HR policies, laws, and regulations.
- Adept at establishing strong communication links with staff to resolve human resources issues.
- Consulted all levels of personnel on 401(k), disability, retirement, and survivorship plans.
- Exhibited HR training abilities conducting weekly new hire orientations for up to 50 staff.
- Demonstrated acute computer skills combined with an extremely dedicated work ethic.

**Project
Management**

- Skilled in managing diverse process re-engineering projects accurately and within deadlines.
- Experienced in the integration of the PeopleSoft system into HR and benefits departments.
- Heavily involved with coaching and educating clients on organizational policies and procedures.
- Created and implemented critical staff analysis reporting formats for multiple facilities.
- Managed performance/compensation review process working with division and department heads.
- Conducted research and implemented process improvements that created efficient operations.
- Handled manpower report analysis functions, divisional transfers, and staff tuition aid process.
- Served as primary liaison coordinating key programs for retired employees and executives.

EXPERIENCE

THE SODA COMPANY - Sunshine City, USA   (9/95-10/97)
Total Compensation Delivery Organization
CLIENT SERVICES, HUMAN RESOURCES DIVISION
Managed critical generalist human resource functions with an emphasis on record-keeping
and employee issues for 2,500 HR, Marketing, and Corporate Affairs employees. Interacted
with assigned client organization to maintain data integrity, interpret benefit plans, and ensure
compliance with pertinent legal and tax regulations. Selected to handle projects requiring close
involvement with upper-level management.

*Selected
Highlights:*

- Processed detailed documents related to stock options, annual incentives, retirements,
  survivorship, and employee transitions in a deadline-oriented and accuracy-driven setting.
- Directed annual open enrollment of health, life, AD&D, and dental benefits; handled policy
  changes related to life status issues utilizing HRIS PeopleSoft.
- Selected to serve on task force assisting with initial PeopleSoft implementation and upgrades.
- Chosen to participate as a key member on numerous special project teams, i.e., rewards and
  recognition, personnel change coding and documentation, and process improvements.
- Provided critical assistance in creating and implementing retired executives' programs.
- Earned sought-after prestigious performance ratings after only 4 months of employment.

EXPERIENCE
(Cont.)

<u>KRESS INTERNATIONAL CORPORATION</u> - Sweetwater, USA   (9/94-6/95)
Corporate Human Resources
HUMAN RESOURCES ASSISTANT
Comprehensively handled diverse aspects of employee relations as well as HR database and records management for a technical-oriented operation. Functions included recruiting, interviewing, and hiring as well as employee benefits administration and compensation control. Also handled wellness program development, job posting management, and newsletter production.

Selected
Highlights:

- Revised company-wide policy and procedures handbook and operations manual.
- Interfaced frequently with attorneys to ensure compliance with EEOC guidelines.
- Evaluated and amended written job descriptions in order to optimize internal efficiencies.
- Utilized computer skills to create and distribute internal forms on an employee network.
- Worked in conjunction with temporary placement agencies to fulfill staffing requirements.

<u>FEDERATED UNITED</u> - Sweetwater, USA   (2/84-4/94)
EXECUTIVE HUMAN RESOURCES STAFF
Oversaw all facets of recruitment, HR development, and system enhancements, which included providing HR support to corporate headquarter executives for a 40-store chain. Managed a $240K operating budget allocated to individual stores and corporate offices, which included monthly reporting. Handled staffing functions, including screening resumes, conducting reference and background checks, completing all documentation, and conducting new employee orientations. Interfaced directly with senior management team.

Selected
Highlights:

- Administered payroll system changes for 300 of company's highest-level executives.
- Co-managed a complex payroll system conversion and created critical new reporting formats.
- Originated an employee profile database and created divisional succession planning reports.
- Maintained accurate and updated personnel files and electronic records.
- Coordinated annual recruitment events that involved a targeted selection hiring process.
- Sensitively handled distribution of executive performance appraisals and exit interviews.
- Handled bi-weekly job postings and staff turn-over activity analysis reporting.
- Served as new employee liaison handling internal/external relocation details.
- Planned and coordinated logistical aspects of diverse employee events.

* Initially hired as Personnel Assistant for largest store in company processing weekly payroll for 500 employees. Hired temporary staff and managed a Safety Task Force that coordinated plans to achieve preventive missions. Promoted to a higher-level HR position.

EDUCATION

<u>REALLY HARD COLLEGE</u> - Brentville, USA **Liberal Arts Major,** 1982

AFFILIATIONS
- Society for Human Resource Management
- Metro Big City High-Tech Personnel Association

COMPUTER
- PeopleSoft HRIS   • MS Word   • Excel   • PowerPoint

REFERENCES AVAILABLE UPON REQUEST

SARAH J. SEARCH

123 Job Hunting Lane
Big Time, USA 10101
(444) 567-8910

CAREER SUMMARY

A results-oriented business consultant with an extensive technical and project management
background which emphasizes business automation projects.

SIGNIFICANT QUALIFICATIONS

Technical Background

- Vast technical knowledge of NT, Windows 95, MS Access, Visual Basic for Applications, MS Office, Geographical Information Systems, Multi-media, Graphics, and CBT.
- Extensive experience in customizing applications, networking, database development, and system programming combined with a particular expertise in MS Access.
- In-depth technical understanding of diverse industries, i.e., hospital management, airline, local government, financial, not-for-profit, power generation, and manufacturing.

Consulting Background

- Proven track record in improving business processes, maximizing efficiency of existing systems, redirecting marketing tactics, and recommending profit enhancement strategies.
- Talented in identifying ways of leveraging technology to reduce costs and improve services.
- Adept at solving problems using in-depth knowledge of database and information management.
- Interface well with both technical and non-technical personnel and skillfully extract critical information from cross-functional teams to assist in organizational change management.
- Fluidly coordinate projects from inception, which includes design, testing, roll-out, and user training while ensuring project control, user acceptance, and system quality.

Sales Background

- Extensive executive sales experience primarily working with senior executives to design risk management programs for major corporations requiring a consultative selling approach.
- Skilled presenter and lecturer at conferences on insurance and risk management topics.

EXPERIENCE

<u>CONSULTING SERVICES, INC.</u>
TECHNOLOGY CONSULTANT

(1/95-Present)
Big Time, USA

Utilize a wealth of business expertise and a broad understanding of diverse industries to provide project-oriented consulting services. Accurately identify clients' short and long-term business needs, uncover client objectives, research possible tools for organizing information, and formulate proposed solutions. Employ astute work process analysis, programming, software development, and specification planning skills. Coordinate each phase of multiple automation projects, including hardware/software recommendations, software development, testing, program roll-outs, and end-user training.

Project Highlights:

- ***Health Care Consultants***: Created a database from ground zero of workers' compensation data, interfacing with a Geographical Information application, utilized as a critical marketing tool that automated the lead generation process.

- ***The Power Source***: Designed unique Intranet software that provides employee access to a corporate pictorial phone directory; intimately involved in all project management functions ranging from testing to roll-out; assisted in selling the concept to executives internally.

- ***VIP Department***: Managed the development of a database to automate environmental inspections/reports and manage storage of site photographs in compliance with EPA regulations.

*Project
Highlights:*
(Cont.)

- ***Physician Services***: Debugged a medical practice management system and fine-tuned the application interface, which included determining network and hardware specifications.

- ***Manufacturing Industries***:   Converted asset tracking from spreadsheets to a relational database, reducing reporting turn-around from 40 days to 3 days for this multibillion-dollar manufacturer.

- ***Wireless***: Produced a quality control tracking program using a relational database system that managed and expedited a wide range of shipping, product return, and inventory processes.

- ***Large Broker***: Designed a system to manage safety inspection and accident investigation reports that expanded reporting capabilities; also consulted internal developers in the creation of industry-specific software.

- ***Multiple Clients***: Created custom software that managed the insurance component of large construction projects, typically known as owner-controlled programs; also developed a network-based training system which delivered just-in-time PC training.

NOAH'S ARK INSURANCE (1/73-12/94)
MAJOR ACCOUNT MANAGER Big Time, USA

One of 25 Major Account Representatives nationwide accountable for selling a full range of commercial insurance products to large corporate accounts with minimum insurance assets of $250M+. Successfully managed and expanded a $15M revenue stream. Steadily progressed throughout a long tenure to the following positions: Assistant to Sales Manager, Account Representative, Senior Account Representative, and Major Account Manager.

- Recognized for producing top volume and earning acknowledgement for new business sales.
- Demonstrated excellent executive presentation skills selling primarily to risk managers and other key decision-makers within senior management.
- Successfully nurtured a long sales cycle requiring multi-tiered, consultative selling.
- Managed a complex, technical sales process which required a strong understanding of diverse buying styles and business processes.
- Conducted formalized sales training and provided peer mentoring in specialized areas.
- Selected as the Field Sales Representative supporting and consulting the National Technology Committee on internal development projects and platform recommendations.

EDUCATION
SOUTHERN STATE UNIVERSITY - Big Time, USA
BACHELOR OF BUSINESS ADMINISTRATION DEGREE

ASSOCIATION
BUSINESS COALITION - Big Time, USA (1997-Present)
TECHNOLOGY LEADER (Volunteer)
Provide critical technology consulting to a non-profit organization focused on collaborating with the corporate community and local/state agencies to assist individuals in effectively transitioning from welfare programs to employment. Advise visible community leaders on methods of automating organizational processes and devising mission-specific strategies.

REFERENCES AVAILABLE UPON REQUEST

JOHN J. SEEKER, JR.
123 Looking Hard Avenue
Top Dog, USA 20202
(555) 678-9101

CAREER SUMMARY

A successful individual demonstrating over 20 years of diverse and highly
progressive experience within the field of law enforcement.

SIGNIFICANT QUALIFICATIONS

- Experienced in evaluating both personnel and departmental policy in a thoroughly unbiased manner.
- Highly proficient administrator especially as related to manpower management and protocol establishment.
- Possess crucial diplomacy skills and effective communications abilities necessary to facilitate team work.
- Demonstrate superior troubleshooting capabilities resulting in cooperative inter-agency relationships.
- Offer over 20 years of dedicated professional service and progressive management responsibility.
- Extremely capable of directing a diverse staff in all procedures while fostering efficient operations.
- Proven ability to interact with a demanding, often critical public regarding various police matters.
- Vast law enforcement experience ranging from undercover narcotics investigations to traffic control.
- Frequently acknowledged for performance excellence as well as professionalism and related expertise.

EXPERIENCE

CITY OF SOMEWHERE - Dangerous, USA   (1973-Present)
CAPTAIN, *Uniform Division,* 1985-Present
Comprehensively manage a staff of 23 Law Enforcement Officers throughout a 3-shift
operation. Effectively delegate shift assignments among personnel. Demonstrate strong
financial skills related to payroll management. Utilize full decision-making authority
to ensure overall efficiency of shift operations.

* Simultaneously to this position, served as **Officer in Charge of Community Policing
   Program**. Created and implemented community-related programs which involved various
   planning, scheduling, and staff supervision for this public relations program. Programming
   included field trips designed for children in the community.

* *Promoted to Captain by the Chief of Police first time eligible, 1985.*

LIEUTENANT - *Uniformed Division,* 1982-1985
Promoted to serve as Watch Commander during the weekend shifts. Handled a vast
array of citizen complaints and assisted in investigations regarding internal affairs cases.
Exhibited strong troubleshooting and issue prioritization skills.

* *Promoted to Lieutenant first time eligible, 1982.*

ASSISTANT TO CITY MANAGER, *Special Assignment,* 1981
Selected to conduct in-depth analysis of compensation rates of 400 employees and calculated
estimated pay increases. Required the utilization of strong analytical/financial abilities.

UNIFORM SERGEANT, 1979-1980
Officer in Charge of Traffic Division
Supervised a staff of 23 Crossing Guards in addition to Motorcycle Officers, Radar
Traffic Unit, and Daytime Business District Patrol. Addressed public concerns related
to traffic issues and oversaw traffic accident investigations.

EXPERIENCE Continued...	**SERGEANT**, *Investigations-Narcotics*, 1977-1978 Conducted undercover investigations for the joint agencies, Somewhere County. Utilized a high degree of resourcefulness and case management expertise within this extremely independent setting. Handled cases from their inception; assisted in case reporting and trial preparation. Established a team approach, utilizing agencies throughout the city, to successfully complete investigations. * *Promoted to Sergeant first time eligible, 1977.* **PATROLMAN**, *Tactical Anti-Crime Unit*, 1975-1976 Selected to participate on a team accountable for the development of a stakeout unit. Duties included coordinating and implementing various undercover assignments. **PATROLMAN**, 1973-1975 Gained initial exposure to numerous law enforcement activities. Received letters of commendation from the public regarding outstanding performance. * Also, previously employed by Universe Department Store, Shopping, USA, 1969-1973.

EDUCATION	<u>SOMEWHERE STATE UNIVERSITY</u> - Somewhere, USA **B.S. Degree in Business Administration** (Candidate) * *Majored in Management* (40 Hours remaining)
PROFESSIONAL TRAINING	• Instructors Training, Somewhere County Public Safety Training Center, 1989 • Law Enforcement Management, Police Academy of Somewhere, 1986 • Police Budget Perception, Police Academy of Somewhere, 1981 • Supervisory Training, Police Academy of Somewhere, 1980 • D.E.A. Training, United States Justice Department, 1977 • Homicide Investigation, University of Somewhere, 1976 • Professional Training, Executive Program - Universe Department Store, 1972/73
INSTRUCTOR	• Taught the following courses at the Somewhere County Training Center: *Criminal Procedure, Criminal History, and Report Writing*
CERTIFICATION	• Certified as a *Promotional Assessor* for the Peaceville Police Department, Corn County Police Department, Wheatville Police Department, and Intown County Police Department; requires serving as impartial evaluator of personnel in line for promotions.
COMMUNITY SERVICE	• Somewhere Youth Baseball Coach, 5 years • Somewhere Youth Baseball League Association, President • Academic Scholarship Board of Directors, 5 years
CIVIC	• Special Sports Competition, Volunteer • Children Charity, Volunteer

---

REFERENCES AVAILABLE UPON REQUEST

JOHN J. SEEKER

123 Looking Hard Avenue
Top Dog, USA 20202
(555) 678-9101

CAREER SUMMARY

Astute attorney demonstrating a successful track record in multiple facets of corporate law with
a wealth of experience in commercial transaction and litigation areas.

SIGNIFICANT QUALIFICATIONS

Transaction
- Broad base of experience in transactional law, including contract development and review as well as business mergers and acquisitions.
- Vast background in commercial law encompassing an in-depth knowledge of employment law.
- Highly skilled drafting, analytical, and interpretive abilities critical to legal counsel.

Litigation
- Proven litigation track record with in-depth trial experience in both jury and non-jury formats.
- Tried litigation cases within a wide array of state and federal courts, including Magistrate, Superior, Appellate, Administrative, U.S. District, and U.S. Court of Appeals.
- Strong case management skills exemplified through commercial and personal injury litigation, including a strong emphasis in business operations and employee-related disputes.
- Skilled in handling trial preparation and court appearances in addition to multi-state cases.

**Business
Management**
- Demonstrated ability to excel in all aspects of new client development and practice management.
- Adept in a wide range of critical business administration functions including office set up, financial record-keeping, expense control, billing, accounting, receivables, and staff supervision.
- Experienced in marketing and promoting legal expertise within a highly competitive market.

EXPERIENCE

SMITH & SMITH
PARTNER

Legaltown, USA
(3/95-Present)

One of 2 attorneys to develop a start-up legal practice which handles primarily
commercial transaction and plaintiff litigation cases. Manage cases from inception with
integral involvement in conducting client interviews, handling legal research, drafting
correspondence and discovery documentation, conducting depositions, filing/arguing
diverse motions, and negotiating settlements with defense counsel. In addition, perform
detailed and often complex commercial transaction work.

*Case
Highlights:*
- Transaction experience includes setting up new business entities and drafting multifaceted contracts/agreements, i.e., shareholder, partnership, stock purchase, employment, non-disclosure, non-circumvention, franchise, sales, trademark, consulting, and lease.
- Litigation experience includes commercial and shareholder litigation, fraud/misrepresentation, general personal injury, property damage liability, restrictive employment covenants and trade secrets, breach of fiduciary duties, directors'/officers' liability, and intellectual property.

- Established a practice from ground zero after relocating to a new geographic area.
- Quickly cultivated a well-respected legal reputation within the business community.
- To date, possess a track record of having won all litigation cases managed in this practice.
- Simultaneously manage over 100 matters with a case load which incorporates varied size disputes with petitioned amounts of up to $250K.
- Increased revenues from existing clients based on strong relationship-building skills.
- Extremely talented at generating new clients and marketing the firm to build a practice.

EXPERIENCE
Continued...

<u>REGULATORY COMMISSION USA</u>   Capitol, USA
ADVISORY ATTORNEY   (8/92-3/95)
Office of General & Administrative Law

Managed all non-energy-related matters for this national regulatory body which governs electric, gas, and water utilities. Provided extensive legal defense related to labor law with a heavy emphasis on discrimination and personal injury cases. Also, during tenure managed a copyright infringement matter.

• Managed civil litigation cases involving the U.S. District Court, EEOC, GSBCA, MSPB, and multiple government agencies.
• Advised upper management and commissioners on preventing ethical violations.
• Reviewed financial disclosure statements to eliminate conflict-of-interest matters in addition to reviewing and revising government contracts.
• Assisted in writing administrative rules and regulations published in the *Federal Register* which impacted the nation's utility organizations.

<u>OFFICE OF THE ATTORNEY GENERAL</u>   Coldtown, USA
LAW CLERK   (4/91-5/92)
Cold State Retirement & Pension Systems

Provided legal defense related to workers' compensation and disability matters through the Appellate and Administrative Courts. Handled all research, drafting, and trial preparation. Additionally, resolved issues involving tax, contracts, and budget implications.

<u>HONORABLE JOHN C. JUDGE</u>   Coldtown, USA
LAW CLERK   (5/91-8/91)
Circuit Court for Coldtown City

Gained exposure to criminal litigation through research, drafting, and courtroom experience.

* *Previously served as a Research Intern with Congressman Good Guy in Washington, D.C.*

EDUCATION

<u>UNIVERSITY OF COLDTOWN SCHOOL OF LAW</u>   Coldtown, USA
J.D. DEGREE (Top 25%)   5/92

Activities: Member of Phi Delta Phi Fraternity; Participant in Trial Advocacy, Client Counseling, and Negotiation Competitions

<u>UNIVERSITY OF STUDY HARD</u>   Study Hard, USA
B.A. DEGREE IN POLITICAL SCIENCE   5/89

Honors: Dean's List, Order of Omega National Honor Society,
Activities: President of Tau Epsilon Phi Fraternity

ADMITTED   • Peach State Bar   • Cold State Bar

MEMBERSHIPS   • City Bar Association   • Cold State Bar Association
       • Peach State Bar Association   • American Bar Association

CIVIC   • Habitat for Humanity, Volunteer   • Community Center, Basketball Coach

PUBLICATIONS   <u>State Business Advisory</u>, *Non-Compete Agreements: Valuable Protection or Mere Deterrent*, October 1996

REFERENCES AVAILABLE UPON REQUEST

SARAH J. SEARCH

123 Job Hunting Lane
Big Time, USA 10101
H - (444) 567-8910
W - (222) 123-4567

CAREER SUMMARY

A highly talented professional with over 20 years of successful paralegal and legal secretarial experience.

SIGNIFICANT QUALIFICATIONS

- Excellent interpretive and analytical capabilities crucial to effectual paralegal production.
- Demonstrated research and investigative efficiency requisite to successful legal-support performance.
- Illustrated ability to accurately, concisely, and efficiently summarize complex legal depositions.
- Superior planning skills and implementation strategies in fast-paced, high-pressure arenas.
- Possess valued administrative and reporting skills necessary for generating voluminous amounts of data.
- Comprehensive understanding of numerous aspects of the law as well as resulting legal policies/procedures.
- Approach all personal and professional challenges with high degree of dedication, motivation, and poise.

EXPERIENCE

THE SODA COMPANY - Slurping City, USA   (1984-Present)
LEGAL SECRETARY, 1/88-Present
Corporate Legal Division/Litigation Department

Prioritize and prepare voluminous legal correspondence, i.e., pleadings, documents, speeches. Respond to incoming calls pertaining to litigation procedures. Analyze and determine nature of new matters, which involves managing an extensive database. Conduct in-depth database searches on legal matters pertaining to relevant cases. Research outside counsel, opposing counsel, and judges, utilizing *Martindale-Hubble* as a major resource. Maintain and update in-house billable matters and generate dollar value, comparison, summary, and annualization reports. Schedule meetings for all levels of management, including inside and outside counsel, which includes organizing domestic and international travel arrangements.

- Extensive knowledge of diverse legal matters, including breach of contract, product liability, antitrust, trademark infringement, and employment discrimination.
- Experience in reviewing thousands of litigation cases involving numerous components, i.e., notice of representations, claim letters, exhibits summons, complaints, interrogatories, and production requests.
- Prepared a diverse range of monthly and quarterly reports which served as a key component in justifying the cost effectiveness of the in-house legal department.
- Report directly to Department Heads, the Senior Litigation Counsel, and the International Litigation Senior Counsel.
- Efficiently compile extensive legal communications, including notebooks, legal directories, policies, and corporate information bulletins.
- Serve as member of *Legal Division Newsletter*, which discusses current topics as well as compiles legal profiles.
- Implemented a major computer conversion from DOS to Windows-based programs.

* Previous positions with The Soda Company include Senior Secretary, External Affairs, 6/86-1/88, and Legal Secretary, Corporate Legal Division/Litigation Department, 9/84-6/86. As a key contributor in the start-up of the in-house legal department, set up the entire legal filing system, developed reporting procedures, and wrote the job description for the legal secretary positions.

EXPERIENCE **Continued...**	<u>LAWYERS ROCK & CAMPBELL</u> - Fighter Town, USA **PARALEGAL**, *Mass Transit Tort Litigation*	(1979-84)

Participated extensively in numerous aspects of litigation. Assisted in witness interviews and served legal documents. Conducted site investigations involving directing photography and measuring/marking functions. Ordered medical subpoenas and analyzed medical records. Developed initial drafts to interrogatories, responses to interrogatories, and requests for production. Aided in jury selection, observed litigation procedures, and interpreted jury response. Prepared exhibits for court proceedings and scheduled depositions. Also worked with clients and interfaced significantly with opposing counsel.

- Summarized 364 depositions throughout a commercial litigation case in one year, which involved reviewing and interpreting depositions ranging from 20-850 pages.
- Cultivated valuable contacts and relationships with various members of court personnel.
- Initially hired to fulfill duties as Legal Secretary earning promotion to Paralegal.

<u>HONORABLE JUSTICE RIGHT, JUDGE</u> - Fair City, USA (1976-79)
ADMINISTRATIVE ASSISTANT
Prepared correspondence with outside parties requiring extensive public interaction. Screened all incoming calls and managed the court calendar. Scheduled attorney appointments and provided support for other judges and court administration.

<u>ATTORNEY SHARP</u> - Quick Minds, USA (1974-76)
LEGAL SECRETARY
Assisted both a real estate and a corporate attorney by preparing copious amounts of incorporation documents. Gained valuable knowledge in incorporation procedures and real estate matters. Developed legal descriptions of property and prepared closing documentation.

MILITARY	<u>THE AMERICAN MILITARY RESERVES</u> - Cadetteville, USA **LEGAL ADMINISTRATOR**	(1979-94)

Screened, hired, and supervised a staff of 3-30 Law Clerks. Conducted training regarding legal administration procedures. Established standards of operating procedures. Prepared memoranda with an emphasis on wills and powers of attorney.

- Designed and implemented a new computer program to streamline operational efficiency.
- Tracked and evaluated staff performance to ensure highest level of productivity.

EDUCATION	<u>THE PARALEGAL TRAINING INSTITUTE</u> - Legalese, USA **ABA Approved Litigation Certificate; Accredited Institution** Graduation, 12/95 * *Full-time employment during this training.*

<u>COUNTY COLLEGE</u> - Local, USA
Associate Degree in Office Administration, 1994

ADDITIONAL **TRAINING**	<u>COMMUNITY COLLEGE OF STUDYVILLE</u> - Studyville, USA **Certificate in Private Investigation**, 1983

COMPUTER	• MS Word	• WordPerfect	• Excel	• Lotus 1-2-3
	• Q&A	• Summation	• Lexus	• Nexus

OTHER   Notary Public

REFERENCES AVAILABLE UPON REQUEST

JOHN J. SEEKER
123 Looking Hard Avenue
Top Dog, USA 20202
(555) 678-9101

CAREER SUMMARY

Results-producing executive leader with an impressive track record in all facets of sales organization development ranging from infrastructure building and strategic planning to product positioning and market introduction within both untapped and saturated markets for manufacturers.

QUALIFICATIONS HIGHLIGHTS

Management
- Skilled in rebuilding organizations and defining/launching undeveloped product lines.
- Experienced in pioneering products and improving underperforming sales organizations.
- Adept in forecasting, developing zero-based budgets, and predicting industry trends.
- Exhibit critical ability to motivate cross-functional teams toward achieving common goals.
- Vastly talented in developing cohesive sales efforts through third-party rep firms.

Sales
- Experienced in multi-tiered selling environments, developing key contacts with architects, designers, facilities managers, end-users, OEMs, and distributors.
- Highly effective in creating sales concepts and marketing programs to increase revenues.
- Strong background in pursuing and developing multifaceted marketing channels.
- Skillfully communicate with key players in a high-profile/image-conscious business.
- Astute abilities in all aspects of solutions, application, and conceptual sales.

EXPERIENCE   TABLE MANUFACTURERS - Top Dog, USA   (3/96-Present)

V.P. OF SALES & DISTRIBUTION
Comprehensively manage a national revenue stream of $22M for this niche manufacturer of height-adjustable tables/open-plan systems which offers AutoCAD design/space planning services. Pursued and negotiated OEM contracts for products sold to national office furniture manufacturers.

Accountability
Highlights:
- Provide executive leadership to 18 rep firms with 50-70 sales reps in North America and Canada.
- Manage 5 regional managers working in concert with rep firms to develop lucrative markets and cultivate key contacts with architectural/design firms, distributors, and corporate end-users.
- Strategically develop primary markets and identify major business development opportunities.
- Maintain critical influence over pricing, contribution margins, dealer discounts, distribution alignment, contractual/national purchasing agreements, and space planning project approval.
- Contributed to product development in conjunction with the executive management team.

Results
Highlights:
- Increased overall net sales by 17% in one year, which represents $2.1M in revenue growth.
- Spearheaded and developed significant growth within a previously untapped OEM market.
- Totally realigned distribution, which included development and implementation of a new strategy which shifted from non-captive to captive distribution.
- Restructured over 50% of the independent rep coverage nationwide and instituted a training program to increase the focus and productivity of the existing rep firms.
- Redefined sales goals, wrote annual business plans, developed forecasting procedures, formulated job descriptions, and created account development/sales tools.
- Dramatically improved the cohesiveness of the sales force by improving field communications.

| EXPERIENCE *continued...* | FURNITURE COMPANY - Super Hot City, USA | (1991-1996) |

REGIONAL MANAGER/SOUTHWEST
Directed the Southwest region for this $1.2B company designated as the 2nd largest commercial office furnishing manufacturer in the world. Significantly strengthened an existing sales organization by providing consistently strong executive leadership.

Accountability Highlights:
- Built an effective sales force by implementing new policies/procedures, infusing insightful sales direction, and fostering cooperative sales and account support efforts.
- Acted as the key regional corporate liaison with full financial accountability for 2 sales offices serving 8 states which included leading 10 direct reports.
- Actively involved in industry-specific events to develop relationships and promote products.
- Developed strategic actions on market development plans for dealer/distributors.

Results Highlights:
- Grew net sales from $28M to $49M for an industry leader with heavy existing market penetration.
- Consistently exceeded sales goals, achieving up to 149% of annual quotas and profitability goals.
- Developed a top-performing team which consecutively earned a top 5 national sales ranking.
- Earned 5 Sales Leadership Awards (Cube Award) for outstanding sales management related to achieving sales volume and profitability objectives within this 250-person sales organization.

COMMERCIAL ITEMS - Somewhere, USA   (1982-1990)

CORPORATE CONSULTANT - 1989-1990
Earned promotion from Regional Sales Director position to a visible in-house industry consultant role for this high-end open-plan/modular commercial furniture manufacturer. Directly interfaced with the highest-level decision-makers of major accounts to define and resolve all pricing, product application, and distribution matters. Critically assisted in overcoming client objections and finalizing sales contracts at the executive level.

REGIONAL MANAGER - 1985-1989
Conceived marketing strategies, promotional tactics, and distribution planning for 350 independent dealer representatives covering the entire Western region of the U.S and Hawaii. Participated in industry-related trade shows and conferences to effectively market products. Provided strong consultative sales support and product training to the direct reports.

- Nurtured key client relationships with several major Fortune 500 accounts.
- Recognized as a driving force behind the sales increases from $18M to $70M during tenure.

MARKET MANAGER - 1982-1985
Hired initially in an outside sales position with full territory management and account development accountabilities. Based on excellent performance, earned increased sales authority.

* Other experience includes brief term with That Corporation as West Coast Regional Manager and employment in diverse industries from 1974 to 1982, including an Account Manager position with Office Interiors, an Account Manager position with Another Company, USA, and a Title Officer position with Title Insurance Company.

| EDUCATION | STATE UNIVERSITY - South State, USA
Bachelor of Science in Public Administration |

| TRAINING | • Spin Selling   • Executive Management   • Contract Negotiations |

REFERENCES AVAILABLE UPON REQUEST

SARAH J. SEARCH
123 Job Hunting Lane
Big Time, USA 10101
(444) 567-8910

SKILLS HIGHLIGHTS

- Highly talented individual with a strong background in all aspects of digital, multimedia production, project management, and business development.
- Extensive knowledge of marketing and advertising, particularly on the Internet.
- Capable of directing projects involving teams of experts in diverse areas, including graphic art, hardware/software engineering, programming, digital audio/video.
- Vast technological expertise related to digital video compression, capture, dubbing, grabbing, and editing as well as CD-ROM development and burning, graphic animation painting, and art/photo scanning.

EXPERIENCE

TECHNOLOGY RACER SYSTEMS - Technotown, USA   (3/95-Present)
Digital Video Producer, Technical Marketing
Manage a diverse range of production projects involving digital video and still photography compression in a low-bit-rate format using fractal-based technology for the Internet. Work closely with high-profile clients including major corporations, strategic partners, distributors, and compression service bureaus. Manage projects from inception to final production, including software testing, to ensure quality and functionality.

- Successfully completed projects for national and international companies in diverse industries, i.e., consumer products, banking, computers, media, telecommunications, professional services.
- Key contributor to new business development and customer retention through the creation and delivery of critical sales presentations and on-site executive demonstrations.
- Conceptualized creative advertising and marketing designs for company's impressive Web site.
- Initiated an acquisition and licensing procedure for video content, which involved working with multiple departments of major movie studios, i.e., Cartoon Films, Movie Brothers.
- Created and produced digital video demos for important trade shows including Computer USA.
- Developed and implemented video capture/compression training classes for various clients.

AMERICAN IMAGES PRODUCTIONS - Producer City, USA   (1/93-12/94)
Production Assistant
Performed a variety of creative and technical functions for this multimedia production company which specialized in the production of interactive and CD-ROM entertainment titles. Served as an integral member of the concept development team. Personally conducted product editing and testing, which included audio and visual aspects, for ultimate market release. Also contributed to press releases and public relations activities.

- Displayed strong production skills which included audition management/talent selection, script/talent contract negotiations, set coordination, and video recording supervision.
- Provided critical decision-making related to final video selection and script editing.
- Solely conceptualized and produced an 8-minute corporate marketing video tool.
- Reviewed and approved foreign translations required to convert scripts of existing titles.

ABC ENTERTAINMENT - Entertainers Village, USA   (6/92-11/92)
Intern
Assisted in script writing and editing of films and music videos for an independent production company. Also developed press packages to pitch movie ideas to investors.

EDUCATION

THE UNIVERSITY OF SUCCESS - Fast Moving, USA
B.A. in Visual Media, 1/93 (Traveled abroad for a Photo Journalism Internship)

COMPUTER

- Macintosh
- Windows 95
- Adobe Premiere
- Vid. for Windows
- Adobe Photoshop
- Macromedia Director

EQUIPMENT

- Truevision's Targa 2000 capture cards • Media 100 • Radius Telecast • Turbo Cube • SGI/Unix

JOHN. J. SEEKER
123 Looking Hard Avenue
Top Dog, USA 20202
(555) 678-9101

CAREER SUMMARY

Dynamic professional demonstrating an 18-year proven track record in all facets of
media planning, brand building, and business development.

SIGNIFICANT QUALIFICATIONS

- Leverage intimate knowledge of all media vehicles to effectively promote client-specific products, image, experience, or services, as well as to build a strong advertising team.
- Proven ability to determine ideally aligned media mix that optimizes advertising investment dollars.
- Key experience with wide range of industries, i.e., healthcare, automotive, package goods, lotteries, alcohol, tobacco, electronics manufacturing, health and beauty, and airline.
- Demonstrate ability to create dynamic, tightknit infrastructures that maximize resources and efficiencies.
- Recognized by peers and clients for exceptional vendor negotiation skills that result in client cost savings.
- Consistently command premium fees by establishing industry-wide reputation for standards of excellence.
- Exceptional talent for cultivating strong relationships with a diverse and extremely demanding clientele.
- Established strong relationships with several major accounts such as Atlantic Shipping, Prestige Cars, Big Utility Co., Best Chemical Products, Sukiyaki Electronics, Greater USA Savings, Med Pharmaceuticals, Red Bottle Beers, Tool Time Taylor, and Pickle & Pickle.

EXPERIENCE   <u>XYZ ADVERTISING</u> - Sweetwater, USA   (11/92-Present)
EXECUTIVE VICE PRESIDENT
Oversee all aspects of media planning and time buying for 7 active clients in the Southeast
U.S. region and 2 international accounts with accountability for $300M in billings. Supervise a
management team and media staff of 55, handling broadcast buying for clients that generate from
$1M to $150M media dollars. Manage numerous process improvement and business development
projects and serve in several community relations capacities. Report directly to the CEO.

Provide staff with extensive knowledge of each type of media category, i.e., newspaper, television,
interactive, radio, magazines, and outdoor, in order to build a well-trained advertising team.
Research/prepare client-specific presentations by geographic areas to develop new business activity.
Identify and aggressively pursue new media-only business prospects utilizing industry tools.
Design and implement business development strategies in conjunction with the Creative, Planning,
Account Management, and Finance Departments.
Handle troubleshooting for key accounts related to problematic pricing issues or program negotiations.

Critical
Accomplishments:
- Acquired $150M telecommunications media-only account due to outstanding program plan, 1996.
- Combined efforts with European team to create and implement a Media Masters training program geared for senior executives with long-term industry track records.
- Reduced outsourced staff recruiting costs by developing and leveraging existing staff talent.
- Spearheaded Media Department Internship Program to recruit students from major colleges.
- Initiated mentor program linking senior staff with new hires as personal career advocates.
- Established substantial clout with numerous media vendors, utilizing relationship-building skills.
- Conduct seminars on brand-building methodologies/strategies as guest speaker at industry functions, the USAU Internship program, and Excel and Big State Universities.
- Member of the XYZ South Board of Directors; initially hired as Senior V.P./Media Director.

EXPERIENCE   XYZ ADVERTISING - (Cont.)

Business   • Conceived and implemented the out-of-home buying-group business from ground zero under
Development   the auspices of XYZ Media Department; realized a positive cash flow since its inception.
Project: Handled budget development, interviewing, staff accountabilities, training, and
                     business expansion strategies. Target a broad spectrum of clients nationwide that
                     generate $5M+ in annual billings.

Training   • Co-developed with Big State Educational Development Team all aspects of an intensive
Project: training program for use in Big City with all levels of media planners and buyers. Handle
                     budgeting, created curriculum content, coordinate all attendees' hospitality needs, and oversee
                     weekly implementation. Approve yearly modifications to curriculum components, including
                     media math, presentation skills, client development skills, and brand strategy development.

JIM DANDY ADVERTISING - Big City, USA   (1988-1992)
SENIOR VICE PRESIDENT/MEDIA DIRECTOR
Managed key aspects of business development, media planning, and buying. Maintained
accountability for $200M+ in annual billings of individual client accounts ranging from
$5M to $100M. Hired, trained, supervised, and evaluated 4 direct reports and staff of 39.
Consulted with multiple departments to determine final budget and staffing needs per account.
Initiated successful internal staff media training program. Reported to Agency President.

• Launched a lucrative media-only start-up operation from inception.
• Captured major Sukiyaki account through innovative media-only strategies.

BAKER & BAKER ADVERTISING - Big City, USA   (1984-1988)
SENIOR VICE PRESIDENT/ASSOCIATE MEDIA DIRECTOR
Directed an 8-member media planning team determining best optimization of media dollars
for 7 national clients with billings of $100M+ annually. Strategically secured new accounts.

• Earned 3 Gold and 1 Silver prestigious industry EFFIE Awards for outstanding professional
  industry contributions to brand building.
• Captured the Big State Lottery, Really Good Toys, and Med Pharmaceuticals accounts
  through remarkable team efforts.

GREAT DEAL ADVERTISING - Big City, USA   (1980-1984)
MEDIA SUPERVISOR
Directed a media planning staff of 4 handling client-specific marketing plans across diverse
industries. Accountable for $50M+ in annual billings.

* Previously employed as Media Planner Intern for large marketing firm, 1979-1980.

EDUCATION   GOOD COLLEGE - Big City, USA
                   B.B.A. in Marketing   ** Concentration: Marketing*

TRAINING   • 4 A's Executive Management Training Program, 1997
                   • Numerous corporate training programs, 1992-Present

AWARDS   • Winner of Three Gold EFFIEs awarded by pharmaceutical product vendors

AFFILIATIONS   • ADDY of Sweetwater Board Member, 1998
                   • Excel Business to Business Program, Participant

COMPUTER   • Persuasion   • PowerPoint   • Excel   • Word

REFERENCES AVAILABLE UPON REQUEST

206

JOHN J. SEEKER

123 Looking Hard Avenue
Top Dog, USA 20202
(555) 678-9101
jseeker@aol.com

CAREER SUMMARY

An experienced executive possessing 20+ years of proven core strengths in the areas of operations and resource management coupled with expertise in strategic planning, reporting, leadership, and training.

SIGNIFICANT QUALIFICATIONS

Operations Management
- Display strengths in articulating mission-critical goals, implementing tactical and strategic actions to achieve success, and maximizing resources within approved budgets and crucial timeframes.
- Vast experience with managing and controlling budgets of $3M+ and assets of $52M+.
- Excel at developing and implementing cost-effective process and procedural improvements.

Resource Management
- Salvaged millions of dollars by maximizing time, equipment, facilities, and personnel.
- Strategic decision-maker and astute asset manager with ability to elicit strong VIP support.
- Key experience supervising management teams of 80+ with accountability for 3,000+ personnel.
- Managed broad range of outsourced contract negotiations, ensuring no favoritism, fraud, or abuse.

Program Planning/ Management
- Coordinated complex operations by sea, air, and rail, meeting extremely critical deadlines.
- Planned and executed all aspects of senior-level executive training conferences held quarterly.
- Championed and initiated several successful management and personnel training programs.

EXPERIENCE

DEPARTMENT OF DEFENSE
EXECUTIVE OPERATIONS MANAGER - 1996-Present
Manage all aspects of critical readiness reporting operations for the re-engineering headquarters. Direct a management team of 15 high-level military and civilian personnel researching and analyzing monthly data reports related to 200,000 U.S.-based personnel. Provide concise summaries to Department of Defense (DOD) for strategic planning and Congressional Testimony purposes, ensuring compliance with stringent accuracy and correctness guidelines of Congressional Reviews and Committees. Report directly to group of chief executive officers.

Critical Accountabilities:
- Maintain detailed and updated personnel, training, and equipment records pertaining to numbers, shortages, specialties, needs, capabilities, and optimum resource operational levels.
- Produce statistical data packets and graphic displays to report operational status.
- Cooperate with CFO to identify/report systemic funding issues for a $304M budget.
- Provide the Strategic Business Planning Re-engineering Directors with critical assessment data.

Selected Highlights:
- Achieved the charter mission by establishing and maintaining exceptional VIP advocacy, including conducting quarterly briefs with top-level DOD personnel and Congressional VIPS.
- Prepare CEOs for Congressional inquiries with exhaustive and accurate operations reports.
- Developed and implemented a new automated process tool that provided global command with efficient accessibility to comprehensive and accurate strategic business planning report data.

TRAINING PROGRAM/OPERATIONS MANAGER - 1993-95
Selected to direct a leadership training program team of 15 senior DOD joint forces consisting of personnel, foreign officers, and high-level civilians. Researched, developed, and presented materials and practical methodologies to be used during joint operations. Simultaneously attended master's-level program on National Security and Strategy. Also accountable for daily operations, general staff training, and supervision functions of a management team of 80 senior officers and federal government employees.

EXPERIENCE

DEPARTMENT OF DEFENSE - (Cont.)

Critical
Accountabilities:

- Served on-call as Operations Manager in Crest-based headquarters performing troubleshooting, and closely monitoring a diverse range of real-world missions and simulated exercises.
- Provided TQM training and formed Process Action Teams to optimize re-engineering efforts.
- Key contact for all government and civilian VIP delegations to observe and discuss operations.
- Coordinated all aspects of foreign American embassy tour for 35 students and faculty.

Selected
Highlights:

- Selected from thousands of Service candidates to attend a Senior Officer Air War College.
- Planned and executed all aspects of quarterly executive training conferences for 30-35 high-level international and U.S. managers at various European facilities, including travel, hotels, food, social and business agendas, security, expense management, and all required negotiations.
- Authored articles on Strategic Leadership selected for a DOD publication.
- Led a DOD delegation to study and internally apply effective Israeli training initiatives.

STRATEGIC OPERATIONS MANAGER - 1989-93
Performed a diverse range of contingency and daily operations as well as personnel management functions related to foreign military crises and post-crisis security. Maintained full accountability for operations budgets up to $3M and up to $52M in aviation, communications, medical, field artillery, armor, and engineering equipment. Trained and supported up to 3,000 personnel. Strategically planned and implemented policies related to financial and resource management, training, and logistics to achieve missions within budget and deadlines.

Critical
Accountabilities:

- Synchronized all aspects of multiple global missions directing a management staff of 20+.
- Fostered government/civilian agency cooperation in order to maximize crisis response resources.
- Established strong public relations and widespread support systems serving as key DOD liaison.
- Astutely channeled salvaged funds into process improvements and equipment enhancements.

Selected
Highlights:

- Spearheaded a new training concept that integrated tactical management training/team-building.
- Developed and initiated comprehensive ongoing training program for a 1,000-member task force.
- Planned and directed several national disaster relief programs, including response to state floods, fires, border security crises, as well as patriot missile site security.
- Coordinated logistics of 3-month rotations of 130 American personnel based on foreign soil.

GENERAL MANAGER - 1986-89
Managed training, process improvements, conference planning, and contract negotiations with accountability for a $75K operations budget. Supervised teams of 25 international and U.S.-based managers and up to 3,000 staff members. Conducted extensive research to write and initiate training policy revisions for 80,000 personnel.

Early Career
Highlights:

- *Served as operations and personnel coordinator for all services requiring excellent resource management skills, handling up to $3M in assets.*
- *Directed training for teams of up to 3,000 with a diverse range of accountabilities.*
- *Conducted high-level leadership and intelligence training of team that trained 14,000 personnel.*
- *Selected as a technical skills instructor for specialized global teams.*

EDUCATION

MILITARY OFFICER UNIVERSITY - Sometown, USA
Master's Level National Security Strategy Program, 1996   Emphasis: Strategic Leadership

UNIVERSITY OF SALUTATIONS - Nextdoor, USA
B.S. in International Relations/Social Psychology

MANAGEMENT TRAINING

- Total Quality Management and Process Action Teams
- Aircraft Assets Operation Management
- Personnel Training and Logistics Management
- Executive Operations Management
- Operations and Training Management
- Advanced Management Training

CREDENTIALS/ COMPUTER

- TQM for Strategic Business Planning Certification, 1993 • Top Secret Security Clearance
- Proficient in numerous data management, graphics, and communications software programs.

208

JOHN J. SEEKER, R.PH., PH.D.
123 Looking Hard Avenue
Top Dog, USA 20202
(555) 678-9101

CAREER SUMMARY

Talented, multi-lingual professional demonstrating 18 years of proven experience as a
pharmacist in upper-level management and scientific research.

SIGNIFICANT QUALIFICATIONS

- Experienced in managing all aspects of both hospital and retail pharmacy operations.
- Internationally recognized scientist noted for discoveries at a renowned research institute.
- Possess valuable marketing and management expertise in U.S. and European pharmaceutical markets.
- Extensive background in maximizing operational efficiency, inventory control, and cash flow.
- Demonstrate excellent strategic planning, resource management, and troubleshooting skills.
- Highly educated executive with broad academic and professional qualifications.
- Proven ability in utilizing strong, multicultural interpersonal skills to impact revenues.

EXPERIENCE

GROCERY STORE PHARMACY - Food City, USA   (1994-Present)
PHARMACY MANAGER
Promoted into a management role while maintaining duties as a Pharmacist.
Comprehensively manage a fast-paced $1M+ retail pharmacy. Handle a diverse
range of managerial duties including prescription preparation and fulfillment,
inventory control, file maintenance, and information management. Review and
order pharmacy products from approved suppliers/distributors. Consult physicians,
hospital staff, and patients. Analyze financial information and ensure
bottom-line profitability.

- Key contributor in facilitating revenue increases of 80% within 2 years.
- Successfully impacted profit margins by up to 29% and immediately decreased
  inventory by 20%.
- Increased department cash flow by strengthening inventory controls.
- Significantly improved customer satisfaction and cultivated strong client relations.
- Upheld maximum efficiency during a major company-wide computer conversion in 1995.
- Maintain vast knowledge of medical terms demonstrated through responsive service time.
- Comprehensive experience with insurance filing procedures and related coding.
- Received letters of commendation from management.

* Presently employed on a part-time basis as a Pharmacist with Prestigious
  University Hospital, 7/95-Present.

STATE BOARD OF PHARMACY - Overseas   (1990-1994)
Southeast District of Pharmacies
DISTRICT MANAGER
Comprehensively responsible for supervising the operational efficiency and profitability
of 24 pharmacies in an assigned district. Personally investigated fraud cases and
financial irregularities on behalf of the government. Resourcefully managed and
distributed pharmacy products among multiple locations in spite of limited resources.
Developed strong relations with pharmacy suppliers and warehouses.

EXPERIENCE
Continued...

- Successfully managed and controlled pharmacy inventory levels of $10M+.
- Instituted improved ordering and distribution methods of the drug supply.
- Impacted district profitability by 15% and increased sales by 60%.
- Possess expansive knowledge of chemistry; capable of mixing/compounding hundreds of different prescriptions.
- Ensured compliance with strict regulating guidelines and operating conditions.
- Selected as Commission Chairman; conducted numerous audits in hospital and retail pharmacies.
- Employed excellent decision-making and troubleshooting skills in this visible position.

ACADEMY OF SCIENCES - Overseas   (1983-1990)
RESEARCH SPECIALIST
Conducted cutting-edge scientific research related to natural resources of medicinal plants. Utilized advanced spectrum analysis, such as nuclear-magnetic resonance, and other physical and chemical research techniques. Produced results with long-term impact.

- Successfully discovered and classified three new chemical structures.
- Identified one chemical; personally named new drug as having antispasmodic activity; hold patent on new drug (Overseas, 1990).
- Awarded a bronze medal for research at a Scientific Exhibition in a Foreign Country, 1985.
- Research is published internationally, including among various U.S. publications.

STATE BOARD OF PHARMACY - Overseas   (1981-1983)
STAFF MEMBER/INSPECTOR
Reported directly to the Chairman of the State Board agency. Directed a staff of 5. Performed management and marketing audits of 200 retail and hospital pharmacies. Researched emergency requests and located medications during extreme shortages. Provided input to manufacturers to affect the production and inventory of drugs needed.

- Improved operational efficiency by enhancing file maintenance and distribution methods.
- Expediently resolved customer problems and strengthened public relations.
- Identified strategies to educate the consumer population on substitute medications.

EDUCATION

ACADEMY OF SCIENCES - Overseas
PH.D. IN BIOLOGY, 1980-1984
Completed Post-graduate Courses in Chemistry and Biology

PHARMACY SCHOOL OF MEDICAL INSTITUTE - Overseas
B.A. IN PHARMACY, 1975-1980

* Passed the Foreign Pharmacy Equivalency Exam, NABPLEX, 1991
* Passed the Test of English as a Foreign Language, TOEFL, 1992

LICENSES

State Pharmacist License, 1997

LANGUAGES

- Fluent in Russian, Azerbaijani/Turkish, Ukrainian, English
- Communication skills apply to many countries in Eastern Europe

COMPUTER

- EDX • UNIX • Zadall • Lotus 1-2-3 • Dbase • Pagemaker • WordPerfect

---

REFERENCES AVAILABLE UPON REQUEST

JOHN J. SEEKER

123 Looking Hard Avenue
Top Dog, USA 20202
H - (555) 678-9101
W - (222) 245-2200

PROFESSIONAL SUMMARY

Talented and results-oriented executive with over 17 years of diverse real estate experience in all aspects of shopping center development, asset management, and consulting for a renowned developer.

QUALIFICATIONS HIGHLIGHTS

- Experienced in many aspects of both commercial and residential design/construction.
- Extensive background in the supervision and coordination of regional shopping center development, including planning, design, and construction/renovation development phases.
- Adept in diverse areas of responsibility, i.e., budget management, property management, reporting, retail lease administration, contract negotiations, personnel supervision, and marketing.
- Display key managerial qualities characteristic of strong executive leadership and direction combined with focus toward achieving organizational objectives and profit goals.

PROFESSIONAL EXPERIENCE

<u>JOHN DOE DEVELOPMENTS</u> - Builders, USA   (1977-Present)

During a long-term association with this internationally recognized real estate developer and consultant, performed a wide array of management functions related to shopping center development, leasing, management, and marketing. Diverse present and previous responsibilities are outlined below:

Design/Construction Coordination

- Coordinate all aspects of development construction including scheduling, deadline management, and extensive troubleshooting.
- Establish and disseminate specifications information as well as review construction documents to ensure compliance with all of the developer's criteria.
- Serve as a key liaison between the developer, general contractors, architects, tenants, and tenants' contractors.
- Successfully ensured a timely grand opening of 25 retail stores within 4 months.

Expansion/ Renovation

- Talented in the areas of project management and owner representation involving major retail stores from design planning to construction phases.
- Effectively orchestrate design teams including Architects, Engineers, and Consultants.
- Experienced in securing design/construction approvals with governing authorities.
- Coordinated expansion projects from design/construction to grand opening, including managing all architectural, engineering, and construction contracts.

Property Management

- Capable of directing an on-site management staff composed of office administrators, maintenance, security, and independent contractors.
- Experienced in managing property operations budgets of up to $200K.

Reporting/ Consulting

- Prepare vital management reports outlining ongoing operational activities.
- Conceptualized and implemented a design/construction report to closely track projects.
- Served as a key contributor during consulting projects involving design construction.

Leasing/ Marketing

- Prepare leasing documentation and negotiate lease agreements to final execution.
- Possess in-depth knowledge of shopping center lease agreements.
- Exhibit diplomacy in communicating between landlord, tenant, and leasing agents.
- Provide design support to marketing teams involved in planning promotions.

Property Disposition

- Provide support during due diligence process for the sale of a regional shopping center, including coordinating property analyses and reviewing related documentation.
- Adept at conducting property tours and responding to prospective buyers' inquiries.

PROFESSIONAL   *Project Highlights:*
EXPERIENCE
Continued...   • Regional Shopping Center, **Shopping Center**, Beachtown, USA - Development,
                         Management, Expansion, and Sale; 60 acres with 600,000+ sq. ft. of total leasable
                         space; included 4 major department stores and 125 mall stores.
                       • Regional Shopping Center, **Shop Til You Drop Mall**, Shopping, USA - Expansion,
                         Renovation, and Merchandising; 50 acres with 770,000 sq. ft. of total leasable
                         space; included 3 major department stores, and 160 mall stores.
                       • Office/Specialty Retail, **555 Pretty Place**, Beautyville, USA - Redevelopment, Expansion,
                         and Merchandising; 150,000 sq. ft. of retail space and 182,000 sq. ft. of office
                         space; included 3-level specialty retail, 16-story office tower, and 50+ stores.
                       • Other key development, redevelopment, and expansion projects included **Lightening
                         Mall**, Beachtown, USA; **Good Luck Mall**, Luckie, USA; **Happy Road Center**,
                         Tall Town, USA; **Western Singing Mall**, Country Town, USA.

APPRENTICESHIP   <u>GOOD GUYS ASSOCIATES</u> - Teaching City, USA   (Summer 1976)
EXPERIENCE

                       Utilized strong drafting and design skills to produce construction documents
                       and various aspects of architectural plans for commercial and residential projects.

                       <u>BEST GENERAL CONTRACTOR</u> - Efficientville, USA   (Summer 1975)

                       Gained practical experience in residential construction as a general laborer.

                       <u>BEACH CONSTRUCTION</u> - Surfs Up, USA   (Summer 1973)

                       Demonstrated effective drafting abilities through the creation of construction
                       documents for this residential design/construction firm.

EDUCATION   <u>TIGER TOWN UNIVERSITY</u> - Winner, USA
                       Bachelor of Architecture Degree, 1977

                       <u>TIGER TOWN UNIVERSITY</u> - Winner, USA
                       Bachelor of Arts in Pre-Architecture, 1975
                       * *Lettered as a Varsity Athlete*

STUDIES   <u>TIGER UNIVERSITY/ABROAD PROGRAM</u> - Overseas, Europe
ABROAD   **Center for Building Research & Urban Studies**, 1976
                       * *Studied architectural landmarks in major cities throughout Europe.*

RELATED   • Shopping Center Management Level I (2-day course)
TRAINING   Sponsored by Shopping Center Association, 1982
                       • Shopping Center Management Level II (2-day course)
                         Sponsored by Shopping Center Association, 1983

PROFESSIONAL   • Shopping Center Association, Affiliate Membership
AFFILIATIONS   • American Land Institute, Company Membership

PERSONAL   • Happy Lane Homeowners Association, Past President
AFFILIATIONS   • Happy Lane Swim & Racquet Club, Past Board Member
                       • Overseas Clan Society, USA, Past Vice President, Board Member
                       • Boys Club of America Fraternity Alumni Association

---

REFERENCES AVAILABLE ON REQUEST

JOHN J. SEEKER

123 Looking Hard Avenue
Top Dog, USA 20202
(555) 678-9101

CAREER SUMMARY

Impressive professional possessing an extensive retail background who demonstrates
acute creative, marketing, purchasing, staffing, and management skills.

SIGNIFICANT QUALIFICATIONS

- Maintain a critical understanding of marketing, market demands, and customer-specific profiles.
- Remain abreast of packaging, product, and merchandising trends as well as competitive product lines.
- Demonstrate a high degree of creativity in designing and developing direct mail marketing pieces.
- Adept purchasing, inventory control, merchandising, and strategic growth planning techniques.
- Strong track record in all facets of product research, sourcing, development, and selection.
- Experienced in recruiting, hiring, training, supervising, and motivating part- and full-time staff.
- Exhibit highly effective project and deadline management skills critical to a fast-paced industry.
- Demonstrate strong quality and cost control of products to achieve target profit margins.

EXPERIENCE   <u>SUPER FOODS</u> - Sweetwater, USA   (1982-Present)

BUYER/CATALOGUE DESIGNER
Collaborate in the design and production of a 4-color, 16-page mail order catalogue with
90,000 subscribers. Oversee product development of customized specialty food and gift items.
Simultaneously direct the purchasing of up to $300K in mail order and gift basket merchandise.
Also manage the purchasing and inventory control of more than $500K in gourmet foods and
specialty chocolates for as many as 7 retail stores. Source and authorize new products
in addition to researching and selecting new suppliers.

- Contributed to catalogue growth from 4 to 16 pages, which resulted in sales growth of
  280% and product growth from 3,500 to 13,500 cases.
- Integrally involved in directing photography sessions, product styling, copywriting, editing,
  and catalogue layout for a marketing brochure spotlighting 54 different products.
- Analyze, identify, and set optimal product pricing and handle sales/product forecasting.
- Utilize knowledge of diverse demographics to evaluate and respond to changing market trends.
- Research new products through industry-related food/gift shows and competitive catalogues.
- Negotiate pricing with 40 vendors and strategically balance critical inventory levels
  during high-volume seasonal business.

Adjunct
Accountabilities: Previously managed the Shipping and Order Processing departments in conjunction with purchasing
and catalogue production accountabilities. Coordinated an inventory of 60 different products
and effectively managed critical production deadlines.

- Reduced warehouse handling time 30% by revising procedures, which improved product
  turn-around and streamlined shipping efficiency of 14,000 items.
- Improved order-processing procedures, which increased staff productivity by 20%.

EXPERIENCE
continued....

DISTRICT MANAGER
Comprehensively managed 4 profit centers with gross sales of $1.5M. Directed a management team of 4 and a staff of up to 60 full- and part-time personnel. Maintained full operations accountability with total authorization for product line development and purchasing. Closely controlled and monitored individual stores' performances.

- Identified a rapidly expanding sugar-free market segment and developed ground-floor revenues which currently represent 18% of district's total confection sales.
- Recognized lucrative new profit center and instituted consumable snack/drink products which ultimately generated 35% of the district's sales.
- Key contributor in creation of name, logo, and product image of the private-label product line.
- Managed the opening of 3 new stores with critical influence over operation's start-up, including layout design, display development, purchasing, staffing, and grand opening implementation.
- Assisted in product selection, copywriting, and advertising photography approval for jointly sponsored direct mail marketing campaigns with a circulation of 400,000.
- Created and wrote employee policies and devised specialized product training programs for staff.

STORE MANAGER
Directed all operations and personnel management functions for one assigned retail location. Based on outstanding results, promoted within one year to multi-store accountability.

WELLMADE SHOES (1978-1982)

MANAGER - Sweetwater; Palm City; Beachtown, USA
Maintained accountability for daily sales operations and personnel activities for this high-end apparel retailer. Supervised all in-store merchandising and inventory control procedures. Personally handled corporate reporting, bookkeeping, and cash management functions. Tightly monitored loss prevention to minimize shrinkage. Acted as a key resource in resolving customer-related issues and providing ongoing sales training.

ASSISTANT MANAGER/
SALES ASSOCIATE - Pleasantville, USA
Promoted into a management role based on exceptional performance. Consistently achieved target goals related to sales and leadership track record.

EDUCATION

UNIVERSITY OF CENTRAL USA - Pleasantville, USA
B.A. IN POLITICAL SCIENCE - 1980
* *Self-financed degree 100% through full-time employment.*

TRAINING/
COMPUTER

- Completed annual management training programs related to Operations, Personnel Management, Staffing, and Project Management.
- Working knowledge of MAS 90 and WordPerfect.

CIVIC/
COMMUNITY

- AIDS Sweetwater Volunteer - *4 years*
  - Earned 2 Outstanding Volunteer Awards
  - Served as Volunteer Phone Recruitment Coordinator
  - Participated in soliciting vendor donations
- AIDS Research Consortium of Sweetwater Volunteer - *3 years*
- Townegate Condominium Board of Directors - *3 years*

REFERENCES AVAILABLE UPON REQUEST

JOHN J. SEEKER
123 Looking Hard Avenue
Top Dog, USA 20202
(555) 678-9101

OBJECTIVE

To obtain a sales position where I may utilize my strong relationship-selling and consultative sales abilities to positively affect corporate revenues.

SKILLS SUMMARY

- Skilled in nurturing an intangible and conceptual sales process with a long sales cycle.
- Adept in strategic identification and planning of aggressive corporate marketing efforts.
- Display acute solutions selling, proposal development, and executive-level presentation skills.
- Capable of selling applications and technology-driven products within a competitive market.
- Proven ability to identify key decision-makers and excel in a multi-tiered selling environment.
- Demonstrate highly persuasive selling skills and closing techniques essential to financial sales.

EXPERIENCE

ABBOTT & COSTELLO - Top Dog, USA (1996-1997)
Branch Development
ASSISTANT VICE PRESIDENT
Worked for an independent broker/dealer serving institutional and retail clients. Pursued and developed relationships with investment brokers, financial planners, CPAs, and attorneys as registered representatives to market the company's full line of financial products. Key contributor in all aspects of new business development.

- Prospected and strategically generated interest in company through multifaceted marketing.
- Structured and negotiated compensation/incentives and successfully closed open-ended contracts; maintained decision-making authority related to contracts based on previous/potential production.
- Collaboratively recruited registered representatives through start-up branch offices which resulted in annualized production of $15M; achieved 125% of projected revenue goals.
- Consulted branch offices, advised on recruiting, business development, and administration aspects.

TRUE COMPETITORS - Top Dog, USA (1995-1996)
Major Accounts Division
ACCOUNT EXECUTIVE
Aggressively marketed business solutions and applications to major Fortune 500 accounts. Pursued long-term competitive win-back business, targeting companies with $25K-$100K per month in telecommunications expenses. Demonstrated strong cost analyses and forecasting skills.

- Gained knowledge of advanced voice, data, and video communications products.
- Expanded existing account revenues and developed new accounts through cold calling.

GOOD INVESTMENT CORPORATION - Top Dog, USA (1992-1995)
MARKETING/FINANCIAL ANALYST
Worked primarily with high net-worth retail clients. Performed financial analyses, identified clients' objectives, developed investment and financial management strategies, executed trades, and prepared performance reports for periodic client reviews.

- Prospected for new accounts and marketed products and services to an existing client base; secured and executed signed proprietary financial planning contracts.
- Experienced in preparing portfolio summaries, asset liability updates, tax and cash flow projections, asset rate of returns, and asset allocation reports.
- Attended national, regional, and local conferences to source recruitment and business opportunities.

* Previously employed with The Best Shoe in management and sales roles, 1986-1992.

EDUCATION

YOUR STATE UNIVERSITY - Top Dog, USA
B.S. in Finance - 1991   ** Self-financed 50% through employment.*
* Includes Certificate in Accounting

COMPUTER

- MS Word   • Excel   • Lotus 1-2-3   • ACT

SARAH J. SEARCH

123 Job Hunting Lane
Big Time, USA 10101
(444) 567-8910

CAREER SUMMARY

Talented educator demonstrating 25 years of total experience in the field of education with a
16-year proven track record in administration of student services in higher education.

EDUCATION

MASTER OF EDUCATION & COUNSELING SERVICES 1989
COLD STATE UNIVERSITY - Frigid, USA
GPA: 4.0/4.0

MASTER OF EDUCATION IN ART EDUCATION 1975
SURFERS STATE UNIVERSITY - Surfing, USA
GPA: 3.9/4.0

BACHELOR OF SCIENCE IN EDUCATION 1971
SURFERS UNIVERSITY - Surfing, USA

**CONTINUING
EDUCATION**

Participated in numerous national and regional workshops and conferences involving
student affairs topics such as disability services, wellness, placement, planning and
evaluation, professional ethics, student retention, and foreign student advisement.

PROFESSIONAL HIGHLIGHTS

Student Services

• Demonstrated knowledge and direct experience in a broad array of student services, including
Career and Personal Counseling, Residence Life, Orientation, Student Activities, Student
Leadership, Foreign Student Advisement, Judicial Affairs, and Alumni Services.

Accreditation

• Participated five times as a visiting committee member of the Regional Association
of Colleges and Schools' College Commission for Accreditation and Reaffirmation Visits
(Section V. Student Development).
• Served as Steering Committee member and Principal Committee Chair for a Self-Study program.

**Management/
Administration**

• Experienced in fostering a team approach among faculty and staff to achieve program continuity.
• Possess a strong combination of professional attributes related to administrative abilities,
including writing skills, reporting, program research, and maximizing internal efficiency.

**Curriculum
Development**

• Outstanding originality in course development to ensure maximized learning and retention.
• Solely coordinated annual Study Tours, including developing creative, effective curriculum.
• Awarded for performance as an advisor to the International Studies Abroad Tours.

Instruction

• Demanding instructor utilizing positive reinforcement and self-esteem-building techniques.
• Demonstrated track record for successfully educating audiences of all ages in diverse topics.

ADMINISTRATION **EXPERIENCE**	<u>Creative College</u> - Fresh Ideas, USA	(1980 - Present)

STUDENT DEAN

Comprehensively manage all student affairs for 980+ student body: Health and Welfare, Residence Life, Judicial Affairs, Student Governance, Student Activities/Study Tours, Career Development, and Alumni Services. In addition, manage budget, compile and edit student handbook, and coordinate orientation. Actively involved in conceiving and implementing program enhancements, including "Student Awards," "Student Service," "Student Survival," and "Meal Plan." Hired initially as an Instructor and promoted several times, which involved increasing levels of accountability and expansion of responsibilities.

- Instrumental in solidifying accreditation for the Creative College.
- As a member of the Accreditation Team, hosted and responded to team visitations.
- Contribute to future directions as a member of the Planning and Management Committees.
- Originated and conducted professional development presentations: "Diversity," "ADA Regulations," and "Drug & Alcohol Abuse: How to Detect It."

DIRECTOR OF STUDENT DEVELOPMENT SERVICES

Solely responsible for counseling students on personal, health, and wellness issues. Oversee disability services, including serving as Compliance Officer for ADA. Develop all drug and alcohol programming.

CAREER DEVELOPMENT COORDINATOR

Successfully developed entire job placement and job referral program from ground zero to provide active and effective role in students' career development. Initiated and developed internship program including supervising program for 10 years, resulting in crucial hands-on training for graduating students. Developed and coordinated numerous career days and educational programs abroad and nationally to further expand educational experiences and impact. Implemented and currently maintain elaborate Alumni tracking system.

TEACHING **EXPERIENCE**	<u>USA Parks & Recreation</u> - Goodtime, USA	(1975 - Present)

INSTRUCTOR

Originated, designed, implemented, and currently instruct a diverse range of enrichment courses and workshop programs for all ages at community arts centers.

<u>Friendly County School System</u> - Niceville, USA   (1973 - 1977)

INSTRUCTOR

Taught at high school and elementary levels. Served on a Curriculum Committee, resulting in the establishment of an exemplary art enrichment program and the redesigning of the county's art curriculum guide.

AFFILIATIONS

- Regional Association for College Student Affairs
- American Counseling Association
- National Association of Colleges and Employers
- State College Placement Council

REFERENCES AVAILABLE UPON REQUEST

SARAH J. SEARCH
123 Job Hunting Lane
Big Time, USA 10101
(444) 567-8910

CAREER SUMMARY

Accomplished professional demonstrating 10 years of successful writing experience and
publication management in both corporate and freelance environments.

SIGNIFICANT QUALIFICATIONS

- Published author possessing an innate talent to conceive, develop, and compose diverse written materials.
- Capable of transforming highly complex, technical information into simplified, comprehensible text.
- Noted for extremely effective writing skills with an acute ability to concisely convey messages.
- Proficiently manage numerous projects simultaneously while working within strict deadlines.
- Uniquely equipped to flourish in creative, unstructured environments as well as corporate arenas.
- Exceptionally professional demeanor and unobtrusive interview style resulting in quality work.

RELATED
EXPERIENCE

WRITER ASSIGNMENTS - Sweetwater, USA   (1990-Present)
Writer/Materials Manager
Contracted by various corporations and non-profit organizations for a diverse
range of copywriting assignments. Consistently handle all phases of development
from conception to composition. Experienced in creating and producing fundraising
support materials, newsletters, marketing brochures, public relations literature,
and special event invitations. Successfully manage project deadlines and interface
effectively with teams of both creative and executive-level professionals.

- Selected as Materials Manager for the Sweetwater PRASAD Volunteer Committee;
  also Chairman of Public Relations/Outreach Committee.
- Produce and manage mass-mail campaigns, coordinate poster/flyer distribution,
  and write press releases/advertisements for Sweetwater PRASAD Volunteer Committee.
- Contracted as a Staff Writer for the SYDA Foundation, Big Time, USA.
- Currently authoring a book, producing text and artistic design.

AMERICAN DISEASE SOCIETY - Sweetwater, USA   (1989-1990)
National Office
Program Support Services Coordinator, Public Education
Comprehensively managed all Public Education and Special Programs materials.
Coordinated audio-visual support for international/national conferences and all
major meetings. Directed the creation of videos and slide presentations, publication
and logo development, materials selection, and event day supervision. Liaisoned
with 10 Department Heads, Senior and Department Vice Presidents, and
Creative Services personnel.

- Personally managed a $1M+ annual budget.
- Controlled over a 2,000-piece inventory of support services publications,
  including revising materials when applicable.
- Composed a nationwide publication for distribution to 57 divisions.

EXPERIENCE
Continued...

- Wrote speech for the Chairman's Update at the Public Education Committee meeting.
- Initiated and instituted automated department procedures to maximize efficiency.
- Reduced operational costs by developing a formal bid process for vendor selection.
- Hired and closely collaborated with a Video and Media Producer.
- Interfaced frequently with the Adult Education Committee composed of a high-profile volunteer staff of national health education leaders.

FINANCIAL SOFTWARE SYSTEMS - Sweetwater, USA   (1987-1989)
Writer, Communication Services
Performed a broad range of writing assignments which targeted the mortgage banking industry. Conducted extensive research and in-depth interviews.

- Wrote feature articles for a marketing and customer publication.
- Primary contributing author of a monthly employee newsletter including article topics ranging from employee profiles to product features.
- Correspondent and contributing author of a headquarters newsletter.
- Gained comprehensive experience as a ghost writer for mortgage banking experts.

XYZ CORPORATION - Sweetwater, USA   (1984-1986)
Associate Analyst, Product Information
Wrote and edited press releases, product promotion packages, and technology bulletins for this financial banking software manufacturer.

- Solely produced a 100-page bi-weekly news clipping publication which required continual and intensive study of national computer and financial publications.
- Assisted in writing and producing a monthly employee newsletter.

COMMUNITY JOURNAL - Sweetwater, USA   (1983)
Intern
Active participant in all phases of publishing for a highly publicized magazine, including staff editorial meetings, story development, research, and copy editing.

- Composed a feature article published May 1984; conceived story line and interviewed 25+ physicians in the recovery field.

* *Previous experience also includes sales and administrative positions.*

EDUCATION

BIRD STATE UNIVERSITY - Robin, USA
Bachelor of Arts Degree in Print Journalism, 1984 **GPA: 3.79/4.00**

COMPUTER

- WordPerfect   • DisplayWrite   • QuatroPro   • dBase

**ACCOLADES/
ACTIVITIES**

- Second-Place Winner, National Magazine Writing Competition, Sponsored by AEJMC (Assoc. of Educators of Journalism & Mass Communications, Entry: "What a Day," Profile of a Disabled Soldier
- Editor of Excel University Literary Magazine

WRITING SAMPLES & REFERENCES AVAILABLE UPON REQUEST

JOHN J. SEEKER
123 Looking Hard Avenue
Top Dog, USA 20202
(555) 678-9101

SIGNIFICANT QUALIFICATIONS	• Possess proven administrative skills, including typing and transcription and an in-depth knowledge of medical terminologies.
	• Demonstrated mastery in all phases of customer service due to resourceful and efficient problem-solving techniques.
	• Outstanding time management and organizational skills, resulting in high levels of productivity.
	• Experienced in various aspects of insurance benefits with an emphasis on filing and reviewing claims; also, possess some bookkeeping experience.
	• Poised in all high-profile interpersonal relations with strong interprofessional ties to the medical, legal, and insurance communities.
	• Capable of performing receptionist duties, including phone management and patient/client scheduling.

PROFESSIONAL EXPERIENCE

PRIVATE PRACTICE - Paris/London, USA
Owner/Practicing Physician   1989-1998

EDUCATION

MORGAN COLLEGE OF CHIROPRACTIC - Collegetown, USA
Doctor of Chiropractic   1988

USA STATE UNIVERSITY - Academic, USA
Undergraduate Studies in Preparatory Medicine   1980-1987

CREDENTIALS

• Licensed, Moontown Board of Chiropractic Examiners   1988
• Certified by National Board of Chiropractic Examiners   1987

CONTINUING EDUCATION

Courses Sponsored through Various Institutions:

• Chiropractic Orthopedics; 320 Hours, Board Eligible for Specialty
• Physical Therapy   • Spinal Reconstructive Techniques   • X-Ray

PROFESSIONAL DEVELOPMENT

Courses Sponsored through Various Organizations:

• CareGivers Renewal; Course Leader Trainee   • Time Management
• Human Relations   • Productivity, Service, and Well-Being
• Communication

AFFILIATIONS

• American Chiropractic Association
• Chiropractic Association of Moontown; Previous Board Member, Secretary/Treasurer
• South Central Moontown Chiropractic Society; Secretary

PROFESSIONAL REFERENCES AVAILABLE UPON REQUEST

SARAH J. SEARCH

123 Job Hunting Lane
Big Time, USA 10101
(444) 567-8910

CAREER OBJECTIVE

To redirect my career within an organization that values experience in counseling, training, human resources, and management.

EDUCATION

MASTER OF ARTS DEGREE IN COUNSELING, 1998
Any State University - Sunshine City, USA

* Self-financed 100% through full-time employment.

BACHELOR OF ARTS DEGREE IN ENGLISH/EDUCATION, 1980
USA College of Education - Pleasant, USA

ADDITIONAL TRAINING

Completed additional courses in the following topics:
• Instruction   • Motivation   • Writing   • Learning Styles

QUALIFICATIONS

Counseling

• Trained in variety of social services issues, including drug and alcohol abuse, pregnancy, parenting skills, conflict management, group management, interpersonal techniques.
• Instructed a graduate course on Psychological Helping Skills that focused on training others how to teach interpersonal skills; responsible for student evaluations.

Training

• Experienced in planning and conducting on-the-job training for supervisors.
• Resourceful and creative individual who develops effective instructional programs.
• Exceptional instructor with effective presentation and communication techniques.

Human Resources

• Experienced in screening and interviewing staff with keen ability to assess skill levels.
• Successfully placed up to 300 employees in companies enrolled in a Youth Services program.
• Counseled employees on career-related issues to ensure consistency of performance.

Management

• Resolve problems quickly, serving as a liaison between educators and parents.
• Demonstrate excellent organizational, time management, and decision-making skills.
• Coordinate and implement various enhancement programs within the educational system.

Professional Profile

• Poised individual who upholds the highest standards of excellence in all endeavors.
• Consistently display a diverse range of talents and overall professional integrity.

EMPLOYMENT HISTORY

TEACHER
BIG COUNTY PUBLIC SCHOOL SYSTEM - Sunshine City, USA   1983-Present

PROGRAM ASSISTANT
SOCIAL DEVELOPMENT COMMISSION - Growing City, USA   1982-1983

TEACHER
XYZ SCHOOL SYSTEM - Growing City, USA   1980-1982

OTHER

• Teacher's Licenses in three states
• Computer literate, LotusWorks
• Member of Adlerian Society

REFERENCES AVAILABLE UPON REQUEST

JOHN J. SEEKER
123 Looking Hard Avenue
Top Dog, USA 20202
(555) 678-9101

OBJECTIVE   A growth-oriented position in a progressive industry where I may utilize my strong customer service, sales, and interpersonal skills as well as proven creative abilities.

QUALIFICATIONS

**Client
Service**

- Highly skilled in determining client needs with an ability to communicate among multiple parties.
- Excel in customer-oriented positions, managing multiple responsibilities in fast-paced environments.
- Provide top-notch guest-support services, including accurate documentation and record-keeping.
- Adept in handling special requests and researching community resources thoroughly and efficiently.
- Positively evaluated by undercover evaluators, which reflects a commitment to service excellence.
- Successfully completed required training courses related to guest-relations management.
- Utilized customer service and time management skills at an upscale restaurant recognized citywide.
- Demonstrate keen troubleshooting and problem-solving skills essential to account management.

**Sales &
Management**

- Sold computer systems, including hardware/software product lines of multiple manufacturers.
- Effectively handled up to 70 inbound calls daily from both corporate and personal end-users.
- Performed customer presentations, developed price quotes, and utilized creative closing skills.
- Analyzed customers' needs and customized systems to accommodate users' requirements.
- Researched individual customer specifications to accurately identify which products to recommend.
- Cultivated strong management skills related to operations supervision, customer management, daily record-keeping, cash management, and loss prevention.
- Gained knowledge of computer-related, application-based, and technologically advanced solutions.

**Quality
Assurance**

- Demonstrate a stringent work ethic with attention to quality and high standards of performance.
- Key contributor to consistent maintenance of department's customer satisfaction ratings hotel-wide.
- Extremely diplomatic and committed employee with exceptional leadership and interpersonal skills.
- Selected as a member of a special task force to communicate between management and employees.
- Experienced in conceptualizing improvements in service standards and employee performance.

EXPERIENCE

MAJOR HOTEL INTERNATIONAL - Sleepwell, USA   (1995-Present)
GUEST SERVICES REPRESENTATIVE

SOFTWARE INTERNATIONAL - Technicaltown, USA   (1995)
SYSTEM SALES REPRESENTATIVE

GOOD DINING - Eat More, USA   (1994-1995)
SERVICE STAFF

** Background also includes a position as an Assistant Manager of a gas
station in Big City, USA, and in-depth experience in retail sales.*

EDUCATION

COLD STATE UNIVERSITY - Frigidtown, USA
Majored in Music; Minored in English

**PERSONAL
PROFILE**

- Experience as a professional actor in dramatic theater
- Member of Actor's Equity Union

JOHN J. SEEKER
123 Looking Hard Avenue
Top Dog, USA 20202 • (555) 678-9101

OBJECTIVE   Position in Customer Service with a focus on outperforming the competition through exceptional service. Long-term goal: Position in Sales.

HIGHLIGHTS OF QUALIFICATIONS

- Reliable and adaptable; learn new systems quickly and take initiative.
- Exceptionally organized and resourceful, with wide range of skills.
- Consistently met and surpassed assigned goals.
- Effective team member who is comfortable with leading or collaborating.
- Strong motivation to advance in a career.

RELEVANT SKILLS & ACCOMPLISHMENTS

Customer Relations
- Thoroughly and tactfully research potential solutions to customers' problems.
- Listen and acquire feedback to be sure customers are satisfied with results.
- Recognize unique customer requirements and resolve individual problems quickly.
- Developed successful, professional approach to providing top-quality customer service.

Sales & Marketing
- Secured major client, which resulted in acquiring $800K in precharge off business.
- Maintained and serviced 115 accounts within assigned sales territory.
- Performed on-site merchandising at individual client locations.
- Managed company-to-client distribution to ensure timely scheduling and disbursement.
- Increased sales volume through: instituted promotion plan on weaker selling items, developed innovative point-of-sale material, promoted closer client relationships.
- Successfully created and instituted a promotional plan for a nightclub that increased patronage by 6%.

Management
- Strengthened unit employees' collection and phone techniques through evaluation and training.
- Reviewed daily reports and advised employees as to weaknesses to improve productivity.
- Set monthly goals for unit in conjunction with department goals.
- Arranged motivation program along with company trainer to increase unit proficiency.
- Conducted one-on-one reviews with each unit member to provide performance feedback.
- Developed more extensive and uniform training procedures for new employees.
- Managed top-producing unit within department.

Accounts Control & Collections
- Provided timely collections for various Fortune 100 companies.
- Convinced delinquent cardholders of necessity to alleviate past-due accounts.
- Initiated tracking procedures for locating accounts considered skip accounts.
- Evaluated legal and bankruptcy proceedings for accounts.
- Reviewed daily figures and goals for employees within my unit.
- Achieved highest percentage total of entire department during first month on the collection system at USA Express.
- Achieved 8% increase over monthly goals compared to previous quarter.

EMPLOYMENT HISTORY

1994-Present	**Flight Attendant**	FLYAWAY AIRLINES	Pleasantville, USA
1993-1994	**Senior Account Manager**	CONE CONE & CONE	Sunshine City, USA
1991-1993	**Team Leader**	GOOD PERFORMANCE CORP	Sunshine City, USA
1989-1990	**Accounts Control Clerk**	USA EXPRESS, OPS	Blueville, USA
1987-1988	**Sales Representative**	DELICIOUS BEVERAGE COMPANY	Sunshine City, USA

EDUCATION   GET AHEAD UNIVERSITY - Toboggan Hill, USA
Industrial Relations/Psychology Major, 1983-1986

TRAINING   • Time Management; Management and Sales Techniques; Motivational Seminar

JOHN J. SEEKER

123 Looking Hard Avenue
Top Dog, USA 20202
(555) 678-9101

OBJECTIVE

To continue my successful career with an organization that values comprehensive operations expertise, keen analytical skills, and critical decision-making abilities.

QUALIFICATIONS

Analytical

- Utilize strong analytical abilities in compiling key information from numerous sources (i.e., flight control, reservations, ramp services) regarding data necessary for balancing flights.
- Experienced in interpreting information obtained from a customized weight/balance system.
- Maintain an understanding of multiple variables that affect weight/balance manipulation, including weather, winds, barometric pressure, and runway selection.
- Capable of analyzing technical and other complex variables (i.e., altitude, fuel distribution destination/departure locations, passenger counts, and cargo volume).
- Skilled in determining exact volume of cargo to ensure properly balanced loading of aircraft.
- Adept at utilizing a comprehensive technical and mechanical guide as a key information resource.

**Operations
Management**

- Efficiently prepare between 60 and 80 weight/balance reports per day for flights worldwide.
- Possess keen decision-making abilities in circumstances with high liability/extreme ramifications.
- Identify discrepancies and ensure timely resolutions under exceptionally stressful conditions.
- Research and develop plausible solutions to weight/balance issues affecting flight departure; utilize strong communication skills to direct ramp personnel in implementing resolutions.
- Possess extensive knowledge of strict regulatory guidelines related to weight/balance factors.
- Work closely with gate agents to assist in monitoring passenger counts; interact with numerous departments in efforts to decrease error percentages/increase passenger service/safety.
- Interface with pilots regarding FAA classified dangerous goods to ensure proper handling.

Supervisory

- Managed 3-4 staff members in loading 5 flights per day within extremely strict deadlines.
- Provided ongoing personnel training; demonstrated flexibility in managing rotating crews.
- Illustrate strong team-building skills while directing an extremely diverse personnel.

EXPERIENCE

ABC AIRLINES - Anytown, USA   (1/83-Present)
Centralized Load Planning
Senior Customer Service Representative
Perform numerous functions related to the efficient and proper handling of aircraft cargo. Utilize information obtained from various departments regarding flight variables and review data acquired from customized weight/balance system. Rely on keen analytical and problem-solving abilities to identify accurate situational adjustments and resolutions. Consistently earn strong employee evaluations based on excellent performance.

** Promoted from Aircraft Load Agent to an area of increased accountability. Held
a variety of other positions during tenure that involved preflight operations.*

EDUCATION

SUCCESS UNIVERSITY - Collegeville, USA
Business Major ** Sigma Alpha Epsilon Fraternity, Member*

REFERENCES AVAILABLE UPON REQUEST

SARAH J. SEARCH

123 Job Hunting Lane
Big Time, USA 10101
(444) 567-8910

OBJECTIVE

A personally and professionally rewarding position in which I can utilize my talents, cultivated skills set, and multifaceted experiences to positively impact an organization.

QUALIFICATIONS

Management

- Experience leading and partnering with teams to develop and implement action plans related to education, community/healthcare issues, and nonprofit groups.
- Demonstrate excellent needs identification, consensus-building, and troubleshooting skills managing issues that frequently involve severe resistance and complex relational dynamics.
- Adept at creating and executing inventory control and loss prevention restructuring initiatives.
- Authored, coordinated, produced, and managed training programs and corporate newsletters.

Community Affairs

- Adept at building public trust and credibility while overcoming misconceptions and controversy.
- Served as corporate representative and in-house trainer for 2 major nonprofit groups.
- Appointed to serve on Program & Development task force due to reputation for achieving results.
- Effective communicator of group-specific needs and programs to a wide cross-section of people.
- Possess sharp observation and listening skills used to assess and interpret behavior/attitudes.
- Work closely with health professionals in providing emotional support to adult cancer patients.
- Handled administrative support functions for a human rights advocacy organization.

Fundraising/ Planning

- Skilled in spearheading and directing multipurpose committees toward goal achievement.
- Demonstrated expertise in fundraising and promotions using strong relationship-building skills.
- Proven success in recruiting and mobilizing large volunteer teams due to positive energy.
- Planned diverse aspects of heavily attended weekly social, religious, and educational events.
- Elicited financial pledges from 60% of targeted individuals using low-key sales techniques.

PROFESSIONAL EXPERIENCE

THE LITTLE CARPENTER - Sunshine City, USA   (Three Years)
Senior Sales Associate/Floor Manager, *Fig Newton Branch*
Managed sales, customer service, and administrative functions for highest revenue producer of 4 branches of premier jewelry operation. Handled business planning, cash control, problem-solving, custom product design, ordering, and visual merchandising. Trained and supervised staff of 15.

NEWS TIME COMPANY - Sunshine City, USA   (One Year)
Freelance Commercial Wardrobe Director
Coordinated and managed wardrobe needs for three on-air TV personalities appearing on weekly news program. Also supported a movie star during filming of special feature presentation. Assisted Costume Manager with live Alien Theater production.

THE STORE - Sunshine City, USA   (Five Years)
Department Manager (In-house French Translator)
Handled marketing, customer service, staff development, and $1.4M in retail sales. Served on several critical corporate committees and as community liaison; coordinated employee programs.

EDUCATION

UNIVERSITY OF OUTER SPACE - Moon City, USA
B.B.A. in International Business   * *Studied in Europe*

NONPROFIT ACTIVITIES

- Find Us International, Office Assistant
- Fun School, Fundraising Committee
- School Theatrical Production, Coach/Reader
- Mute High School, Athletic/Fundraising Teams
- Cancer Home, Volunteer

LANGUAGE/ COMPUTER

- Conversant in French
- MS Office 97
- Dual Citizenship-U.S./Australia
- Quicken

JOHN J. SEEKER
123 Looking Hard Avenue
Top Dog, USA 20202
(555) 678-9101

OBJECTIVE

A position where I may utilize the full scope of my athletic background, project management skills, marketing and promotions abilities, and personnel supervision experience.

**ATHLETIC
ACCOLADES**

- Somewhere Regional Soccer Team, 3 years
- USA Soccer Team (Alternate Player), 1 year
- State Select Soccer Team, 5 years
- University of Birdstate Team, 4 years (1 of top 10 teams in nation)
- Peachstate Steamers, Semi-Professional League, 2 years

QUALIFICATIONS

**Professional
Profile**

- Performed well within a fast-paced, deadline-oriented arena with strong seasonal fluctuations.
- Consistently received superior ratings from management on performance reviews.
- Highly capable of working closely with clients to identify exact needs and expectations.
- Self-directed individual, experienced in managing priorities while traveling to competitions.

**Marketing/
Communications**

- Experienced in developing marketing/promotional materials necessary to increase client base.
- Proven ability to solicit new business through effective client relationship-building techniques.
- Provided critical information to corporate buyers related to shipment activities/quantities.
- Gained extensive familiarity with product manufacturers, i.e., Runners Inc., Shoe City, Sportswear Enterprises, High Tops USA; consistently interacted with management teams.
- Utilized strong troubleshooting/interpersonal skills in communicating with office staff members.

**Project
Management**

- Possess keen project management skills evidenced through efficient coordination of receiving functions, including voluminous paperwork and ensuring accuracy of orders.
- Capable of efficiently fulfilling orders for over 18 different retail operations.
- Supervised warehouse personnel and delegated responsibilities regarding inventory control.
- Serve as a key member of a team in charge of various renovation projects, including Always Safe Airlines, Restaurantville, Parcels USA; projects range from $100K to $350K.
- Maintain on-site supervisory responsibilities throughout construction process.

**RELATED
EXPERIENCE**

THE ATHLETE'S SPOT - Buffsville, USA   (1991-1994)
Inventory Control/Warehousing Specialist
Supervised numerous functions related to merchandise receiving, shipping, and warehousing. Gained significant exposure to key sports apparel manufacturers.

**OTHER
EXPERIENCE**

BULLDOZER CONSTRUCTION COMPANY - Dirtsville, USA   (1994-Present)
Commercial Construction

LOVINGLY LAWN CARE - Dirtsville, USA   (1995-Present)
Owner/Manager, *Part-time*

** College experience included position as Valet, Hotels USA; Bellman, Luxury
   Hotel Inc.; and Warehouse Staff, Big Tee Incorporated.*

EDUCATION

THE UNIVERSITY OF SMARTS - Honorsville, USA
Bachelor of Science Degree, 8/90 * Received full athletic scholarship

REFERENCES AVAILABLE UPON REQUEST

SARAH J. SEARCH
123 Job Hunting Lane
Big Time, USA 10101
(444) 567-8910

**CAREER
SUMMARY**

Multitalented professional demonstrating a proven track record and
outstanding skills in marketing, training, and management.

SIGNIFICANT QUALIFICATIONS

Marketing
- Possess 8 years of marketing experience and undisputed professional expertise.
- Currently conducting in-depth research for ABC Company identifying selling solutions.
- Improved product performance by 30% due to exceptional marketing strategies.
- Instituted an invaluable customer satisfaction survey for a national audience.
- Extensive involvement and proven track record in strategic and marketing planning.
- Exhibit excellent research, communication, presentation, and writing skills.

Training
- Possess comprehensive training experience from program inception to implementation.
- Experienced in conducting Train-the-Trainer modules for a major corporation;
  successfully trained 250 trainers over a 7-week period for ABC Company.
- Oversaw a national training program spanning 73 districts for 1,700+ employees;
  delegated staff to monitor and ensure quality of program.
- Continually attend training classes related to sales, marketing, and training.

**Curriculum
Development**
- Conceived a highly visible sales training program from ground zero, including
  formatting program, creating collateral materials, and developing training agenda.
- Experienced in utilizing interactive, participatory training format.
- Recognized by upper management for creating dynamic and unsurpassed training program.
- Assisted in producing an internationally awarded motivational training video.
- Talented in directing the creative efforts of outside marketing/communication firms.

Sales
- Exhibit extensive sales training and knowledge of the sales process.
- Persuasive individual with proven ability to motivate others into action.
- Contribute to sales presentations and account relations in conjunction with sales staff.
- Effectively teach a consultative sales approach with an emphasis on relationship-building;
  attend sales meetings to disseminate crucial product information.
- Created and produced numerous sales presentations and various promotional literature.

EXPERIENCE

ABC COMPANY - Sweetwater, USA   (1992-Present)
Marketing Manager

FASCIMILE - Sweetwater, USA   (1986-1990)
**Director of Industry Marketing/
Senior Research Analyst**

GAS COMPANY - Horseville, USA   (1985-1986)
Operations Supervisor

* Other experience includes a part-time Adjunct Professor position with Mitchell University,
  1988-1991, and Credit/Collection Analyst position for Green Money Bank, 1982-1984.

EDUCATION

EXCEL UNIVERSITY, **M.B.A in Marketing**, 1985 **GPA: 3.4/4.0**

UNIVERSITY OF LEARNING, **B.A. in Medical Sociology** (Emphasis in Communications)

**AFFILIATIONS/
COMMUNITY**
- Toastmasters International • American Marketing Association • Women's Network
- American Society for Training & Development • American Assn. of Women
- American Business Women's Association • Renaissance Business Associates
- American Cancer Society Speakers' Bureau • Who's Who in America
- Sierra Club • United Way Neighbor to Neighbor, Volunteer • Hospital, Volunteer

SARAH J. SEARCH
123 Job Hunting Lane
Big Time, USA 10101
(444) 567-8910

CAREER SUMMARY

Uniquely qualified professional with extensive clinical experience in a medical teaching/training
environment combined with a public relations background.

SIGNIFICANT QUALIFICATIONS

**Training &
Management**
- Demonstrate ability to conduct thorough and well-planned training to diverse medical personnel.
- Adept in creating comfortable, safe, and productive learning environments during training process.
- Experienced in developing highly professional job-specific training materials.
- Managed orientation of a high volume of staff in operating room techniques and neurospecialty area.
- Key member of task force that streamlined rotation and orientation procedures for new employees.
- Skilled in developing standards module for neurosurgery cranial service, contributing to
  employee performance evaluations, and supervising nursing professionals.
- Chaired an employee-based education council that coordinated all aspects of in-service programs.
- Possess strong analytical and decision-making skills essential to quality case management.

**Public
Relations**
- Experienced in organizing special events and coordinating volunteer and departmental teams.
- Utilized responsive, people-oriented strengths during a 6-year tenure in public relations.
- Effective rapport-builder with physicians, nurses, administration, and patients.
- Edited and published a weekly new bulletin for a large service-oriented healthcare facility.
- Displayed excellent communication skills as an author of articles for medical publication.
- Demonstrate extensive planning and organizational skills in fast-paced, demanding environments.

**Medical
Background**
- Possess 10 years of strong clinical experience working with extremely complex and high-tech cases for
  a prominent teaching hospital, displaying in-depth knowledge of equipment and aseptic requirements.
- Demonstrate technical proficiency in operating room procedures, particularly cerebral aneurysms.
- Highly skilled in use of Philips EasyGuide Neuro System, CUSA, Midas Rex, Hall and
  Codman drills, and PCA machines.
- Expertise in scrubbing/circulating for major neurosurgical procedures, handling all preliminary surgical
  preparation, charting patient records, coordinating surgical supplies and detailed instrumentation,
  assessing equipment requirements, and preparing patients.
- In-depth experience in IV therapy administration, including hyperalimentation and chemotherapy.

EXPERIENCE

EXCEL UNIVERSITY HOSPITAL - Sweetwater, USA   (1993-Present)
REGISTERED NURSE - OPERATING ROOM - 1995-Present
Serve as team leader for cranial portion of neurosurgery service responsible for supervising nursing
staff, developing training materials, and performing wide array of perioperative surgical care.

STAFF NURSE - SURGICAL FLOOR - 1993-1995
Managed complexities of surgical care for high-acuity patients. Set up and utilized medical
equipment, administered medications, and performed complex wound care.

SINGING RIVER HOSPITAL - Pleasantville, USA   (1990-93)
PUBLIC RELATIONS ASSISTANT
Utilized strong writing, organizational support, and event planning skills. Published
a weekly news bulletin and authored articles for monthly hospital publication.

EDUCATION

UNIVERSITY OF LEARNING - Pleasantville, USA
B.S. in Nursing, 1990 *Magna Cum Laude*
B.S. in Business Administration, 1980

AFFILIATIONS
- AORN - Local & National Member
- RN - State of the South, #R076822

JOHN J. SEEKER
123 Looking Hard Avenue
Top Dog, USA 20202
(555) 678-9101

SUMMARY   Extremely successful professional illustrating a proven track record in diverse sales arenas.

QUALIFICATIONS

Securities Sales

- Over 10 years of successful institutional sales experience selling to highly visible accounts.
- Comprehensive understanding and cutting-edge knowledge of rapidly changing products and markets.
- Superior sales ability evidenced by top production and national recognition with a leading company.
- Demonstrated ability to cultivate a widespread client base of upper-level and key decision-makers.
- Crucial negotiating techniques developed through years of highly competitive sales experience.
- Excellent financial skills crucial to establishing customer credibility and loyalty.
- Utilize a persuasive selling approach to market products involving volatile risk/reward parameters.
- Successfully educate customers on complex product variables and foster long-term relationships.
- Self-directed and focused individual who excelled on a 100% incentive-based compensation plan.

Technical Sales

- Over 4 years in a high-end technical sales arena that required in-depth product comprehension.
- Utilized effective feature/benefit selling skills to impact revenues in direct and third-party markets.
- Exhibited strong relationship development, product demonstration, and executive presentation skills.
- Achieved a #1 national ranking based on outstanding sales performance in a specific product group.
- Consistently exceeded performance of peers and earned acknowledgments based on results.
- Displayed excellent territory management and strategic planning abilities vital to success in sales.
- Employed strong account management and follow-up skills in coordinating product implementation.
- Talented in all aspects of new account development through aggressive cold calling and prospecting.
- Motivated wholesalers' sales representatives and trained them in various field sales strategies.

SECURITIES SALES

INTERNATIONAL BANK   More Money, USA
Vice President, *IB Securities Subsidiary*   10/94-Present
One of 7 sales executives recruited nationally to spearhead a start-up marketing
program targeting the regional corporate bond market for this major banking institution.

SECURITIES TRADERS, INC.   Traders, USA
Vice President, Fixed Income Sales   2/90-10/94
Successfully marketed high-grade taxable investment products. Primarily targeted
insurance companies, savings and loans, investment advisors, and trust departments.

BIG DOLLAR FUNDS   Wealthytown, USA
Vice President, Taxable Fixed Income Sales   3/84-11/89
Aggressively developed top-tier and secondary accounts. Acknowledged nationally for
$5M production and recognized as #1 High-Yield Sales Representative within the region.

* Other experience includes **Corporate Planner** with American Engineers, 3/80-2/84, and
  Senior Analyst with Investors USA, 6/79-3/80.

TECHNICAL SALES

ENGINEERING EXPERTS   Technical Town, USA
SALES ENGINEER   (6/73-8/77)
Strategically sold electrical distribution equipment to a sophisticated engineering market
consisting of consulting engineers, contractors, and distributors. Utilized strong consultative
selling skills to market custom-designed and premanufactured products. Displayed strong
needs identification, product education, sales training, and relationship development skills.

EDUCATION

UNIVERSITY OF SMARTS, *Hard Graduate School*   Smartsville, USA
MASTER OF BUSINESS ADMINISTRATION   1979

INSTITUTE OF TECHNOLOGY BRAINS   Brainy, USA
BACHELOR OF SCIENCE IN MANAGEMENT   1973

Sarah J. Search
123 Job Hunting Lane
Big Time, USA 10101
(444) 567-8910

CAREER SUMMARY

Dynamic professional with a successful track record in all phases of sales and management.

SIGNIFICANT QUALIFICATIONS

Sales & Customer Service
- Consistently a top performer, including attainment of a million-dollar sales designation resulting from superior salesmanship abilities.
- Demonstrated effectiveness in lead generation, product presentation, contract negotiation, and sale closings.
- Resourceful and creative sales professional who impacts company profitability.
- Strengthened client relations by providing exceptional service and follow-up.

Personnel Management
- Comprehensive sales management experience with accountability for hiring, training, and motivating staff of 6 to achieve corporate objectives.
- Successfully planned, organized, and conducted sales meetings to affect performance.
- Assisted sales force in the procurement of new clients and sales support functions.
- Conceived and implemented excellent promotions and incentives to increase sales.

Operations Management
- Conducted feasibility and demographic studies to identify untapped target markets.
- Effectively qualified purchasers, secured lending institutions, and negotiated loans.
- Resolved problems quickly, serving as a liaison between builders and purchasers.
- Presented strong decision-making skills by contributing sound design decisions.
- Initiated dynamic advertising strategies; conducted extensive cost analyses.

Professional Profile
- Poised and professional individual who upholds the highest standards of excellence.
- Consistently displays a diverse range of talents and overall business integrity.

EMPLOYMENT HISTORY

COMMERCIAL/	
RESIDENTIAL REAL ESTATE SALES	
HOME REALTY - Sunshine City, USA	1990 - Present
PROJECT MANAGER	
WELL BUILT HOMES - Sunshine City, USA	1983 - 1987
SALES/SALES MANAGEMENT	
MORE SOLD - Sunshine City, USA	1981 - 1982
REAL ESTATE SALES	
HOME REALTY - Sunshine City, USA	1979 - 1981

EDUCATION/LICENSES

College City University - Cottontown, USA   **Bachelor of Arts Degree**

- *Who's Who in Colleges & Universities*
- State Real Estate Brokers License
- Crimson Key Honorary
- State Real Estate Sales License
- Student Council Officer

AFFILIATIONS/VOLUNTEER

- National Association of Realtors
- SIDS Foundation, Volunteer
- County Boards of Realtors
- State Political Campaign, Volunteer
- State Alumni

SARAH J. SEARCH

123 Job Hunting Lane
Big Time, USA 10101
(444) 567-8910

OBJECTIVE

To secure a position where I may utilize the full scope of my expertise, especially in the areas of sales support, account management, and purchasing/inventory control.

QUALIFICATIONS

**Sales/
Support**

- Provide comprehensive support to 32 sales representatives, especially in matters of inventory.
- Gained significant experience in all aspects of sales while training under a leader within the industry; adept at identifying customer needs, product presentations, and price negotiations.
- Demonstrated proven closing and customer follow-up skills through 5-year sales track record.
- Successfully prioritized leads and qualified clients; generated $850K per year in gross revenues.

**Purchasing/
Inventory**

- Extremely efficient in utilizing a network database that incorporates a nationwide inventory.
- Maintain a high degree of powerful decision-making authority that impacts bottom-line profits.
- Contributed to overall record-breaking sales increase by ensuring the proper product mix.
- Possess extensive market knowledge; monitor sales movement of products with multiple features.
- Recognized by management as a key contributor in facilitating highest sales in dealer's history.
- Highly resourceful in researching inventory and locating specific product at customer request.
- Experienced in negotiating product exchanges; analyze product and determine market value.

**Project/Account
Management**

- Highly capable and efficient in calculating/processing complex performance/income reports.
- Effectively interface with upper-level management, business owners, sales, and technical staff.
- Utilize a broad range of effective administrative skills; efficiently handle 60-80 calls per day.
- Illustrate superior project/account management skills and effective personnel supervision abilities.

**Customer
Service**

- Demonstrate outstanding diplomacy skills in maintaining positive relations among dealers.
- Illustrate effective customer relations skills in efforts to increase profits through future contact.
- Possess keen financial acumen/customer service expertise as evidenced by highly progressive tenure within the banking industry; full accountability for daily balance of $750K+.

EXPERIENCE

CAR DEALER USA - Automotive Haven, USA   (4/84-Present)
Inventory Sourcing/Exchange
Selected by management to fill a newly created inventory-related position due to overall performance excellence. Coordinate numerous functions related to overall sales support and inventory management with an emphasis on product exchanges, negotiations, and selection. Utilize extremely effective account management abilities coupled with highly efficient administrative skills to contribute to significant sales increase.

* Also gained 5 years of experience as a Sales Representative as well as previous employment within the finance office as a Clerical Assistant.*

BANKERS OF AMERICA - Money City, USA   (8/82-4/84)
Head Teller
Received 4 promotions throughout this tenure based on management recognition of outstanding customer service, operations management, and staff supervision abilities.

COMPUTER

- Knowledge of Lotus 1-2-3 and WordPerfect applications.

REFERENCES AVAILABLE UPON REQUEST

SARAH J. SEARCH
sarah@aol.com

123 Job Hunting Lane   Big Time, USA 10101   (444) 567-8910

OBJECTIVE   To utilize my proven training, program management, organizational, and team-building skills combined with my strong leadership and communication abilities to impact organizational growth.

QUALIFICATIONS

**Training/
Public Speaking**
- Display team-building and mentoring skills training new hires in all policies and procedures.
- Utilized exceptional communication skills conducting diverse county-wide curriculum training.
- Designed objectives and methodologies and trained 50+ staff on educational software programs.
- Developed skills and strategies to effectively deliver training on specific curriculum/objectives as key participant in textbook company product knowledge meetings.
- One of 10 teachers chosen out of 300 candidates based on performance record to train peers on a specific program's policies and procedures in order to ensure strict government compliance.
- Voluntarily helped 30 peers develop individualized plans using broad knowledge of regulations.

**Management/
Leadership**
- Structured and instituted a facility-wide behavior management plan, including reporting formats.
- Key needs identifier/idea contributor on Strategic Planning for School Improvement Committee.
- Coordinated and managed all aspects of Awards Program, i.e., assembly planning/public relations.
- Organized, launched, and managed a county-wide innovative Peer Mediation Program, 1997.
- Skilled at mentoring and developing talent, structuring and implementing individualized educational plans, directing effective staff teams, and heading local/county-level committees.
- Exhibit exceptional leadership attributes and ability to motivate others toward top performance
- Promote self-improvement philosophy by personally exceeding continuous education requirements.

**Professional
Profile**
- Skilled at persuading peers to adopt new programs due to positive integration presentations.
- Utilize core competencies in needs identification and creative problem-solving to achieve goals.
- Proven abilities as a key liaison among peers, administrators, professionals, and parents.
- Detail-oriented, multitasking professional who displays a disciplined and efficient work ethic.
- Possess strong interpersonal and rapport-building skills as well as diplomacy and professionalism.

EXPERIENCE   FOWLER COUNTY SCHOOLS - Fowler, USA   (1989-Present)
SPECIAL EDUCATION TEACHER
Big Mountain Elementary, 1996-Present; *Forest Elementary*, 1989-1996
Plan, develop, and manage all daily classroom activities and individualized discipline and instructional programs for up to 12 2nd- to 6th-grade special needs students. Mentored student teacher and directed paraprofessional. Conduct formal testing throughout the year and informal daily assessments to develop, implement, and evaluate 12 separate curriculum plans.

- Coordinate, conduct, and mediate 2 annual IEP meetings for each student, attended by parents, related teachers, administrators, and outside professionals.
- Manage all critical documentation, ensuring strict compliance with government regulations.
- Repeatedly demonstrated strong program management and team-building skills in several highly accountable leadership roles, i.e., Team Leader (5 years), Student Mentor Program (9 years), Educational Computing Specialist (5 years), numerous training roles, and committee chairmanships.

EDUCATION   BIRD STATE UNIVERSITY - Robin, USA * *Taught full-time while pursuing degree.*
M.S. in Education, 1992   **Dean's List, 2 years**
B.S. in Education, 1989   **Summa Cum Laude**

AWARD   • Forest Elementary Teacher of the Year, 1996 (Peer-Selected)

COMPUTER   • MS Works   • MS Office   • Print Shop   • PowerPoint   • Internet

REFERENCES AVAILABLE UPON REQUEST

SARAH J. SEARCH

123 Job Hunting Lane
Big Time, USA 10101
(444) 567-8910

CAREER SUMMARY

Highly skilled professional with a unique set of training, consulting, staff development, and counseling qualifications earned while pursuing a long-term career with a Fortune 500 organization.

PROFESSIONAL QUALIFIERS

Management/ Personnel Development

- Successfully handled all aspects of maximizing staff productivity and operational efficiency.
- Competent in implementing change management programs in multi-tiered organizations.
- Demonstrated strong project management skills that incorporated policy development aspects.
- Experienced in organizing and managing multifaceted projects with far-reaching impacts while achieving all deadlines within various budget constraints.
- Served on highly visible strategic planning teams in cooperation with management.
- Selected as a Board of Directors member for the ABC Association subsequent to an internship.

Training/ Consulting

- Co-created and delivered an in-depth 2-week training course for high-tech staff which included authoring an accompanying handbook.
- Extremely accomplished at identifying methods of establishing critical student rapport.
- Experienced developer and facilitator of professional development workshops related to career and personal transitions as well as self-empowerment.
- Capable of educating, training, and mentoring technical and nontechnical personnel.
- Extremely committed to individual training and continuing education on a personal level.
- Offer highly effective presentation development and delivery skills.

Counseling/ Outplacement

- As a former upper-level manager for a multimillion-dollar company, utilized strong interviewing, career pathing, and skills assessment abilities in developing personnel.
- Experienced in working with a nonprofit organization in formulating and implementing effective re-engineering strategies to better achieve predefined missions.
- Talented at forming internal task forces and directing the attainment of objectives.
- Possess a strong background in counseling through graduate-level studies.
- Knowledgeable about various assessment tools and personality tests (i.e., Myers Briggs and DISC).

Professional Profile

- Integrate rapidly into diverse settings, including highly structured corporate settings.
- Firmly committed to assisting and motivating others toward higher levels of achievement.
- Demonstrate a broad-minded perspective and a creative approach to problem resolution.
- Successfully blend a focused, accomplishment-oriented mind set with a humorous attitude.

CORPORATE HIGHLIGHTS

BIG COMPANY TELECOMMUNICATIONS   (1973-1995)
Littletown, USA; Lazyville, USA; Cityslickers, USA
Earned steady promotions throughout a long-term career based on continuous top performance and a high degree of professional dedication and flexibility.

MANAGER, *Strategic Planning & Support*
Comprehensively managed a 9-state territory which involved directing a staff of 27 in a variety of technological, engineering, and administrative-based functions. Directed a 3-year re-engineering process that encompassed centralization of numerous processes and managing a $1.5M budget.

EXPERIENCE
Continued...

STAFF MANAGER, *Procurement, Property & Services*
Created and implemented standardized procedures that created uniformity among the field operations. Reviewed and selected product vendors, which included assessment of manufacturing operations and contract negotiations.

ASSISTANT STAFF MANAGER, *Network Operations*
Directed various business operations, which included supervising union employees. Demonstrated excellent personnel development and leadership skills, leading to numerous achievements that related to productivity and efficiency objectives.

* Previous positions within the company included various management support and administrative positions prior to management

INTERN

CITYSLICKERS RECOVERY RESIDENCES - Cityslicker, USA   (1995)
COUNSELOR
Counseled individuals in crisis and developed methods and strategies of addressing drug, alcohol, and other chemical addictions.

EDUCATION

HEALTHYVILLE SCHOOL OF PROFESSIONAL PSYCHOLOGY
M.A. DEGREE IN PSYCHOLOGY, 1995   SPECIALTY: COUNSELING
* Completed graduate program while working full-time.

LONG JOHN SILVER UNIVERSITY
B.S. DEGREE IN BUSINESS MANAGEMENT, 1987
* Completed undergraduate degree while working full-time.

AFFILIATIONS

- Healthyville Recovery Residences (HRR), Board Member
  Selected for Board of Directors after completing a student internship.
- Organizational USA Alliance, Member
- USA Training & Development Society, Member
- All Business Women's Association, Vice President
- Women's Psychology Network, Member
- Healthyville School of Professional Psychology, Vice President of Student Cabinet

TRAINING SUMMARY

- Effective Personnel Management
- Communications Workshop
- Diversity Awareness
- Stress Management
- Problem Solving & Decision Making
- Excellence Through Teamwork
- Facilitation Skills Training
- Ethics Awareness Workshop
- Computer Literacy
- Manager Development Training
- Managing Your Way to Excellence
- Affirmative Action
- High-Performance Living
- Managing Interpersonal Relationships
- Developing Peak Performance
- Strategic Performance
- Business Finance
- Jeff Justice's Comedy Workshop

REFERENCES AVAILABLE UPON REQUEST

234

JOHN B. SEEKER
123 Looking Hard Avenue
Top Dog, USA 20202
(555) 678-9101

CAREER SUMMARY

A dynamic professional demonstrating outstanding leadership and training techniques, effective writing abilities, and creative curriculum-development skills.

SIGNIFICANT QUALIFICATIONS

**Curriculum/
Program
Development**
- Led a pilot study to assess the use of laptop computers among elementary school teachers.
- Planned and implemented highly successful enrichment programs within the community.
- Received award from major publication for establishing an innovative educational program.
- Created programs to reward staff excellence and facilitate a team philosophy.
- Initiated and developed a preschool facility from ground zero with full responsibility for curriculum/program development to further academic readiness and social skills.

Writing
- Solely conceived and authored 3 books and 13 published articles relating to education and other cutting-edge subjects.
- Spearheaded an effort to publish a student literary magazine for Little River School.
- Selected as a panel judge for the Hope County Writing Fair in 1990.

**Public
Speaking**
- Experienced public speaker with a 15-year track record addressing diverse audiences throughout the Eastern region.
- Poised speaker exhibiting an engaging and effective presentation style.

Training
- Taught college-level courses in Language Arts, Science, and Social Studies at Great State; also taught two education courses at the University of Smarts.
- Supervised the instruction of interns and student teachers enrolled in college programs.
- Experienced educator at the elementary level, including extensive knowledge of teaching students with learning disabilities, behavioral disorders, and mental retardation.
- Conducted training programs on self-esteem, family relationships, and personal power.

**RECENT
EXPERIENCE**

<u>Little River Elementary</u> - Sweetwater, USA   (1993-Present)
Learner Support Strategist   (*Confidentiality Requested*)
Act as a curriculum director and manage all aspects of teacher training. Conceive and implement staff development programs. Position emphasizes parent and teacher workshops.

<u>South Park Elementary</u> - Sweetwater, USA   (1987-1993)
Assistant Administrator/Learner Support Coordinator
Coordinated daily operations and school administration functions. Maintained strong parent and teacher relations. Developed various academic and enrichment programs.

EDUCATION

<u>BALD STATE UNIVERSITY</u> - **Pursuing an Ed.S. in Administration and Supervision**

<u>UNIVERSITY OF LEARNING</u> - **M.Ed. in Special Education**, with Distinction

<u>BRIGHT UNIVERSITY</u> - **B.S. in Elementary Instruction**

OTHER
- Delta Pi Kappa (Honorary)   • Association for Supervision & Curriculum Development
- State Association of Educational Leaders • *Who's Who in the South & Southwest*
- *Who's Who in American Education*   • Proficient in WordPerfect and Q & A.

REFERENCES AVAILABLE UPON REQUEST

SARAH J. SEARCH
123 Job Hunting Lane
Big Time, USA 10101
(444) 567-8910

OBJECTIVE

To pursue a challenging interior design position where I may fully utilize
my related education, creative talents, and strong interpersonal skills.

EDUCATION

THE FASHION COLLEGE FOR THE APPLIED ARTS - Fashion City, USA
B.A. in Interior Design, 1994 * *Industry Accredited*   **Overall GPA: 4.0/4.0**

THE UNIVERSITY OF LEARNING - Studyville, VA
B.A. in Art History, 1987   **Dean's List 1986-87**

ST. HOPE'S SCHOOL - Faithville, USA - Attended 1970-83

**STUDIES
ABROAD**

Rolling College Abroad - Overseas, Europe - Fall 1985
Lived with a French family and completed courses taught entirely in French.

**HONORS/
AFFILIATIONS**

• Recipient of the Interdisciplinary President's Award for Most Exemplary Senior
• Awarded Most Outstanding Interior Design Student
• Honored with the Interior Design Alumni Award
• Awarded the Jane C. Smith Scholarship by the Peachstate Chapter of IDA
• Member of Dean's List, Each Consecutive Quarter
• Interior Designers of America, Student Chapter; President, 1993-94

**DESIGN
EXPERIENCE**

THE DESIGNING PARTNERSHIP - Creativetown, USA   (1994-1995)
Interior Designer
Handled a variety of tasks including space planning, finish selection, construction
rendering, and design presentation. Interfaced frequently with clients, providing
consultation on design ideas. Acted as a liaison between clients and dealers.
Demonstrated both creativity and excellent client relations skills.

FURNITURE UNIVERSITY - Tableville, USA   (1994)
Interior Design Student
One of 25 students selected through a national competition to participate in a newly
developed interactive scholarship program. Analyzed the business of design with an
emphasis on work process, space planning, team design, business strategy, product,
lighting, and color. Program addressed conceptual, theoretical, and practical applications.

RUGS & COMPANY - Carpetown, USA   (1994)
Design Assistant, *Part-time*
Performed commercial design support functions such as drafting, presentation
preparation, document management, library maintenance, and client interaction.

**PREVIOUS
EXPERIENCE**

John Smith & Associates - Attorneytown, USA - **Paralegal**   (1991-92)
Bird & Bird - Nesting Hills, USA - **Head Paralegal**   (1989-91)
Cheaper & Cheap - Costlyville, USA - **Paralegal**   (1989)
Investors America - Dollarville, USA - **Sales Assistant**   (1988-89)
Rolling Valley Ranch Camp - Sunshine, USA - **Camp Counselor**   (Summers, 1984-87)

Skills Gained from the Above Positions:
• Proven ability to excel in team environments while employed as a paralegal.
• Highly developed organizational skills reflected through litigation
  preparation, information management, and cross-referencing materials.
• Effective management techniques exhibited as Head Paralegal.
• Dynamic leadership and creative abilities demonstrated through planning and
  implementation of wilderness expeditions for teenagers.

COMPUTER

Proficient in AutoCAD, MacWrite, and WordPerfect

PORTFOLIO AVAILABLE UPON REQUEST

JOHN J. SEEKER
123 Looking Hard Avenue
Top Dog, USA 20202
(555) 678-9101

OBJECTIVE

To launch and build a successful career with a major investment firm where I may fully utilize my diverse sales and relationship-building skills to contribute to revenue growth.

EDUCATION

COLLEGE OF LEARNING - Pleasantville, USA
B.A. in Corporate Communications, 1996   *Minor: Business*

Leadership Experience

Ep Pi Siga:
- *Treasurer* - Created and managed operations budget, maintaining full accountability for $60K annually. Handled all financial aspects related to 40 members and facility, including payment of dues, insurance, and utilities.
- *Social Chairman* - Planned and coordinated fundraising and hospitality events for fraternity members. Worked in conjunction with Greek system leadership to plan campus-wide events.

Intrafraternity Council:
- *Rush Chairman, 1994* - Organized and directed rush activities campus-wide for 8 fraternities. Planned and conducted orientation seminars for parents and new students. Oversaw bidding system to ensure fair standards and practices.

RELATED EXPERIENCE

JACK WHITE & CO. - Pleasantville, USA   (Spring 1996)
INTERN
Provided stocks and mutual funds research assistance to clients and brokers at branch of investment industry leader. Established rapport by effectively training clients to optimally use company's forerunning on-line trading and portfolio management software. Created a database incorporating over 1,000 new and existing clients.

JEFFERSON FINANCIAL SERVICES - Pleasantville, USA   (Summer 1995)
INTERN
Facilitated the development of new business by cold calling prospective clients. Provided leads with strategies and services offered for college financial planning, i.e., insurance and annuities. Identified client-specific interests and distributed sales-generating informational packets.

SALES EXPERIENCE

SPECIAL FIXTURE & SALES COMPANY - Sweetwater, USA   (6/96-Present)
ACCOUNT REPRESENTATIVE
Manage sales and service of restaurant equipment and supplies to major hotels, country clubs, and retirement communities in the Mid-Southern USA area for award-winning and largest Southeastern-based distributor. Participate in weekly sales meetings and selling seminars to develop in-depth knowledge of high-volume lines and manufacturers. Utilized networking connections to maximize new business development throughout the Southeast.

- Generated product sales of $300K in first year in an extremely competitive and mature market.
- Received Goal Achiever Award for accomplishing daily business objectives in first year.
- Captured 2 new major accounts in first year that created $350K in additional company revenues.
- Leveraged exceptional relationship-building skills to generate new business and drive sales.

COMPUTER

- Proficient in MS Word, Excel, Windows 95, and Outlook

REFERENCES AVAILABLE UPON REQUEST

J. JOHN SEEKER
123 Looking Hard Avenue
Top Dog, USA 20202
(555) 678-9101

OBJECTIVE

To continue a career in the insurance industry where I may utilize my related experience, education, and strong professional skills to impact company profitability.

QUALIFICATIONS

Education

SUCCESSVILLE UNIVERSITY - Happy, USA
B.B.A. Degree in Risk Management/Insurance 1999   Major GPA: 3.5/4.0

Coursework

- Employee Benefit Planning
- Commercial Insurance
- Insurance Company Operations
- Life and Health Insurance
- Risk Management Insurance Series
- Contract and Consumer Law Courses

Credentials

- Passed INS-23 Exam, Commercial Insurance Segment
- Passed Property Casualty Licensing Examination, 1999
- Currently preparing for the Chartered Property Casualty Underwriter (CPCU-1) and Associates of Fidelity & Surety Bonding (AFSB 151) Exams.

Computer

CLS...Lotus 1-2-3...Microsoft Word...Windows 3.1...Prowrite...Excel

Skills & Strengths

- Knowledgeable of the insurance field and dedicated to excellence.
- Demonstrated time efficiency and strong organizational skills.
- Proven analytical and problem-solving abilities.
- Effective salesmanship and customer relations techniques.

EXPERIENCE

Insurance of America - Risky, USA   (4/99-Present)
Underwriter, Small Business Specialist
Review insurance applications for property and casualty coverage with annual premiums of up to $30,000. Evaluate potential policies, assess risk factors, and code and establish policy rates according to actuarial guidelines. Maintain decision-making authority on new and renewal policies.

- Effectively manage a workload consisting of 80-200 cases per month.
- Act as the primary underwriting liaison for 22 agencies in Government Land, Surf State, and Freezertown.
- Successfully completed an 8-week training program.

COLLEGE EXPERIENCE

Fun County Parks & Recreation Department - Goodtime, USA   (Summers 1995-98)
Grounds Personnel
Performed a diverse range of labor-intensive landscaping and grounds-maintenance duties throughout various metropolitan parks. Traveled to 35 playing fields, handling field preparation and lawn care services.

More Toys - Tonkertown, USA   (Holidays 1996-98)
Customer Service Staff
Completed 13-hour shifts during fast-paced holiday seasons. Primarily stocked shelves and merchandised displays. Assisted customers.

REFERENCES AVAILABLE UPON REQUEST

JOHN J. SEEKER
123 Looking Hard Avenue
Top Dog, USA 20202
(555) 678-9101

OBJECTIVE	To obtain a position as a litigation attorney where I may utilize my effective case management, analytical, public speaking, and interpersonal skills toward future success.
SIGNIFICANT SKILLS	• Exhibit strong writing, research, and investigation techniques essential to case development. • Persuasive and persistent individual demonstrating distinctive communication and writing skills. • Proven entrepreneur possessing critical analytical, problem-solving, and follow-up abilities. • Self-directed, focused, and ambitious professional who interfaces well with diverse individuals.
EDUCATION	LAW SCHOOL OF AMERICA - Attorneyville, USA **Juris Doctorate Degree** - 1/98 *GPA:* 3.0/4.0 * *Personally financed 100% of degree through full-time self-employment.* USA POLYTECHNIC INSTITUTE & STATE UNIVERSITY - Academic, USA **Bachelor of Arts Degree in English** - 5/92 Minor: History * *Self-financed 50% of educational expenses.*
ADMITTANCE	State Bar of Peaches
MEMBERSHIPS	• Legal Fraternity - Vice President/ Secretary
RELATED EXPERIENCE	PMBR - Study Hard, USA (1997-1998) **BAR REVIEW COURSE REPRESENTATIVE** Promoted Bar Review curriculum, selling course memberships through active networking. JOHN SMITH, ATTORNEY - Attorneyville, USA (Summer 1996) **LEGAL INTERN** Provided legal support to a criminal defense attorney handling primarily personal injury and negligence cases. Drafted interrogatories and briefs. Assisted in case research and file/document management.
OTHER EXPERIENCE	LANDSCAPING USA - Scapes, USA (1997-Present) **OWNER/PRESIDENT** Oversee landscape design operations for company specializing in high-end landscape development projects. Direct a team of employees and manage all accounting, bookkeeping, and hiring/ supervision of subcontractors. Spearheaded business from ground zero to $100K in revenues with accountability for marketing, contract negotiations, project management, and cost-control functions. LANDSCAPING AMERICA - Landscapers, USA (1994-1996) **GENERAL PARTNER** Developed and managed residential landscape design business with an emphasis on new business development and contract negotiations. Arranged general liability insurance and secured initial business licensing. Established profit margins, project pricing, and bid development. Handled purchasing and inventory control as well as accounting and records management duties. * *Previous work history from 1990 to 1994 encompasses sales and service-oriented positions, including Academic Tutoring for University Athletes from 1987 to 1990.*
COMPUTER	• Westlaw • MS Word • WordPerfect • Excel • Lotus • Quicken
LANGUAGES	Working knowledge of Spanish

SARAH J. SEARCH
123 Job Hunting Lane
Big Time, USA 10101
(444) 567-8910

OBJECTIVE

To secure a challenging position where I may apply my current related legal studies, acute professional abilities, and proven business administration experience.

EDUCATION

THE USA PARALEGAL TRAINING CENTER - Legalville, USA
A.B.A. Approved Lawyer's Assistant Certificate, 8/98 (General Studies Program)
* *ACICS Accreditation * Electives: Family Law and Real Estate Law*

STUDY HARD UNIVERSITY - Learningville, USA
Bachelor of Business Administration Degree, 1995 (15 Hours Remaining)
* *Included Business Law Studies*

RELATED COURSEWORK

- Introduction to Law
- Computer Literacy
- Civil Litigation
- Environmental Law
- Legal Research/Writing
- Real Estate
- Family Litigation
- Estates, Trusts, and Wills
- Business Organizations
- Debtor-Creditor/Bankruptcy
- Criminal Litigation

QUALIFICATIONS

Organizational/ Administrative

- Utilize keen analytical abilities/problem-solving techniques in identifying plausible solutions.
- Possess crucial needs identification skills vital to providing strong administrative support.
- Demonstrated ability to creatively reorganize existing systems to improve operational efficiency.
- Highly effective in a detail-oriented atmosphere that involves efficient records management.

Management

- Extensive operations management background requiring strict financial and inventory control.
- Illustrated expertise in creating marketing materials/advertising programs to increase revenues.
- Capable of implementing effective personnel procedures/policies that foster top performance.

Professional Profile

- Experienced in establishing superior credibility/confidence among high-level clientele.
- Extremely motivated and articulate individual with an unwavering standard of professionalism.
- Proven ability to manage multifaceted responsibilities as well as extensive client contact.

EXPERIENCE

CONSULTANT - Fashion City, USA   (1993-Present)
Independent Fashion Consultant
Comprehensively manage all aspects of a highly personalized consulting service, including coordinating, selecting, and consolidating client wardrobes. Also maintain accountability for new business generation through marketing and advertising campaigns.

FASHION WEAR - Fashion City, USA   (1991-1993)
Manager
Supervised start-up procedures for a 2,000 sq. ft. facility. Ensured a successful opening, including layout development, inventory management, promotional implementation, and personnel recruitment and training. Also assisted in buying and financial record-keeping.

OVER PRICED RETAILERS - Brokesville, USA   (1985-1991)
Commissioned Sales Coordinator
Participated in numerous aspects of the sales process from display coordination and special ordering to record-keeping and customer service. Contributed to merchandise selection, vendor interaction, and overall administrative support functions.

WOMEN'S CORNER - Splurging, USA   (1980-1985)
Assistant Sales Manager
Assisted Store Manager with bookkeeping, sales training, hiring, and overall supervision of a staff of 12. Consistently achieved a #1 ranking for sales within the region.

COMPUTER

- Lotus 1-2-3 • WordPerfect • Windows • DOS • Westlaw • dBase • Inmagic

JOHN J. SEEKER

123 Looking Hard Avenue
Top Dog, USA 20202
(555) 678-9101

OBJECTIVE

To obtain a challenging, growth-oriented position where I may utilize my strong aptitude in the areas of sales, customer service, and management toward impacting future profits.

EDUCATION

GROWING STATE UNIVERSITY - Sweetwater, USA
Bachelor of Business Administration Degree, 12/96 Emphasis in Management

* Worked while attending school in order to self-fund education.

AFFILIATION

- Member of Pi Phi Pi Business Fraternity

COMPUTER

- Windows 95 & 3.1
- Power Point
- WordPerfect 6.0
- Lotus 1-2-3
- Excel
- Corel Draw

SKILLS HIGHLIGHTS

- Acute interpersonal and relationship-building skills critical to successful business development.
- Extremely focused and motivated to achieve in competitive, fast-paced work environments.
- Possess keen troubleshooting and client relations skills essential to effective account management.
- Demonstrate strong project coordination, leadership, and task management capabilities.

EXPERIENCE

HERSHEY CONSTRUCTION COMPANY - Chocolate Town, USA   (1990-Present)
Intermittently employed by this $80M commercial and industrial contracting company in several positions while attending college. Gained an overview of all operations from on-site construction development to operations management.

Project Liaison
Assist in job estimating by conducting thorough research of material costs. Remain abreast of company strategies by regularly attending management meetings. Serve as management liaison, communicating closely with Project Foremen to effectively monitor project status and ensure deadline achievement. Interface closely with different specialties to guarantee that adequate levels of raw materials are maintained.

Customer Service Representative, *Concrete Plant*
Efficiently handled order-processing functions, including driver dispatch. Interfaced extensively with customers, performing critical relationship-building with new and existing clients.

Construction Team
Operated heavy machinery at existing construction sites and participated in the development of major office buildings, industrial facilities, and retail projects throughout Southeast U.S.A.

AUTO COVERS - Sweetwater, USA   (Summer 1993)

Sales Support
Sold auto accessories to retail accounts. Processed customer orders, which required managing mass-merchant clients. Handled details of data entry and coordinated product shipping.

OUTFIELD SALES COMPANY - Chocolate Town, USA   (1989-1990)

Maintenance Staff
Handled repair and refurbishment of existing equipment for a food product distributor. Coordinated distribution of vending machines to locations throughout the Best County area.

REFERENCES AVAILABLE UPON REQUEST

JOHN J. SEEKER
123 Looking Hard Avenue
Top Dog, USA 20202
(555) 678-9101

OBJECTIVE

To secure a marketing position where I may fully utilize my graduate-level education and strong professional skills toward future contributions.

SKILLS SUMMARY

• Possess a high degree of creativity as well as critical writing abilities.
• Demonstrate financial and analytical skills crucial to the marketing field.
• Exceptional team player with fundamental and cooperative leadership qualities.
• Display an unwavering commitment to top performance and an admirable work ethic.

EDUCATION

<u>SUCCESS STATE UNIVERSITY</u> - Success-driven, USA
MASTER OF BUSINESS ADMINISTRATION IN MARKETING, 8/97

* Simultaneously working over 40 hours per week.

<u>STATE UNIVERSITY OF APPLEVILLE</u> - Fruit City, USA
BACHELOR OF SCIENCE DEGREE IN BUSINESS ADMINISTRATION, 5/94
Concentration: Marketing

* Self-financed 100% of educational expenses.

SPECIAL PROJECT

Computer-Simulated Marketplace Assignments
• As Team Leader, managed an in-depth group project that involved long-term market planning, new product development, and financial analysis. Gained practical experience in marketing, pricing, budgeting, promotions, and advertising.
• As a project participant, demonstrated strong forecasting, statistical modeling, and proforma development skills. Utilized effective analytical and decision-making abilities to impact key business areas, including labor, inventory, procedural, and financial.
• Earned two #1 project rankings based on overall excellence.

RELATED EXPERIENCE

<u>SALLY, DICK & JANE</u> - Runsville, USA   (1995-1996)
ASSISTANT ACCOUNT EXECUTIVE
Participated in various advertising support functions, which included the management of Yellow Page advertising campaigns on behalf of 2 international accounts. Interfaced with 1,000+ of the clients' dealers, consulting on aspects of print advertising, such as text, pricing, and placement. Prepared bi-monthly progress reports. Demonstrated strong troubleshooting and account management skills.

OTHER EXPERIENCE

<u>THE PRESTIGIOUS HOTEL</u> - Expensivetown, USA   (1994-Present)
FINE DINING WAIT STAFF
Utilize proven interpersonal and customer service skills in servicing upscale clientele.

<u>PICTURES OF AMERICA CORPORATION</u> - Snapshot City, USA   (Summer 1992)
DEPARTMENT ASSISTANT
Provided internal support to the medical department, which required the delivery of highly confidential medical information and other documentation.

* Additional experience as Waiter with the Olive Garden in Cold City, 1991-1992.

REFERENCES AVAILABLE UPON REQUEST

SARAH J. SEARCH
123 Job Hunting Lane
Big Time, USA 10101
(444) 567-8910

OBJECTIVE   To utilize my political experience, international exposure, and strong interpersonal skills
to pursue a career that will reward professional dedication and top performance.

QUALIFICATIONS

Education   College of Excellence - Pleasantville, USA
B.A. Degree in Political Science and Portuguese (Double Major), 12/98

Alamo College - Battleville, USA
Undergraduate Studies, 1994-1996

University of Fitztown - Fitztown, USA
Semester at Sea Program (Toured 13 Countries), Fall 1996

Activities &   • Political Science Club, Member   • Ambassador Club, Member
Affiliations   • Language Club, Member   • Students Against Gun Violence, Member

Languages/   • Fluent in Portuguese
Computer   • Knowledgeable of Macintosh

Skills &   • Significant international contact with impressive fluency in a foreign language.
Strengths   • Proven marketing talent demonstrated through support techniques and fundraising efforts.
• Positive attitude and commitment to excellence regarding all facets of the work environment.
• Excellent organizational and time management skills used to enhance promotional endeavors.

EXPERIENCE   BRIGHT ADVERTISING - Pleasantville, USA   (5/98-8/98)
Administrative Assistant
In association with the campaign for governor, provided support for the candidate
by distributing campaign literature, attending fundraising events, compiling information
on key political contacts, and providing research to update the communications database.

SELNIK FOR GOVERNOR CAMPAIGN - Pleasantville, USA   (5/98-8/98)
Internship
As task leader for the gubernatorial campaign of Mayor Bob Selnik, managed and distributed
campaign mailings to contribute to the election. Provided vital assistance to campaign
managers through volunteer coordination, advertising, and maintenance of statistical
information. Personally secured media advertising time, including both radio and
television exposures.

THREE PIGEON INN OF INDIAN SPRINGS - Indian Springs, USA   (Holiday 1997)
Server/Bartender
Assisted with the implementation of special events for this upscale catering service.
Provided food and beverage service involving strong interaction with clientele.

RALPH FACILITIES - Polo, USA   (Summer 1996)
Swim Team Coach/Lifeguard
Comprehensively developed program with responsibility for recruiting swimmers,
developing practice plans, soliciting support of members' parents, and organizing
competitive meets. Taught swimming lessons and trained the next head coach.

WINDWARD SAILING SCHOOL - Windy Villa, USA   (Summers 1992-94)
Instructor/Dispatcher...Taught all levels of sailing; handled rental operations.

REFERENCES AVAILABLE UPON REQUEST

SARAH J. SEARCH
123 Job Hunting Lane
Big Time, USA 10101
(444) 567-8910
sarahsearch@aol.com

OBJECTIVE

A position in the field of advertising or public relations where I may utilize a high degree of creativity combined with strong communications, organizational, and account management abilities.

**SKILLS
SUMMARY**

- Possess strong writing skills highlighted by an understanding of publicity and event promotions.
- Results-oriented individual who excels in fast-paced and demanding project-driven settings.
- Exhibit keen analytical skills, essential presentation abilities, and proven computer aptitude.
- Display highly effective planning, scheduling, implementation, and event management skills.

EDUCATION

UNIVERSITY OF STUDYING - Autocity, USA
Bachelor of Arts in English - May 1997
GPA: 3.4/4.0 - *Earned Honors Convocation*

**STUDIES
ABROAD**

FOIS DE GRAS - Paris, France
Culture and Language Studies - 1992

GISE HIGH SCHOOL - Shalom, Israel
History and Cultural Studies - 1991

EXPERIENCE

RIGHT ON LINE - Good Town, USA   (1995)
Intern
Reported directly to an Account Manager of this advertising and strategic consulting agency. Assisted in creative brainstorming sessions and coordinated internal campaign traffic which required interdepartmental communications. Maintained client contact and performed account-related record-keeping functions. Researched celebrity contacts for participation in ad campaigns during special athletic event.

BIG GOVERNMENT OFFICE - Sweetwater, USA   (1993)
Intern
Researched cultural and community resource information. Communicated details about Montreal and Sweetwater to international travelers, often utilizing French language skills. Handled office administration functions as well as written correspondence.

**ACTIVITIES/
AFFILIATIONS**

- **Tau Tau Sorority -**
Assistant Philanthropic Advisor - Successfully organized fundraising events with up to 200 attendees. Demonstrated leadership skills in coordinating volunteer teams.

  Treasurer - Handled cash flow management of social, philanthropic, and individual funds for a 150-member organization. Managed financial record-keeping and dues collections.

- **International Program** - Participated in a 2-year internationally focused curriculum.

- **National Honor Society**

VOLUNTEER

- Services for Students with Disabilities
- Women's Initiative for Self-Employment
- Home for the Aged
- Snow Valley Humane Society

COMPUTER

- Microsoft Word
- Windows
- Macintosh Word

JOHN J. SEEKER

123 Looking Hard Avenue
Top Dog, USA 20202
(555) 678-9101

OBJECTIVE

To secure a position where I may utilize my proven abilities in the key areas of sales, sales support, customer service, and account management.

EDUCATION

INSTITUTE OF TECHNOLOGY BRAINS - Genius, USA
Bachelor of Science Degree in Management * *Concentration in Economics*
* *Dean's List (2 Quarters)* * *Simultaneously worked while attending school*

ACTIVITIES

• Fraternity Boys of the Nation, Member
  Social Chairman and Vice President

COMPUTER

| • Apple | • Macintosh | • WordPerfect | • Lotus 1-2-3 | • DOS |
| • Excel | • MS Word | • PowerPoint | • Claris Works | • Freelance Graphics |

PRIMARY EXPERIENCE

BREWERY U.S.A. - Barley, USA   (1999)
Sales and Promotions Representative
Completed a contract assignment promoting Dark Lager beer throughout a 3-state region including Peachstate, Southern State, and Country Singer State. Targeted both retailer and distributor accounts. Assisted distributors with sales calls, providing the sales team with manufacturer support and comprehensive product knowledge. Created staff incentives and tracked effectiveness of promotions. Utilized multi-tiered selling techniques while interacting with several different organizational levels within the account base.

• Scheduled, organized, and supervised over 200 successful end-user account promotions.
• Demonstrated strong territory management skills, which included generating weekly/monthly expense reports, strategic sales planning, and promotion/market recaps.
• Assisted in securing over 100 new placements as well as increased sales in existing accounts.
• Facilitated a 33% increase in sales for the Peach State, and specifically increased sales in Peachie Town by 64% within less than one year.

OTHER EXPERIENCE

THE ATHLETIC CLUB OF AMERICA/
REGIONAL ATHLETIC CLUB - Peachville, USA
Sports International Club (Parent Company)
Fitness Trainer, 1999-Present
Perform a wide range of consultative functions for a highly diverse clientele; evaluate existing fitness condition, identify objectives, formulate a customized program, and monitor performance. Utilize effective selling strategies to establish the need for these services. Successfully establish professional credibility and develop positive customer relations.

Sales Representative, 1998
Conducted heavy prospecting and new business generation through extensive cold-calling procedures. Created individual marketing programs and contributed to the club's overall marketing strategy. Successfully sold higher-priced, high-end services to a demanding customer base. Consistently achieved/exceeded monthly quotas; established a 50% closing rate within the member referral program.

Front Desk Supervisor, 1997-1998
Interviewed, hired, and trained a staff of 10. Maintained accountability for payroll, budgets, profit tracking, and operational efficiency. Created a highly successful food/beverage service. Promoted from Front Desk Associate within 4 months; earned award for excellence.

* *Previous employment includes position as Restaurant Manager, Eatery, Inc., 1991-92.*

REFERENCES AVAILABLE UPON REQUEST

JOHN J. SEEKER

123 Looking Hard Avenue
Top Dog, USA 20202
(555) 678-9101

OBJECTIVE

To pursue a sales position in highly competitive industry where I may utilize
my proven sales abilities and undisputed tenacity to achieve top performance.

EDUCATION

SUCCESS STATE UNIVERSITY - Studyville, USA
B.S. in Political Science, Expected Graduation: March 2000
* Initially attended The University of Parties, 1994-97.

**LICENSES/
COMPUTER**

• Series 7, 63
• WordPerfect 6.1; Lotus 1-2-3; Windows 95; Internet

**ACTIVITIES/
AFFILIATIONS**

Party Dogs Fraternity:
• *Vice President* - Provide direction to a team of 6, conduct committee meetings,
  and retain decision-making authority regarding organizational policy.
• *Membership Development Chair* - Pursued and developed a guest speakers bureau
  that increased awareness of key student, life, and welfare issues; increased
  member participation through excellent program planning and promotion.

University Senate:
• *Standards & Admissions Committee* - Singularly selected as a student member with
  contribution toward evaluating student petitions regarding academic matters.
• *Student Life & Development Committee* - Review organizational applications for
  school charters and formulate various student-related policies.
• *Athletic Committee* - Monitor compliance of governing departmental regulations.

Student Government Association:
• *Senator & Bylaws Committee Chair* - Rewrite specific committee bylaws.

Interfraternity:
• *Interfraternity Council Delegate* - Regulate fraternity activities campus-wide.
• *Greek Week Chair* - Successfully plan and implement major fundraising and social events.
• *Expansion Committee* - Analyze and authorize the addition of new campus fraternities.
• *Order of Excellence National Honor Society Member*

Incept Team, New Student Orientation:
• Honored as one of 11 students to conduct in-depth campus tours to groups of up to 50.

**SALES
EXPERIENCE**

STOCKBROKERS BIG TIME - Bondsville, USA   (1/98-3/98)
Stockbroker Assistant
Performed critical lead-generation and client-support functions for one of the
top brokers. Handled a variety of sales functions, including client presentations.
Also, managed and serviced a personal portfolio of investment clients.

HIGH ROLLER INVESTORS COMPANY - Risk Takers, USA   (8/97-1/98)
Stockbroker
Developed a client base from ground zero through aggressive cold calling and selling
techniques. Generated an investment portfolio that exceeded $250K+. Utilized strong
consulting skills and financial acumen in optimizing individuals' investment strategies.

**OTHER
EXPERIENCE**

SUCCESS STATE UNIVERSITY - Goal Setters, USA   (6/98-11/98)
• *Welcome Center Staff*, Conducted campus tours and served as liaison to the public.
• *Health Science Department Assistant*, Provided department administrative support.

POLITICAL

• Local Bi-Partisan Student Organization - Developed and managed registration drives.
• Statewide Bi-Partisan Student Organization (President) - Contributed to Presidential campaign.

SARAH J. SEARCH
123 Job Hunting Lane
Big Time, USA 10101
(444) 567-8910

OBJECTIVE

To secure an outside sales position where I may utilize my tenacity, interpersonal skills, and management experience toward impacting profits.

EDUCATION

SUCCESS STATE COLLEGE - Anytown, USA
B.S. Degree in Psychology, 8/95 **GPA: 3.4/4.0**
Concentration: Business Emphasis: Sales

HONORS/ ACTIVITIES

- Dean's List: 1993, 1994, 1995
- Platinum Key National Honor Society of America
- USA Psychology Association, Member

SPECIAL PROJECTS

- Participated in an extensive sales project that required the selection of a consumer product and the identification of its numerous selling points. Created presentation materials, including brochures, competitive ranking outlines, and product statistics.

SKILLS HIGHLIGHTS

- Illustrate extremely effective relationship-building and interpersonal skills.
- Hard-working, self-directed individual who possesses an unwavering drive toward success.
- Possess crucial communication/persuasive skills necessary to succeed in sales arena.
- Experienced in handling a wide range of personalities within a high-stress atmosphere.
- Highly proficient in managing multiple, complex tasks simultaneously while upholding the highest standards of professionalism.

EXPERIENCE

ABC COMMUNICATIONS - Anytown, USA   (1996-Present)
Commercial Account Representative
Aggressively implement new business development strategies, which include extensive cold calling and referral development. Target diverse industries and generate accounts nationwide. Conduct account analyses, determine clients' needs, develop proposals, and negotiate contracts. Hired to drive sales and facilitate rapid growth for a start-up office.

- Consistently exceeded monthly quotas by 28% based on number of orders and revenues.
- Provide excellent customer support and service standards to ensure customer retention.
- Ranked as one of the top 2 producers in the City Commercial Division.
- Utilize strong closing skills and persuasive selling techniques to impact sales.

CAKE FACTORY - Delicious, USA   (1994-1996)
Corporate Trainer
Selected out of 200 staff members to travel to new locations and train employees/ management. Administer tests, perform evaluations, and provide one-on-one feedback. Trained over 45 staff within 9 weeks; recognized by upper-level management for excellence. Initially hired as hostess, promoted subsequent to graduation.

MAIL STOP, INC. - Pickup, USA   (1993-1994)
Sales Manager
Supervised 8 staff members in all aspects of daily operations. Entrusted as a key holder and maintained accountability for opening/closing duties. Assisted in hiring, vendor relations, and product selections. Strengthened customer service and increased sales by 56%. Initially hired as Sales Clerk, promoted within 90 days.

PERSONAL

Willing to relocate and travel.

REFERENCES AVAILABLE UPON REQUEST

SARAH J. SEARCH
123 Job Hunting Lane
Big Time, USA 10101
(444) 567-8910

OBJECTIVE

An elementary-level teaching position where I may utilize my experience, which reflects strong curriculum development, classroom management, and parent/teacher communications.

EDUCATION

UNIVERSITY OF COLD WEATHER - Chillytown, USA
Bachelor of Arts Degree in Psychology, 1995 GPA: 3.4/4.0

**STUDIES
ABROAD**

COLLEGE OF INTERNATIONAL STUDIES - Overseas, Europe
Semester Abroad, Studied French, Spring 1993

LICENSES

Certification in Elementary Education, May 1996

**STUDENT
TEACHING**

BEACH TOWN ELEMENTARY - N. Beachtown, USA   (8/95-12/95)
First Grade
Key contributor in all aspects of preschool planning, curriculum implementation, and student development activities. Effectively utilized an authentic and integrated teaching approach. Consistently applied conflict-resolution strategies. Created literature-based programs and employed creativity in selecting teaching materials. Served as County Reading Council member.

• Developed pilot introducing portfolio assessment techniques to school; strategically fostered parental acceptance of this highly successful method, which demonstrates learning progression.
• Established portfolio assessment video that is serving as a role model by expert Dr. Roger Farr.
• Created the curriculum for an interdisciplinary thematic unit; researched topic, formulated lesson plans, utilized learning centers, and engaged administration in student presentations.
• Cultivated cooperative parent/student/administration relations; maintain ongoing student relations.
• Assisted in addressing critical self-esteem issues with students using role-playing techniques.
• Demonstrated initiative in spearheading and organizing an after-school Environmental Club.
• Experienced in the application of Bloom's Taxonomy in developing lesson plans.

**PRACTICUM
EXPERIENCE**

STUDY HARD ELEMENTARY - Chillytown, USA   (Spring 1995)
Second Grade
Prepared daily observational journals. Taught mathematics and maintained reading records. Worked with special education team for students with Attention Deficit Disorder.

FUNTIME MIDDLE SCHOOL - Chillytown, USA   (Spring 1995)
Sixth Grade
Taught interdisciplinary Social Studies, using a thematic teaching approach.

**ADDITIONAL
EXPERIENCE**

UNIVERSITY OF COLD WEATHER - Chillytown, CO   (Fall 1994)
Teaching Assistant, *Undergraduate Psychology*
Planned curriculum, developed testing materials, and evaluated progress. Utilized rubrics to develop grading system and employed interactive learning techniques that offered students an opportunity to assess and defend their own performance.

• Successfully applied portfolio assessment at college level.
• Customized curriculum to empower students with decision-making and critical thinking skills.
• Initiated and conducted weekly mentoring and support meetings with other Teaching Assistants.

ELEMENTARY SCHOOL SYSTEMS OF BIG ROCK - Chillytown, USA   (1991-1995)
Volunteer Teaching Assistant, *First-Fourth Grades*
Served as teacher support during activities. Taught lesson plans in 6 different schools.

AFFILIATIONS

- Professional Association of Chillystate Educators   - International Reading Association

* Authored a children's book used as a class discussion tool.

JOHN J. SEEKER

123 Looking Hard Avenue
Top Dog, USA 20202
(555) 678-9101

OBJECTIVE	To secure a position in publishing where I may utilize my proven writing, proofreading, and research abilities as well as creativity, computer skills, and cultural diversity.

EDUCATION	THE ACHIEVER'S UNIVERSITY - Positivetown, USA **Bachelor of Arts Degree in Philosophy**, 1995 * *Completed a Senior Thesis* * *Dean's List*

ACTIVITIES	• *Partytime Fraternity*, **Rush Chairman, Athletics Chairman, and Historian**; Designed and produced a forerunning marketing piece to attract new members. Authored editorial articles that outlined group's profile and philosophy. Wrote interfraternity correspondence and articles for the national publication. • *Achiever's Review*, **Editorial Assistant** Provided editorial recommendations and reviewed poetry selections.

COMPUTER	• Microsoft Office	• WP 5.1/6.0	• Claris Works
	• Lotus Smartsuite	• Dbase	• Q&A
	• Adobe Illustrator	• Quark	• Superbase

QUALIFICATIONS

Writing	• Possess superior proofreading skills, effective editorial abilities, and proven creativity. • Experienced in writing articles for publication while verifying critical content accuracy. • Completed a writing workshop under the auspices of a well-respected writer.
Management/ Administration	• Utilize a wide range of administrative and leadership skills to ensure organizational productivity. • Capable of researching, managing, and quickly interpreting complex, detailed information. • Efficiently and accurately track and prepare detailed information in support of management teams.
Professional Profile	• Demonstrated ability to handle client service functions requiring strong interpersonal skills. • Perform extremely well within a multitask-oriented, deadline-specific atmosphere.

RELATED EXPERIENCE	INTERNATIONAL PUBLICATION - Overseas, Asia (Summer 1992) **Publications Assistant** Created a publication that targeted foreign students in Japan. Researched, wrote, and edited articles for publication. Assisted in production of annual calendar through solicitations and ad space sales. Provided support for the office hot line and performed a vast array of computer functions, including record-keeping and database management.

OTHER EXPERIENCE	CONSULTING & ACCOUNTING - Numbersville, USA (1995-1996) **Reception**, *Temporary Contract Position* Provided overall administrative, information management, and client relations support. FOREIGN COUNCIL - Overseas, Europe (1995) **Program Assistant**, *Temporary Contract Position* Conducted extensive project planning for events related to educational program exchanges. Wrote correspondence and compiled copious marketing materials for program introduction. Promoted within 1 month; managed a temporary staff and delegated administration. USA LAW STUDENTS IN COURT - Attorneytown, USA (1993-1994) **Legal/Office Assistant** Gained valuable exposure to criminal/civil justice system while conducting in-depth case research, fielding public inquiries, and providing overall office support. Handled document filing; closely tracked productivity. Also assisted in planning major fundraiser.

LANGUAGE/ PERSONAL	• Competent in French • Extensive international travel; overseas residence for 6 years, Asia.

JOHN J. SEEKER

Present Address:
123 Looking Hard Avenue
Top Dog, USA 20202
(555) 678-9101

Permanent Address:
321 Job Hunting Lane
Big Time, USA 10101
(444) 567-8910

OBJECTIVE

A position that demands a strong environmental and economics background combined with proven analytical, problem-solving, and leadership skills.

EDUCATION

EXCEL UNIVERSITY - Sweetwater, USA
B.A. Degree in Economics - Graduation: May 1998
Co-Major: Human and Natural Ecology (Includes Senior Thesis)

* *Attended prestigious international boarding and precollegiate institutions throughout South Africa, Asia, and the United Kingdom.*

COURSE HIGHLIGHTS

- Conservation Biology
- Water
- Global and Natural Ecology
- Environmental Issues
- Politics and the Environment
- Energy, Resources, and Environmental Changes

RELATED EXPERIENCE

LION GAME RESERVE - Kenya   (5/98-8/98)
WILDLIFE MANAGEMENT TRAINEE
Gained in-depth academic understanding of soil, wildlife, vegetation, and plant life. Conducted tours of the reserve involving various outdoor activities, including canoeing, bush walking, and scuba diving. Educated visitors and fielded inquiries. Utilized strong customer service and public relations skills in ensuring guest satisfaction. Assisted with diverse land-management functions, which required coordination of local workers related to bush clearing, boundary reconstruction, water supply management, and burn-control projects.

* Other employment includes a seasonal Wait Staff position in Asia (1993/1994). Demonstrated strong customer service, suggestive selling, and organizational abilities.

CAMPUS AFFILIATIONS

STUDENTS INVOLVED WITH THEIR ENVIRONMENT, **MEMBER**
Spearheaded and managed a successful recycling campaign. Participated in clean-up projects of river areas, nature trails, roads, parks; attended guest lectures.

STUDENT ENVIRONMENTAL COUNCIL, **MEMBER**
Attended weekly meetings focused on developing organizational strategies to raise environmental awareness. Key contributor to special projects involving clean-up, planting, and recycling.

KIWIS CLUB, **VICE PRESIDENT**
Conduct meetings and manage organizational functions. Assist in planning and overseeing social and fundraising events, recruiting project volunteers, and delegating responsibilities.

ALPHA OMEGA FRATERNITY, **MEMBER**
EXCEL BUSINESS CLUB, **MEMBER**

ATHLETICS

EXCEL RUGBY CLUB, **TEAM COACH**
REBELS RUGBY CLUB (State Sponsored Team), **TEAM MEMBER**
YOUTH SOCCER TEAMS (Scotland), **TEAM COACH**

COMPUTERS/ LANGUAGES

- Computer literate, including knowledge of Windows 95
- Languages: French, Fluent; Spanish, Communicative

REFERENCES AVAILABLE UPON REQUEST

SARA J. SEARCH

123 Job Hunting Lane
Big Time, USA 10101
(444) 567-8910

PROFILE

Extensive background in all facets of event planning, fundraising, committee leadership, and mission management for a wide array of nonprofit organizations.

SIGNIFICANT QUALIFICATIONS

- Strong leadership skills with an acute ability to inspire excellence and build effective teams.
- Talented in creating, leading, and mobilizing committees, improving both structure and direction.
- Vast experience in successful event planning and management despite frequently limited resources.
- Proven track record in site/vendor selection, event design, and agenda/sponsor development.
- Detail-oriented, efficient, and accuracy-focused individual with exceptional organizational skills.
- Adept administrative and word processing skills and the ability to perform in high-pressure settings.

EXPERIENCE   NONPROFIT COMMITMENTS   (1984-Present)

Leadership   **QUICK LEARNING SCHOOLS** - Leadership Roles Included:
Highlights: *Executive Committee* (1992-96); *Secretary* (1992-94)
- Prepared and produced summary reports from executive meetings.
- Collaborated on developing and presenting a formal evaluation of the Board of Trustees.

Long-Range Planning Committee, Chair (1994-96)
- Spearheaded the development of "The Mission and Goals" of the Planning Committee.

Development & Special Events Committee Member (1993-94)
- Assisted in planning fundraising events that resulted in producing $3M+.
- Critically contributed to the coordination and execution of seated dinner events for up to 300, which involved creating presentations and all event management functions.
- Produced highly visible events, i.e., tributary and honorary programs and receptions.

Education Committee Chair (1992-94)
- Formalized committee structure and established a purposeful, revitalized focus.
- Conceived and instituted a lecture series, open to the public, involving expert educators speaking on leading-edge educational trends.
- Instrumental in the creation of Quick Learning Sampler, a new format involving student panels, rotational presentations, and receptions to introduce parents to the school system.

Recruitment & Architect Search Committees (1996, 1993)
- Critical contributor in the selection of a new Head Master and Director of Admissions as well as the Architect accountable for a major construction project.

JOHN DOE CENTER - Leadership Roles Included:
Board of Directors (1 year); *Fundraising Committee*
Key participant in a joint fundraiser that resulted in raising over $100K in donations utilized to procure the John Doe Collection.

CHAMBER PLAYERS USA - Leadership Roles Included:
Board of Directors (1 year); *Fundraising Committee Chair*
Directed all aspects of planning and implementing a paid concert series event for a group of Chamber Musicians.

SMART COLLEGE ALUMNAE - *Board of Directors*
PRESTIGE THEATER - *Board of Directors* (6 years)

EXPERIENCE	<u>NONPROFIT COMMITMENTS</u> - (Cont.)

Event Planning:

- **The History Center of America** - *Hospitality/Advisory Committee Chair* (1989-Present)
  Create and launch holiday and volunteer appreciation parties for over 300 people. Manage all event details including decorations, invitations, and attendee correspondence. Also, planned menus for a series of events in conjunction with the new building grand opening. Won the Volunteer of the Year Award (1993).
- **State Trust for Historic Preservation** - *Committee Co-chair* (1993, 1994, 1996)
  Developed and executed a Preview Party Fundraiser, including Silent Auction and first-time raffle event prior to the American Craft Show.
- **The Big Ball for State Gardens,** *Committee Chair* (1995)
  Directed a team for menu planning and food/beverage implementation.
- **The Society Ball for The History Center of America,** *Committee Chair* (1991)
  Spearheaded the menu planning and selection of catering vendors.
- **The Ballet Fundraising Dinner Party,** *Committee Chair* (1990)
  Planned and organized an exclusive dinner party with a $200 per couple cost. Coordinated menu planning, guest list development, and records management.
- **Civic Association Annual Event** and innumerable **Fundraiser Events,** *Volunteer*

<u>PROFESSIONAL COMMITMENTS</u>   (1971-1980)

SMITH & SMITH, INC. - Importers, USA
Administrative Assistant

Assisted in planning and implementing art exhibitions for art dealers specializing in international art. Contributed to the production of catalogues that showcased the company's unique artwork. Provided assistance with accounting-related record-keeping, file management, and client correspondence preparation. Significantly improved the internal efficiency and organization of the business.

DOE, ROE, & KNOW - Attorney, USA
Executive Secretary/Paralegal

Worked under the auspices of a Partner within the Commercial Real Estate Department. Handled extensive document production, including compiling and drafting closing documentation in addition to coordinating details of property closings. Responded to clients' requests. Provided executive support and acquired diverse knowledge of commercial real estate.

OVERSEAS SECRETARIAL AGENCY - Overseas, Europe
Temporary Staff

Completed temporary assignments utilizing a variety of reception, administrative support, and clerical skills. Positions included a long-term assignment with The Hospital for Children as a rotational Administrative Assistant. Worked under the auspices of one of the top Hospital Administrators.

EDUCATION	<u>UNIVERSITY OF SMARTS</u> - Thinker, USA

B.S. in Zoology, *Summa Cum Laude* **GPA: 4.0/4.0**
- Member of Phi Beta Kappa and Phi Kappa Phi Honoraries

<u>GOOD STUDENT COLLEGE</u> - Study, USA
B.A. in Art History Dean's List   GPA: 2.2/3.0
- Earned honorable recognition for an Independent Study on Japanese Architecture and for comparative art studies in Overseas, Europe.

* Completed a Secretarial course with Secretary Institute.

REFERENCES AVAILABLE UPON REQUEST

252

SARAH J. SEARCH

123 Job Hunting Lane • Big Time, USA 10101 • (444) 567-8910

CAREER SUMMARY

Talented professional demonstrating extensive background in education and a diverse range of volunteer experience.

EDUCATION EXPERIENCE

<u>GOOD PRESCHOOL</u> - Sometown, USA   (1986-1997)
Co-Founder/Instructor
Assisted in the founding of this institution to educate preschool-age students; current enrollment of 200. During tenure, experienced in instructing as a self-contained and specialty teacher (music).

• Elected Chairman of the Board with accountability for conducting quarterly board meetings
  to address policy, curriculum, financial, and personnel issues.
• As Group Coordinator, led weekly special activity and directed annual holiday pageant.

<u>SUBURB HIGH SCHOOL</u> - Suburb, USA   (1980-1986)
Instructor, Taught English to 9th-grade students. Evaluated student progress.

VOLUNTEER EXPERIENCE

<u>LARGE PARISH</u>, 1980-1993
Largest Parish in the United States

• Chosen for a 5-member Vocational Testing Committee; assess vocational aptitudes of people.
• Served on the Altar Committee as Chairman, 1992-93, and Co-chairman, 1991-92. Responsible
  for preparing Large Parish, The Chapel, and Kingdom for a total 22 regular weekly services,
  which include liturgical readings, consecrated elements, and all necessary supplies. Direct
  and schedule 78 volunteer committee members.
• Member of volunteer staff of the city homeless shelter.
• Twenty-year member of a women's volunteer organization, Daughters of Service.
• Experienced in directing Vacation Bible School and as a Sunday School Teacher.

<u>HEALTHY CARE HAVEN</u>, 1980-1993
• Conducted a weekly sing-along session to entertain residents; annually
  coordinate and host a holiday party.
• Entertained at a monthly celebration for residents; assist
  in administering monthly services.

<u>SOMETOWN JUNIOR LEAGUE</u>, 1970-Present
• Volunteered at Medical Hospital, Sometown Speech School, New Store, and Opera Office.
• Member of the SingSongs, singing group performing at charitable organizations/civic events.
• Assisted in developing a children's nature guide program on the West Town River.

<u>PARENT-TEACHER ORGANIZATION</u>, 1971-1986
• Active volunteer at three schools; held numerous leadership positions.

<u>FLOWER GARDEN CLUB</u>, 1970-Present
• Co-chairman of the Garden at the Sometown History Center; directed a 2-year
  garden project. Co-editor of the *Garden Guide.*

EDUCATION

<u>LEARNING UNIVERSITY</u> - Sometown, USA
GRADUATE SCHOOL OF SOCIAL WORK, 1992   GPA: 3.6/4.0

<u>UNIVERSITY OF STUDENTS</u> - Big City, USA
BACHELOR OF ARTS DEGREE IN ENGLISH, 1980
* Recruited by colleges for early entry due to academic excellence.

Licenses/ Certifications

• Licensed Real Estate Agent, 1992 (Scored 94 on State Exam, "A" Grades in Sales I, II, III)
• Certified by State Professional Standards Commission as an English Teacher, 1993
• Secondary Teaching Certificate, Great State
• Completed qualifying coursework for temporary library certification ("A" Grades)

SARAH J. SEARCH
123 Job Hunting Lane
Big Time, USA 10101
(444) 567-8910

CAREER SUMMARY

A multi-talented individual demonstrating a strong background in program management
and project coordination for nonprofit civic organizations.

SIGNIFICANT QUALIFICATIONS

Program Management
- Managed and administered an $80K budget, reporting directly to a 35-member board.
- Directed the efforts of 23 committees related to fundraising, service, community, and financial matters; delegated responsibilities to Committee Chairs.
- Personally supervised the activities of 4 fundraising and financial committees with accountability for allocating school funds.

Project Coordination
- Successfully implemented community projects for nonprofit organizations, i.e., Blue Flight, Baby Hospital, Cook Hospital, and Kaye Rite Hospital, through the Junior League.
- Experienced in all phases of directing a volunteer staff of up to 125.
- Directed and participated in a variety of fundraising campaigns for organizations such as St. Jude's Children's Hospital, American Heart Society, and Sweetwater Music Club.
- Talented at managing multifaceted projects from inception to completion.

Professional Profile
- Interface extremely well with Administrators and other highly visible personnel.
- Demonstrate outstanding troubleshooting and crisis management abilities.
- Possess strong public speaking, writing, organizational, and time management skills.

EXPERIENCE

Sweetwater High School - Sweetwater, USA   (1995-1996)
Office Administrator
Handled a diverse range of administrative and clerical duties on a volunteer basis. Provided ongoing support to administrative personnel.

Goodbody & Company - Sweetwater, USA   (3 years)
Sales Assistant
Provided administrative and sales support to one of the nation's top 10 producing brokers. Worked closely with a high-profile customer base of 500+, monitoring accounts and resolving problems. Prepared marketing letters, correspondence, and detailed record-keeping. Reviewed commission reports for 17 sales executives.

CIVIC INVOLVEMENT
- Parent Association, The Good School, President
- State Association of Independent Schools, Representative for The Good School
- Sweetwater High School, Special Events Chairman, Booster Club
- Junior League, Community Project Chairman Coordinator/Sustainer
- Good Shepherd Center, Chairman Volunteer Committee
- Hospital Auxiliary, Chairman, Financial Committee
- Twigs, Treasurer; Project Chairman; Committee Chair
- Fortress Center Alliance, Board Member
- Sweetwater Music Club, President Elect; V.P.; Treasurer; Secretary
- Garden Tour, Chairman (A Fundraising Event)
- Youth Council; Chairman of Nominating Committee for UMW
- *The Town Crier*, Editor/Publisher

EDUCATION

HIGH CALIBER UNIVERSITY - Sweetwater, USA **B.A. Degree in Fine Arts (English)**

Cover Letter Library

Cover Letters are categorized in alphabetical order
according to a variety of professions

SARAH J. SEARCH
123 Job Hunting Lane
Big Time, USA 10101
(444) 567-8910

In the interest of obtaining a consulting position with your organization, I have enclosed a resume for your review. It will provide valuable details regarding my employment history as well as highlight my significant qualifications.

As you will notice, I am currently employed as a Medical Consultant for Medical Auditing, Inc. In this position, I am accountable for reviewing medical bills and records to ensure their accuracy as well as handling negotiations to achieve maximum claims reimbursements with various insurance companies and managed care organizations. Not only do I reconcile billing discrepancies and provide patient assistance related to understanding medical procedures and their related charges, but I also conduct managed care audits to ensure contract compliance.

During a role as the Project Lead for a highly visible Focus Review Project, I structured, managed, and implemented significant procedural changes to maximize Medicare reimbursements in an organization requiring severe internal reform. Similarly, in a previous consulting role, I conducted audit reviews which required scrutinizing both medical records and workers' compensation charges in order to ensure medical procedures were aligned with the claimants' injuries. As a result of each of my consulting projects, I have become highly skilled in analyzing complex policies, reimbursement guidelines, and medical information on behalf of healthcare providers, insurance companies, and managed care organizations.

At this juncture, I am interested in securing a position within a successful consulting firm where I may continue to utilize my proven skills and medical background toward mutual benefit. I am confident that I would become an immediately contributing member of your already existing team. Aware, however, that a resume can only partially illustrate the scope of my abilities, I am requesting a personal interview to further define my relevant qualifications. Thank you in advance for your time and consideration. I look forward to meeting with you.

Sincerely,

Sarah J. Search

JOHN J. SEEKER
123 Looking Hard Avenue
Top Dog, USA 20202
(555) 678-9101

In the interest of pursuing employment opportunities with your organization, I am enclosing a resume for your review. It will provide valuable details regarding my extensive experience in counseling, human resources, training and development, and event planning.

As you will discover, I possess a diverse professional background in both entrepreneurial and corporate environments which has allowed me to develop fundamentally sound skills in several crucial areas. Having started my career in the military, I acquired an excellent foundation in operations and personnel management which I have continually utilized throughout my career. Under the auspices of an $80 million corporation, I successfully structured and expanded an entire training department to provide top-notch professional development programs for a company consisting of 2,500-plus employees. As a result, I gained extensive experience in all phases of meeting planning with an excellent knowledge of highly detailed planning, event implementation, and logistics coordination.

As I advanced further in my career, I became one of two key managing personnel in a state-approved educational institution and counseling center. During this experience, I expanded my knowledge of the human resources field through this multifaceted position which required extensive recruiting, training, instructing, troubleshooting, staff relations, and employee record-keeping. Finally, as a successful entrepreneur, I have developed a well-respected private practice which allowed me to further extend myself in all aspects of marketing, promotions, business administration, public speaking, and corporate consulting. At this juncture, however, my goal is to assimilate into an organization that can utilize the full breadth of my experience to assist in achieving corporate objectives.

Although I am confident that my numerous accomplishments are well represented, I realize that a resume cannot portray any individual entirely. Therefore, I am requesting a personal interview where we might discuss my qualifications in greater detail.

Thank you in advance for your time in reviewing my credentials. I look forward to speaking with you soon.

Sincerely,

John J. Seeker

SARAH J. SEARCH
123 Job Hunting Lane
Big Time, USA 10101
(444) 567-8910

I am submitting my resume for your consideration in the interest of securing an interior design position with your firm. It includes a brief summary of my training, significant qualifications, and related professional skills.

Please note that my current experience includes a variety of challenging design-related projects and demonstrated skill within the interior design field. As indicated, I have exhibited an acute ability to manage an assortment of projects and responsibilities while performing complex design functions with creativity and efficiency. Previously as an interior design student at the American College for the Good Arts, I displayed the necessary drive and self-direction required to manage the demands of a rigorous school curriculum while maintaining ongoing employment. My ability to excel in all phases of the design process is evidenced by repeated involvement with interior design projects under the auspices of advertising, architectural, and interior design firms.

In addition to my proven design abilities, I possess excellent interpersonal and client relations skills that are essential in all client-oriented environments. At the same time, I am proficient in the utilization of CAD and also possess a strong knowledge of blueprints, crucial skills that will assist in my advancement within this rapidly changing industry. Furthermore, I have demonstrated a high level of talent in drafting, space planning, and selection of fabrics and finishes that further demonstrate my highly developed design abilities. Essentially, I am confident that my proven skills combined with my personal commitment to excellence would allow me to immediately become productive within your firm.

Realizing that a resume can only partially represent an individual, I am requesting a personal interview in order to present my qualifications in more depth. I hope to meet with you as soon as possible to discuss how I might contribute to the success of your organization. Thank you in advance for your time and consideration in reviewing my qualifications.

Sincerely,

Sarah J. Search

JOHN J. SEEKER
123 Looking Hard Avenue
Top Dog, USA 20202
(555) 678-9101

In the interest of exploring executive management opportunities with your organization, I have enclosed a resume that provides a concise overview of my distinctive skills and experience.

Please note that I have a proven track record in all aspects of operations management, training, sales, and customer relations. By facilitating shared ownership of business objectives and accomplishments, I have built staffs that are extremely productive, committed to standards of excellence, and able to achieve peak performance levels. Not only have I leveraged my knowledge to make critical contributions in several highly competitive industries, but I have spearheaded and initiated numerous processes and procedures that have had profound impact on operational effectiveness and corporate revenues. As the Director of Customer Relations for Tool Time, I successfully launched a centralized call operation supported by advanced technical solutions and a proficiently trained staff. Consequently, I ensure delivery of maximum efficiency and quality in service as well as meet or exceed all revenue goals.

In previous roles, I further demonstrated my ability to manage multifaceted, corporate-wide projects that achieved measurable successes. For Liveworld, I generated significant revenue savings and optimized resources by merging operations through technology. Similarly, I pioneered an innovative call center facility that received national publicity not only for its high corporate rate of return, but for its multiple contributions to society. I have proven my ability to dramatically improve organizational training effectiveness as well as skillfully apply conflict mediation and negotiation skills in the private and public sectors, including not-for-profit organizations. I handled dispute resolution and consensus building within diverse groups using systematic procedures and leadership skills. In essence, I am confident that I possess crucial characteristics that will enable me to rapidly become a valuable team player, leader, and innovator within your organization.

At this juncture, I am committed to pursuing continued career challenges in an executive leadership role so I can further engage my versatile talents and unrelenting quest for personal and organizational excellence. Therefore, I am requesting a personal meeting to discuss mutually beneficial opportunities and my broad qualifications in greater detail. Thank you for your time and consideration. I look forward to speaking with you soon.

Sincerely,

John J. Seeker

JOHN J. SEEKER
123 Looking Hard Avenue
Top Dog, USA 20202
(555) 678-9101

Confidentiality Requested

In anticipation of gaining the opportunity to immediately impact your company's future profitability, I have enclosed a resume which briefly outlines my outstanding management credentials, extensive technical background, and versatile qualifications.

As indicated, I am currently an Application Engineer with a U.S. subsidiary of a European-based global leader in engine manufacturing. In this highly customer-oriented and technical position, I have proven my critical leadership and project management skills directing multiple internationally based project teams simultaneously throughout the full cycle of design and market implementation. By utilizing acute analytical and prioritization skills, I facilitate timely and cost-effective project development. Also, I effectively communicate with all levels of internal/outsourced personnel, as well as 20+ OEM customers and 50+ vendors. My efforts have played a vital role in the company earning industry-wide commendations for peak product performance and undisputed service excellence as well as steadily rising corporate revenues. At the same time, being a highly motivated, tenacious, and creative manager, I have taken the initiative to design and develop several successful industrial engine field component packages.

Previous to becoming a permanent resident of the United States, I demonstrated my wide range of technical expertise in the areas of aerospace engineering, lightweight design, computer programming, and materials science managing various projects related to engines, emissions, thermodynamics, and technical mechanics. I was also intimately involved with the creation and implementation of a critical water-supply problem-detection system for a local South American government entity. My highest level of personal satisfaction has always been derived from creating new and advanced product solutions for mission-critical projects. As a results-oriented professional with strong academic credentials combined with extensive international-level project management success, I am confident that I will quickly become a valuable asset on your existing management team.

Aware, however, that a resume can only partially illustrate the scope of my qualifications, I would like to meet with you at your earliest convenience to discuss my abilities in greater depth. Thank you for your time, and I look forward to speaking with you in the near future.

Sincerely,

John J. Seeker

JOHN J. SEEKER
123 Looking Hard Avenue
Top Dog, USA 20202
(555) 678-9101

In the interest of pursuing a challenging opportunity with an organization that would capitalize on my ability to strategically and competitively position businesses for growth, I am enclosing a resume for your review. It will provide an overview of my numerous qualifications.

As you will discover, I possess an excellent track record and a strong combination of talents in the areas of financial modeling, business development, and relationship-building crucial to my effective account management, which has generated a significant increase in division revenues. In my current position with a $350B global banking operation, I skillfully manage a sizable portfolio of major Fortune 500 accounts by negotiating innumerable complex investment transactions. By utilizing acute analytical skills, syndication strategies, and financial modeling expertise, I not only accurately identify my clients' capital needs and glean essential data from credit and financial statements, but also originate, competently structure, and finalize millions of dollars in underwriting commitments. At the same time, I achieve the maximum allocations due to my stringent work ethic and results-oriented deadline management skills.

Throughout my career I have consistently demonstrated an ability to establish rapport and build solid business relationships with major accounts by fostering mutual respect, providing personal service, and offering strategic financial consulting. Based on my strengths in communication, decision-making, and solutions-selling as well as my educational background and distinctive credit training with one of the most renowned programs in the industry, I am confident that I could provide any firm or individual with solid financial direction in building realistic and lucrative business plans, planning business growth, and securing corporate finance needs. I offer a strong versatile skills set that could meet the needs of large-scale corporate structures crossing many industries as well as small business operations.

Realizing that a resume cannot portray any individual entirely, I am requesting a personal meeting so that we can discuss mutually beneficial opportunities and my qualifications in greater detail. Thank you in advance for your time and professional consideration in reviewing my credentials. I look forward to speaking with you soon.

Sincerely,

John J. Seeker

JOHN J. SEEKER
123 Looking Hard Avenue
Top Dog, USA 20202
(555) 678-9101

In order to initiate a career in financial services and to promote my ideally aligned qualifications as a candidate for your training program, I have enclosed a resume for your review.

As you will discover, I am a uniquely talented and highly motivated individual who is eager to demonstrate my proven sales and client relations abilities to your organization. In the two years following graduation from the College of Learning, I have managed sales and service of industry-specific equipment and supplies working with a diversity of clients and accounts. Not only did I achieve a personal best of $300K in sales in my first year in an extremely competitive market utilizing solutions-selling skills, but I captured two new accounts which generated additional revenues of $350K. Through tenacious customer service, integrity, and extensive knowledge of a heavy volume of products and manufacturers, I forged strong business relationships with clients, resulting in numerous networking referrals.

Previously, I gained financial services experience during my association with Jack White & Co. and Jefferson Financial Services. By providing research, on-line training, and financial planning assistance to clients, not only did I facilitate growth in portfolios and new business, but I acquired a broad range of product knowledge and investment strategies. I found it extremely satisfying to provide clients with the tools to help them build secure futures, inspiring even greater desire to enter and succeed in the financial services arena. As an adjunct to my sales experience, I assumed diverse leadership positions during college which provide further evidence of my financial management, decision-making, and interpersonal skills.

As a resourceful, investment-savvy, and highly motivated individual, I am confident that I will positively impact your company's growth and bottom-line profitability. Therefore, I am requesting a personal meeting to further address why I am an ideal candidate for your training program. Thank you for your time, and I look forward to speaking with you soon.

Sincerely,

John J. Seeker

JOHN J. SEEKER
123 Looking Hard Avenue
Top Dog, USA 20202
(555) 678-8910

In the interest of pursuing employment opportunities with your organization, I am enclosing a resume for your review. It provides valuable details regarding my extensive experience in human resources, training and development, counseling, and event planning.

As you will discover, I possess a diverse professional background in both entrepreneurial and corporate environments which has allowed me to develop fundamentally sound skills in several crucial areas. Having started my career in the military, I acquired an excellent foundation in operations and personnel management which I have continually utilized throughout my career. Under the auspices of an $80 million corporation, I successfully structured and expanded an entire training department to provide top-notch professional development programs for a company of 2,500-plus employees. As a result, I gained extensive experience in all phases of meeting planning with an excellent knowledge of highly detailed planning, event implementation, and logistics coordination.

As I advanced further in my career, I became one of two key managing personnel in a state-approved educational institution and counseling center. During this experience, I expanded my knowledge of the human resources field through this multifaceted position which required extensive recruiting, training, instructing, troubleshooting, staff relations, and employee record-keeping. Finally, as a successful entrepreneur, I have developed a well-respected private practice which has allowed me to further extend myself in all aspects of marketing, promotion, business administration, public speaking, and corporate consulting. At this juncture, however, my goal is to assimilate into an organization that can utilize the full breadth of my experience to assist it in achieving corporate objectives.

Although I am confident that my numerous accomplishments are well represented, I realize that a resume cannot portray any individual entirely. Therefore, I am requesting a personal interview where we might discuss my qualifications in greater detail.

Thank you in advance for your time in reviewing my credentials. I look forward to speaking with you soon.

Sincerely,

John J. Seeker

JOHN J. SEEKER
123 Looking Hard Avenue
Top Dog, USA 20202
(555) 678-9101

In the interest of pursuing employment with your organization, I am providing a resume for your review. It provides essential information concerning my background, experience, and skills.

As you will notice, I have extensive experience in the field of computer technology. Currently, as the Founder and President of my own computer consulting firm, I am interested in exploring career pursuits with a larger organization where I may fully utilize my extensive information systems background in a management role. As reflected, I possess a comprehensive knowledge of systems integration and development which encompasses vast experience in a wide array of operating systems, networks, and programming applications. Not only does my technical background reflect strong experience with mainframes, mini-computers, and a variety of PCs, but I have acquired valuable knowledge of leading communications technologies such as the Internet.

In my role as a consultant, I have demonstrated an ability to perform multiple support tasks simultaneously while remaining focused on my primary goal of design and development. My success in project management results from my keen ability to select the proper personnel, develop effective teams, and coordinate project components in order to ensure efficient production and accurate results. In essence, I presently remain apprised of technological advances that affect all existing systems, and I maintain an awareness of new design concepts and systems integration methods. Therefore, I am confident that I possess a number of attributes that could positively impact your organizational effectiveness on both an immediate and a long-term basis.

Realizing, however, that a resume cannot portray any individual entirely, I am requesting a personal interview where we can further discuss my qualifications. Thank you for your time reviewing my credentials. I look forward to hearing from you soon.

Sincerely,

John J. Seeker

JOHN J. SEEKER
123 Looking Hard Avenue
Top Dog, USA 20202
(555) 678-9101

In response to a transition in my current partnership, I am considering opportunities which may be of mutual benefit. Therefore, in order to introduce my qualifications, I have enclosed a resume which briefly highlights my professional background in various legal environments.

As indicated, I possess a wealth of legal experience in the areas of commercial transaction and civil litigation. Throughout my career, I have demonstrated astute legal skills in all facets of case management, ranging from client interviews and discovery to settlement negotiations and trial preparation. As an experienced attorney currently in a partnership practice, I have displayed a range of expertise related not only to the management of diverse legal matters, but also to client development and business administration.

Having relocated to the Sweetwater area in 1995, I demonstrated a high degree of focus and drive in establishing a successful start-up plaintiff law firm in this competitive metropolitan market. As a result, I have cultivated a solid reputation among my clients and have managed a diversity of matters related to business entities and commercial contracts/agreements as well as a host of commercial and personal injury litigation cases. Being extremely efficient, I have managed as many as 100 matters simultaneously and to date have achieved a 100% success rate by winning all the litigation cases opened while in private practice. At the same time, I have exemplified the critical business skills necessary to operate and manage a profitable law firm.

As indicated by my previous background with a national regulatory agency and a state Attorney General's office, I have also gained valuable experience in serving as legal defense counsel. Having held an Advisory Attorney role with the Federal Utility Commission, I further broadened my proactive legal skills in protecting the organization's integrity and preventing ethical or conflict-of-interest disputes. Similarly, during my employment with the State Office of the Attorney General, I expanded my knowledge base related to workers' compensation and disability matters through Appellate and Administrative Courts. In essence, I am a well-rounded attorney with proven case management, drafting, research, and litigation skills who is certain to become an immediate asset to one of your client's legal teams should we determine that a mutually beneficial opportunity exists.

In closing, thank you for your time in reviewing my enclosed professional profile. I would be interested in arranging a personal meeting once you have considered how my qualifications may be of potential value to your firm. I look forward to speaking with you at your earliest convenience.

Sincerely,

John J. Seeker

JOHN J. SEEKER

123 Looking Hard Avenue
Top Dog, USA 20202
(555) 678-9101

In order to explore career opportunities where I can leverage my exceptional management and training abilities combined with my dental industry expertise, I have enclosed a resume which highlights my successful employment history and proven qualifications.

Please note that I have a 19-year proven track record managing technical support and professional training operations. Not only have I demonstrated an acute ability to handle diverse personnel issues in an equitable manner that commands respect and loyalty, but I have spearheaded numerous system, program, quality control, and procedural improvements that have continuously maximized all resources. In fact, my career has historically reflected strong staff leadership, initiative, and innovation, all of which are well documented. Currently, as Technical Advisor for two prominent dental divisions of the United States Military and the Surgeon General, I have been successful in managing all aspects of a broad-reaching service and technical repair operation where I quickly tripled operational efficiency. At the same time, I possess hands-on expertise in critical maintenance, installation, equipment fabrication, and product modification areas combined with practical dentistry experience as a Dental Assistant.

Previously, in other management roles I further demonstrated my leadership skills in project management, purchasing, technical support, and staff development. For instance, not only have I directed the build-out of three new clinics from the ground up, but I possess in-depth technical knowledge regarding all types of multiple manufacturers' dental and medical equipment. In addition, through innovative equipment specification, aggressive maintenance programs, and improved staff training, I maximized competence levels, increased staff productivity, and dramatically reduced costs. In short, I am considered to be a highly persuasive and dynamic leader who always puts forth that extra effort and who has earned many prestigious awards and commendations which validate my innumerable professional skills and contributions.

At this juncture in my career, I am interested in utilizing my proven abilities to build solid infrastructures and increase revenues in order to benefit your organization. Confident that I would quickly become an asset to your existing team, I am requesting a personal meeting to discuss my broad qualifications. Thank you in advance for your time, and I look forward to speaking with you soon.

Sincerely,

John J. Seeker

JOHN J. SEEKER

123 Looking Hard Avenue
Top Dog, USA 20202
(555) 678-9101

In order to secure a position where I may utilize my skills in the areas of sales and management, I have enclosed a resume for your review. It provides valuable details regarding my employment history as well as my relevant qualifications.

As you will notice, I recently completed my Bachelor's Degree in Business Administration with a focus in Management. Currently, I am employed as a Project Liaison by Big Builders Construction, an $80 million commercial and industrial contracting company. In this position, I assist in a variety of management support functions, including materials cost research, which contributes to the job-estimating process. In addition, I communicate closely with various Project Foremen in order to monitor project status and ensure deadline achievement. Throughout my education, I held a diversity of positions with Big Builders Construction, serving in capacities which focused on customer service roles as well as on-site construction development.

To further broaden my experience base in the area of client relations, I was formerly employed by Auto Covers in a Sales Support role which allowed me to gain practical sales and account management experience involving mass merchant customers. At this juncture, I am interested in securing employment with an organization where I may continue to develop my skills in the key areas of management and sales while offering unwavering dedication and a high degree of professional talent. I am confident that, given the opportunity, I would immediately become a contributing member of your already existing team.

Aware, however, that a resume can only partially illustrate the scope of an individual's skills and abilities, I am requesting a personal interview to discuss my relevant qualifications in greater detail. Thank you in advance for your time, and I look forward to speaking with you.

Sincerely,

John J. Seeker

SARAH J. SEARCH
123 Job Hunting Lane
Big Time, USA 10101
(444) 567-8910

In the interest of pursuing employment opportunities with your organization, I have enclosed a resume for your review. It provides valuable details regarding my diverse qualifications.

As you will discover, I possess a proven track record in various phases of program management and project coordination for a variety of civic and nonprofit organizations. Although I have spent a number of years out of the work force, I have demonstrated a wide array of professional talents which will effectively translate into the corporate arena. As reflected, I have held numerous leadership positions within the community which exemplify my management skills. Not only have I recruited and coordinated large teams of volunteers, but I have managed program budgets of up to $80K. As President of the PTA for The Good School, I have had the opportunity to direct the efforts of multiple committees while remaining accountable to a 35-member Board. During each of my volunteer experiences, I established a proven track record in maximizing program efficiency and facilitating the achievement of all organizational objectives. Being in highly visible volunteer positions has afforded me the opportunity to further develop and refine my public speaking and writing skills as well.

At this juncture, I am keenly interested in re-entering the work force and applying this broad range of skills toward a successful career. In essence, I am confident that I will become a valuable asset, if allowed the opportunity. Therefore, I am interested in arranging a meeting where we could discuss my qualifications in greater detail.

Thank you in advance for your time and consideration. I look forward to speaking with you soon.

Sincerely,

Sarah J. Search

JOHN. J. SEEKER

123 Looking Hard Avenue
Top Dog, USA 20202
(555) 678-9101

In the interest of exploring career opportunities with your company, I am enclosing a resume for your review. It provides valuable details of my 18 years of proven experience in the media planning and advertising field.

Please note that I possess a consistent record of directing and developing media planning and broadcast-buying management and media teams, offering them the wealth of my expertise with all media vehicles. Having continually progressed to increased levels of accountability and highly demanding assignments, I presently demonstrate extensive industry experience in business development, strategic planning, campaign execution, and media placement. Currently, as the Executive Vice President with XYZ Advertising, not only have I captured the largest Southeast account through an outstanding media-only plan, but I have launched a successful start-up operation that generates $5M in annual revenues. In addition, I have developed and implemented strategic processes and training programs that consistently produced staffs with exceptional credentials in media planning and buying. Consequently, we have a reputation industry-wide for producing the best professional teams in the business.

In each phase of my career, I have demonstrated strategic vendor negotiation abilities and client needs identification skills that resulted in the creation of mutually beneficial media and buying plans. Similarly, I am extremely adept at identifying new methods to capture the competitive edge and facilitate significant revenue growth. One of my greatest strengths is my ability to establish rapport and credibility with all levels of personnel both with the company and with major domestic and international accounts. Due to the vast network of client relationships I have traversing numerous industries, I have in-depth experience in successfully promoting a diversity of products, images, experiences, and services. Therefore, I have become an industry expert presenting seminars on brand-building methodologies and strategies at university internship programs and at various industry functions. At this juncture, I am seeking an organization where I may fully engage my areas of expertise in an executive management or consulting role to enhance revenue growth and the bottomline.

Realizing, however, that a resume is limited in its ability to portray the full capabilities of any individual, I am requesting a personal meeting to discuss my qualifications in greater detail. Thank you for your time in reviewing my credentials. I look forward to speaking with you.

Sincerely,

John J. Seeker

SARAH J. SEARCH
123 Job Hunting Lane
Big Time, USA 10101
(444) 567-8910

In the interest of utilizing my clinical background to benefit your organization, I have enclosed my resume for your review. It briefly highlights my medical and public relations experience in combination with a variety of highly developed professional qualifications which would translate well into both sales and training positions.

As indicated, I possess over ten years of practical nursing experience, primarily in the operating room and surgical areas. Consistently throughout my career, I have demonstrated strong relationship development skills, diverse technical proficiencies, and proven case management abilities. Currently, as a Registered Nurse for a nationally recognized teaching hospital, I have gained a wealth of medical expertise and leading-edge operating room equipment knowledge which will assist me in immediately excelling within your organization. At the same time, having worked as a primary care nurse managing high-acuity patients, I have acquired specific experience in treating diverse skin care conditions as well as performing various care-related procedures involving fistulas and ostomies.

During my successful tenure with Excel University Hospital combined with a prior public relations background, I have demonstrated strong presentation and hands-on training skills which are critical to marketing high-tech product lines successfully. I am extremely well versed in functioning as a team leader, establishing rapport with diverse personnel, and relating to demanding surgeons during high-stress, intense neurosurgery procedures. At the same time, my background incorporates experience in formulating training materials and coordinating in-service programs.

In essence, I believe my proven medical track record in conjunction with a versatile transferable skills set would allow me to become an immediate contributor within your organization. Realizing the limitations of a resume in portraying the full scope of my abilities, I am requesting a meeting to discuss my qualifications and relevant experience. Thank you in advance for your time and consideration. I look forward to speaking with you in the near future.

Sincerely,

Sarah J. Search

JOHN J. SEEKER
123 Looking Hard Avenue
Top Dog, USA 20202
(555) 678-9101

In the interest of exploring employment opportunities with your organization, I have enclosed a resume for your review. It provides valuable details regarding my diverse qualifications.

Please note that I possess a wide array of professional talents in the areas of management, public and community relations, public speaking, and writing. As reflected, I have excelled in diverse professional environments based on my overall business acumen and unwavering dedication to success. Having worked for a Fortune 500 company, I exhibit effective techniques in managing operations, personnel, training, and public relations programs. During my extended tenure with Flyaway Airlines, I have truly demonstrated the flexibility to integrate my skills as both a leader and a team player. Alternatively, I have excelled in academic settings and community-based organizations such as the Chamber of Commerce. As a result, I display an excellent ability to educate diverse populations as well as foster key political and corporate relationships to achieve common goals.

In addition, my previous experience incorporates a special emphasis in the media. Not only have I directed programming for a highly publicized radio station, but I have managed the editorial and production responsibilities for a company-sponsored magazine. To further broaden my qualifications, I possess a law degree and practical legal experience which serves as an excellent resource of knowledge within the business community. In essence, I am certain to become a valued member of your organization if allowed to utilize the full scope of my abilities toward future contributions.

Realizing, however, that a resume cannot portray any individual entirely, I am requesting a personal interview where we might discuss my qualifications in greater detail. Thank you in advance for your time in reviewing my credentials. I look forward to speaking with you soon.

Sincerely,

John J. Seeker

CLOSING COMMENTS

Now that you have completed the exercises in this program, you should have learned how to describe yourself in a positive light. If so, we hope that you are ready to market yourself aggressively and to pursue your career dreams with great passion. We deeply believe that the resume and other career-related materials you developed will help you achieve much success in the future.

If, after completing this program, you feel that seeking professional resume-writing assistance would be helpful, keep these important issues in mind. The resume-writing industry is unregulated and therefore does not have a nonprofit organization that enforces standards. The burden of judging quality remains with the consumer.

Before selecting a resume writer, ask to see samples of his or her work, review a printed price sheet, and request client references. The value of working with a professional service can be immense. Many times a job hunter is too close to his or her background to focus on the most important, sellable points. Prioritizing information, strategically planning the format, and formulating powerful wording may feel overwhelming. In these instances, the time and investment in working with a resume-writing expert can far outweigh the expenses incurred, particularly if it assists the job seeker in attaining his or her professional goals.

If you are interested in learning more about resumes or need special assistance in writing your resume, please contact America's Best Resumes, Inc., at (404) 233-1467 or (888) 9-RESUME.

Remember, you can accomplish whatever you put your mind to if you are committed to the result and believe in yourself. Make sure you never forget how valuable you are, and never stop reaching for the stars. After all, only you can create your future.

ABOUT THE AUTHOR
GAYLE OLIVER-LEONHARDT

Gayle Oliver-Leonhardt is an established entrepreneur in the Atlanta area who specializes in resume preparation and career-related correspondence. Since December 1989, her business has produced high-quality resumes that have assisted a broad range of job seekers through all phases of the search process.

As President of America's Best Resumes, Inc., formerly known as Buckhead's Best Resumes, Gayle has developed a sterling business reputation. Based on the quality of her service, she has maintained a referral rate that exceeds 48 percent and has extended her services to an ever-expanding national and international client base.

Gayle's current and previous affiliations include Georgia 100, the Georgia Speakers Association, the Georgia Association of Personnel Services, Chambers of Commerce, the Referral Exchange (former director, executive board member, and elected official), Ali Lassons Leads Club (former director), the Atlanta Women's Network (former newsletter editor, board member), the Strategic Employment Coalition, and the National Association of Female Executives. Through each of these organizations, she has gained a comprehensive perspective on business in the 1990s and on the many changes expected to occur in the new millennium.

Gayle has also established a reputation as an outstanding speaker and instructor. She has been an invited speaker for groups at multinational corporations and civic organizations as well as universities and colleges.

In addition to having appeared on multiple radio and television programs, Gayle is one of the founders of the High Impact Job Search program, a concise three-hour seminar detailing the strategies of an effective job search.

You may contact Gayle Oliver-Leonhardt at (404) 233-1467 or (888) 9-RESUME.